PSYCHOPATH
AND ADAPTATION
IN INFANCY
AND EARLY CHILDHOOD

Principles of Clinical Diagnosis
and Preventive Intervention

Clinical Infant Reports:
Series of the National Center
for Clinical Infant Programs

Sally Provence, M.D., *Editor-in-Chief*

Editorial Board

Peter Blos, Jr., M.D. Stanley I. Greenspan, M.D.
Selma Fraiberg Peter B. Neubauer, M.D.
T. Berry Brazelton, M.D. Leon J. Yarrow, Ph.D.

PSYCHOPATHOLOGY AND ADAPTATION IN INFANCY AND EARLY CHILDHOOD

Principles of Clinical Diagnosis
and Preventive Intervention

by

STANLEY I. GREENSPAN, M.D.

INTERNATIONAL UNIVERSITIES PRESS, INC.
NEW YORK

Library of Congress Cataloging in Publication Data

Greenspan, Stanley I.
    Psychopathology and adaptation in infancy and early
childhood: principles of clinical diagnosis and preventive
intervention.

    (Clinical infant reports: series of the National Center
for Clinical Infant Programs; number 1)
    Bibliography: p.
    Includes indexes.
    1. Infant psychiatry. 2. Infant psychology.
3. Child psychiatry. 4. Child psychology.
5. Child psychopathology — Prevention. I. Title.
II. Series. [DNLM: 1. Adaptation, Psychological —
In infancy and childhood. 2. Mental disorders —
Diagnosis. 3. Mental disorders — Prevention and
control. W1 MO567BW v. 1 / WS 350 G815p]
RJ502.5.G73   618.92′89   81-19282
ISBN 0-8236-5660-8   AACR2

Manufactured in the United States of America

Contents

Acknowledgments

This work represents the preliminary clinical impressions and constructs of an ongoing clinical research study of intervention with high-risk infants and their families being conducted at the Clinical Infant Development Program at the Mental Health Study Center, NIMH, and in collaboration with the Clinical Infant Development Program at Family Services, Inc., of Prince George's County, Maryland.

Reginald S. Lourie, M.D., conceived many of the ideas and directions for the field of clinical approaches to infants and their families a number of years ago, planting the seed for the current study. Together with Robert A. Nover, M.D., and myself, Dr. Lourie has collaborated in the creation and ongoing implementation of this study, as well as a series of articles leading to this monograph. Mary Robinson, who joined the planning group in its formative stages, has also been instrumental in the planning, organizing, and implementation of this study.

Serena Wieder, Ph.D., has superbly carried out her responsibility for the overall supervision of the major component of the services-research effort as well as the generation of innovative clinical and research approaches. Her predecessor, Patricia Allison, Ph.D., currently implementing a related program with premature infants and their families, was quite as instrumental in our success.

Alicia Lieberman, Ph.D., responsible for the research component of this study, has contributed significantly to the formulation and implementation of our systematic assessment approaches and the development of innovative frameworks and instruments to quantify complex clinical phenomena.

Perhaps most crucial to the success of this services-research effort, however, have been the primary clinicians and infant specialists who work directly with the participants. Joan Castellan, who has been extraordinarily dedicated and innovative in developing special patterns of care for challenging infants; Diana Denboba, who has been uniquely sensitive to the special needs of our high-risk families; Euthymia Hibbs, who has worked with the most disturbed mothers, fathers, and families in an intense and sensitive manner.

Eva Hollingsworth, in addition to helping in the overall management of the clinical services program, brought exceptional understanding to the concrete needs and environmental conditions of our participants.

Edward Turner has contributed the skills of a veteran clinician. His subtle understanding of psychodynamic processes and their relationship to family and social structure has been of much assistance. He has recently taken on a leadership role in developing a special program component for adolescent parents and their offspring. Deloise Ward, seasoned in community social service approaches, brought a combination of assets: an understanding of infant and early childhood development, combined with an unusual degree of dedication to her work. Delise Williams has brought to this program an exceptional ability to work systematically and intensively with some of our most challenging participants in order to help them reach a more integrated level of functioning. Carol Pollock, Sandra Schuler, and Diane Elliston, while not presently active in this study, also contributed to the clinical care of our participants.

Alfred Scheuer, M.D., our pediatric consultant, brought a rare combination of skills reflecting his ability to plan assessment and treatment strategies at the physical, cognitive, and social-emotional levels. He has made a major contribution to the planning and continuing refinement of our program.

Conducting our developmental testing, and conceptualizing and analyzing our emerging data, were Julie Hofheimer, Ph.D., and Susan Poisson, whose dedication and capacity to work at the complex interface of clinical service and research were remarkably helpful.

Martha Esch has been invaluable for her technical skills and intuitive grasp of clinical purpose in planning, coordinating, and implementing the audio-visual recording portions of the assessment, training, and communications programs. Curtis Powell, who worked in this area as well, also contributed greatly to our understanding of the social context of our participants.

Patricia Findikoglu was responsible for organizing and coordinating our infant observation center, and brought infinite patience and unusual sensitivity to the multiple demands inherent in her task.

Joining us more recently have been Freda Meyerowitz, who brought to this program her considerable management skills and experience; Katherine Jacobs, Ph.D., an experienced clinician and researcher with both infants and parents; and Kathleen O'Leary, a dedicated clinician.

Collaborating with us on related programs at the Mental Health Study Center were Malcolm Gordon, Ph.D., who brought his skill and experience in the areas of language and cognitive assessment; Susan Dowling, who worked closely with Dr. Gordon; Coryl Jones, Ph.D., whose contributions on environmental design and early development were remarkable in their own right, and promise to add an important dimension to our program; and Thais Fisher, who facilitated the integration of the Family Services of Prince

George's County component of this program with the other programs at Family Services, Inc., and whose sensitivity to family and community issues enhances our weekly conferences.

I would like to express my special gratitude to Etta Stern, whose editing, organizing, and refining of this manuscript from its preliminary draft has been phenomenal.

Nick Cariello of International Universities Press has not only further edited the manuscript quite skillfully, but has also made suggestions for changes and additions, often rewriting major sections to bring in a broader theoretical perspective from the author's earlier works. He cannot be thanked enough for his extraordinary dedication, skill, and creativity.

I would also like to thank Betty Albaugh for managing the preparation of this manuscript along with her many other responsibilities. She and her excellent staff, consisting of Hilde Hofmann, Nettie Shapiro, and Karen Freeman, carry out these responsibilities so exceptionally well that such efforts as this are possible.

Special thanks should go to Nathan Nackman, Executive Director of Family Service of Prince George's County, Inc., whose vision and flexibility have helped us to embark on our clinical research endeavors; the voluntary participants in our program, from whom we have learned so much concerning the needs of infants and their families; and all of the health and mental health agencies in Prince George's County which have cooperated so effectively with this and other Mental Health Study Center research efforts for the past 32 years.

Foreword

The work of Dr. Greenspan and his colleagues with infants and parents represents a timely and significant contribution to the fields of mental health and child development, so that it is a pleasure for me to introduce this monograph, the first in a series on infancy planned by the National Center for Clinical Infant Programs.[1] The series will present previously unpublished research and clinical studies relevant to work with infants and parents.

As one who has long been interested in infant mental health and clinical applications of research in early development, I welcome this volume and the serious commitment both to research and to clinical intervention that it reflects. There is increasing acceptance of the importance of early

[1] The National Center, a non-profit scientific organization incorporated in 1977, was founded by leaders in the fields of mental health, pediatrics, child development, psychoanalysis, philanthropy, and public interest programs. As Dr. Reginald Lourie described its aims (1980), they are (1) to facilitate optimal health and mental health through preventive clinical approaches in the earliest years of life, (2) to provide a forum for the exchange of information emanating from clinical infant and early childhood programs, (3) to stimulate and coordinate research, (4) to encourage the training of personnel on a wide interdisciplinary basis, and (5) to foster the dissemination of information and the development of public policy in the important and growing field of therapeutic measures for infants and parents.

intervention as a means of preventing and alleviating conditions (biological and experiential) that lead to developmental deviation and psychopathology. It is true that in some instances infants with vulnerabilities and maladaptive behavior in the first year of life may improve in functioning without intervention, or, at least, without the sort of intervention that we can identify specifically. The fact that this occurs, that many infants are resilient and that many parents improve as nurturers, leads some to discount the importance of providing help early in the life of the child. And yet, other infants and parents fare far less well: Early dysfunctions may crystallize into maladaptive, psychopathological patterns that not only interfere with current development and parent-infant relationships, but exert long-lasting adverse effects as well. Older children and adults with psychological disorders and problems of adaptation often have histories of early childhood disturbances and traumatic or depriving experiences during infancy. Unfortunately, however, prospective studies have often not reliably predicted future development and adaptive capacity. One is impressed with two probable explanations for this: In spite of the fact that a great deal is known about infancy and the relationship between early experience and later functioning, there is still much to be learned, particularly about those factors, biological and psychosocial, that promote *healthy* development. In addition, earlier models of study isolated variables and proposed linear relationships between early experience (or early biological characteristics) and later outcome that were not adequate to the task of understanding the complexity of human development and behavior. The infancy research of Dr. Greenspan and his colleagues is a fine example of the current recognition of the need for a multivariate approach to study and of more concerted efforts to approach issues of how biological factors and early experience interact.

The translation of theory and empirical data into effective practice with infants and parents is no easy matter.

Greenspan's interweaving of research data and theoretical propositions represents a giant step toward developing, as he puts it, a clinically based conceptual framework with identifiable landmarks for assessment, intervention, and evaluation. He points out that barriers to the needed comprehensive approach reside in the fact that much of our knowledge about individual lines of development, much of our data from experimental, observational, clinical, and theoretical approaches, and much of our thinking about symptoms and diagnostic techniques remains largely unintegrated. His presentation tackles the major task of integration, using adaptation as an organizing theme and articulating a set of principles of clinical diagnosis and preventive intervention. Greenspan's "developmental structuralist" approach focuses on how an individual organizes experience at each stage of development. Six experiential organizations, or structures, are described, corresponding to the six stages of emotional and cognitive experience that Greenspan delineates: (1) homeostasis, (2) attachment, (3) somatic-psychological differentiation, (4) behavioral organization, initiative, and internalization, (5) capacity for organizing internal representations, and (6) representational differentiation and consolidation. That other investigators might choose different names for these stages is unimportant: Greenspan's thorough descriptions allow the student of early development to recognize the familiar characteristics and sequences of each stage. One of the strengths of Greenspan's developmental structuralist approach is its consistency with empirical research on early development. His description of the stage-specific capacities and tasks of infants conforms to the now accepted position that timetable and sequence refer to points at which such characteristics become of special significance, not that they are totally absent earlier or later on. Adaptive and pathological formations, in varying degrees, are possible at each of these stages. Greenspan's definition of the adaptive infant as one who can organize experience and achieve a state of comfort and harmony is an essential point.

The detailed examples of adaptive and maladaptive states and behavior and the characterizations of growth-promoting and growth-inhibiting environments are a necessary orientation for the appreciation of the material that follows.

Another strength of the presentation resides in the richness of the data from its longitudinal clinical study of "high risk" and normal infants and their families. Infants and parents are seen in their natural surroundings and in the setting of the Infant Center. Based on systematic observation in a service context, this is action research in which the behavior and reactions of the investigators are part of the field of observation and of the process being studied. Service-centered studies such as this one provide an especially productive opportunity for the investigation of personality development and its deviations. Moreover, involvement with the same infants and parents over time is enormously valuable in that it not only provides rich data but also keeps investigators appropriately humble. It keeps before them the marvelous if sometimes frustrating intricacy of development and the need for careful consideration of the multiple factors involved in developmental outcome. To remain aware of how much there is still to be known and still to be able to provide useful therapeutic experience for infants and parents requires an understanding of the current state of the art. In this connection, Greenspan's experience as a clinician leads him to remind the reader that it is essential that approaches be based on the special characteristics of the individual child and his family, as well as on the general principles of prevention and early intervention. He then describes, for each of the six stages, infant capacities, environmental characteristics, and relevant principles of preventive intervention and treatment. With the clinical illustrations that follow these make a circumscribed and integrated presentation that can be turned to whenever the clinician needs a "quick review." For each of the stages, the author describes the new capacities and characteristics, referring to their antecedents, and then indicates their importance for later development. Clinical illustrations demonstrate the relation of the theoretical constructs to practice.

The case illustrations for each of the stages provide useful and vivid details. Some readers will wish for more information about *how* the work was done, but that must await more detailed case reports. The emphasis here is on the *principles* of intervention. What is of special importance in the case illustrations is the way in which they reflect the real lives of parents and infants and the remarkable variety of situations and conditions of which clinicians must be aware in order to work most effectively with them. The material makes that point very effectively and provides a refreshing contrast to the expectations of some "early intervenors" that there are recipes and shortcuts for such complex situations. The clinical experience and sophistication of the research group are evident not only in the case illustrations but also in the depth and richness of the discourse. Oversimplification of complex issues, happily, is avoided. This is not a book for those seeking easy answers. In providing an approach and a way of thinking that can guide practice, it is a valuable, mind-stretching contribution to the understanding of infant development and clinical applications of child development knowledge.

Sally Provence

Introduction

An important challenge to the increasingly promising field of preventive intervention and treatment approaches for infants and their families is to develop a clinically based conceptual framework with identifiable landmarks for assessment, intervention, and evaluation. Optimally, such a framework would address the full range and variation in human functioning (normality to pathology) and encompass the clinically relevant lines of human development, including physical and neurological development, cognitive development, the development of human relations, and the development of capacities for organizing and differentiating experience (adaptive and coping strategies).

Several existing developmental frameworks (Freud, 1905; Erikson, 1959; Piaget, 1962; Sander, 1962; A. Freud, 1965; Kohut, 1971; Kernberg, 1975; Mahler, Pine, and Bergman, 1975), as well as much recent empirical research, have provided enormous understanding of the different lines of development in infancy and early childhood. These foundations, together with the rapidly growing body of clinical experience with infants and their families (Fraiberg, 1979; Provence, 1979; Provence, in press), pro-

1

vide direction for a much needed integrated approach encompassing the multiple lines of development in the context of adaptive and disordered functioning.

The major impediment to the creation of a truly integrated developmental theory has been the difficulty in reconciling our knowledge of development based on emotional experience with that based on cognitive or impersonal experience, and our knowledge of these two areas with emerging empirical research on the neurophysiological, behavioral, and social development of infants and young children. The development of human relationships and individually different capacities and styles for organizing and differentiating emotional experience (adaptive and coping styles) as well as the manner in which human experience becomes a part of the personality and the foundation for a number of such basic personality functions as reality testing, impulse regulation, mood stabilization, a delineated sense of self, and a capacity for focused attention have all been the subject of various experimental, observational, clinical, and theoretical approaches in the area of emotional experience. Similarly, the development of sensorimotor schemes, means-ends relationships, preoperational use of symbols, and eventually the capacity for logical thinking have been the subject of equally diverse approaches in the area of cognitive or impersonal experience. Not only the content of these areas but the divergent approaches to them remain to be integrated.

Moreover, traditional approaches to classification of adaptive and disordered functioning, as well as to intervention, have tended to be either symptom-based or etiologically based. While necessary, these approaches are in themselves insufficient, founded on partially observed but not fully understood clustering of certain symptoms or on the identification of etiological factors in a disorder. They have not led toward an integrated developmental model of diagnosis and intervention. The same etiological factor, for example, can result in different behavioral outcomes or symptoms. Thus a reaction to a given allergen or stress may differ depending on individual differences in response proclivity; e.g., one individual may become dizzy or develop peripheral neuropathy, another may develop hives, and yet another a gastrointestinal disorder. At the same time, several different etiological agents may result in the same set of symptoms; a given allergen, infectious agent, or a series of stresses can all produce a similar gastrointestinal disturbance.

In many fields of medicine we have learned enough about pathological and adaptive pathways to understand the intervening processes between etiological factors and response patterns. An understanding of allergic mechanisms, for example, suggests that one individual may be having a common allergic reaction, while another may be experiencing a different set of bodily processes, even though the final outcome — a gastrointestinal disturbance — is the same for both.

As of yet, however, we do not have a complete framework for delineating the pathogenic and adaptive processes of personality development. From this perspective, then, there is a need for another dimension in our classification that would focus on the organism's individual way of processing, organizing, and differentiating experience, that is, on the pathways that lead to certain behavioral outcomes. The "final common pathway" unique to each individual connects the influence of multiple etiological factors with varying outcomes, suggesting something fundamental about the organism's manner of organizing its experience of its world, internal and external, animate and inanimate.

This monograph applies a new integrated approach to the classification of adaptive and pathological personality organizations and behaviors in infancy and early childhood. It discusses the implications of such an approach, based on a developmental structuralist framework (Greenspan, 1979), for understanding the growth-promoting and growth-inhibiting environments of adaptive and maladaptive development. Finally, it suggests principles of preventive intervention based on such an approach.

The developmental structuralist approach focuses on how an individual organizes experience at each stage of development. Experience is defined broadly to encompass emotional experience as well as experience with the inanimate or impersonal world. The experiential organization of the individual is the final common pathway for multiple determinants of behavior (environmental, biological, etc.), and can be studied in relation to a specific line of development, whether it be that of human relationships, emotions, or cognition. The principles governing the means by which the human organism simultaneously organizes and processes experience related to the emotional and cognitive aspects of human functioning have been presented elsewhere (Greenspan, 1979) and will only briefly be commented on here.

The developmental structuralist approach is founded on two assumptions. One is that the organizational capacity of the individual progresses to higher levels as the individual matures (Piaget, 1962; Greenspan, 1979). Thus, phase-specific higher levels of development imply an ability to organize an ever-widening and more complex range of experience in stable patterns. Consistent with our integration of the theories of cognitive and emotional development, this experience is conceptualized in terms of stimuli generated from both within the organism (drives, affects, internal self- and object representations) and without (affect-laden relationships and stimuli from the impersonal environment). The active and experiencing child uses the maturing capacities of his central nervous system to engage his internal and external worlds in ever-changing, ever more complex ways: Stimuli of greater complexity are integrated by structures of parallel complexity.

The organizational level of experience can be delineated along a number of dimensions. First, one can determine if the organizational level is *age or phase appropriate*. For example, has an infant by eight months of age attained the expected organizational capacity whereby he or she can engage in reciprocal interchanges with the caretaker? Does the infant perceive mother's signal (a smile, for example), process it in a rudimentary form, and respond to the signal (with a smile or by reaching his hand to mother's face, etc.)? Do such reciprocal interchanges, suggesting a capacity for a cause-and-effect type of relating, characterize the mother-infant dyad? Or is the character of their communications random and chaotic, lacking the purposeful cause-and-effect type of patterns?

Second, the organization of experience may be described according to the *range* and *depth* of experience incorporated into the desirable organizational structure. Some eight-month-old infants, for example, will interact purposefully with the inanimate world but not with the animate. They may pull a string to ring a bell but not respond to or initiate purposeful social and emotional interchanges. Within each domain of experience the range may be further elaborated according to the specific types of experiences accommodated at the expected organizational level: One eight-month-old may engage in reciprocal interchanges only around "low-key" pleasurable pursuits (e.g., a feeble smiling exchange), and become disorganized around assertive themes. Thus, if this youngster wants the red ball which mother holds out, he will cry or just stare rather than reach for it. A more advanced eight-month-old may be capable of reciprocal interchanges with both animate and inanimate experiences and in the context of a range of deeply felt emotional themes such as intense pleasure, curiosity, assertiveness, and protest.

Third, the organization of experience may be described according to the *stability* of the behavioral and emotional patterns or, put another way, their resilience to stress. Some eight-month-olds may lose their capacity for purposeful communication when frustrated, tired, or mildly ill, while others retain these capacities and become even more purposeful under stress.

Fourth, the organization of experience may be described in relation to an emerging *personal uniqueness* in which all of the above patterns are incorporated. Often the personal signature of these patterns is not clear until a youngster is older or, as parents will say, a "little person." In fact, this signature is in evidence from birth onward. The question with respect to this dimension is whether the organization of experience incorporates the infant's individual differences adaptively. These include his special abilities for fine motor coordination, social interactions, self-comforting, etc.

The second assumption of the developmental structuralist approach is that for each phase of development there are certain characteristic tasks the organism must accomplish before advancing to the next stage of development. These tasks are conceptualized in terms of principles of organization available to the child by which he orders his experience of internal and external stimuli. When we say that a child has surmounted a phase-specific task, we mean that he has acquired a principle of organization by which he can order the stimuli of that developmental phase, a principle of organization that will then serve as the foundation for further, more complex organizing principles by which he can order the more complex stimuli of subsequent stages. Thus our second assumption suggests that there are certain characteristic *types* of experience that must be ordered by means of the organizational structure available to the child. These types of experience are typically expressed in specific affects and behavior patterns at first, and in thoughts, wishes, fears, and so forth at later stages of development. The type of experience organized is, in a sense, the drama the child is experiencing, while the organizational level of his activity might be viewed metaphorically as the stage upon which this drama is played out. To carry this metaphor a step further, it is possible to conceive of some stages which are large and stable and can therefore support a complex and intense drama while, in comparison, other stages may be narrow or small, able to contain only a very restricted drama. Still other stages may have cracks in them, crumbling easily under the pressure of an intense, rich, and varied drama.

Thus the developmental structuralist approach proposes a biological-adaptational model of development in that the adapting individual develops his or her unique experiential organizations and contents from an interplay in which maturational progression and its phase-specific interests and inclinations operate on and are responded to by the environment. At each phase of development there are certain characteristics that define the experiential organizational capacity: the stability and contour of the stage. At the same time, there are certain age-expectable dramas, themes characterized by their complexity, richness, depth, and content.

We can thus consider the manner in which experience is organized at each developmental stage according to the characteristics which define the particular stage-specific experiential organization. The developmental structuralist approach applied in this monograph defines these experiential organizations (conceptualized as structures [Piaget, 1962, 1968]) at each stage of emotional as well as cognitive experience (Greenspan, 1979).

Further examples from early infancy will help illustrate the approach. One of the infant's first tasks is to be able to adapt to the external environment in the context of maintaining a state of internal equilibrium. The organism relies predominantly on the use of neurophysiological aspects of the human body, including state regulation and such basic rhythms as sleep/wake, hunger cycles, etc. (Sander, 1962; Brazelton, Koslowski, and Main, 1974). This capacity may be viewed as a stage-specific structural capacity to achieve homeostasis (Greenspan, 1979; Greenspan, Lourie, and Nover, 1979). Some infants, by virtue of individual constitutional differences and environmental influences, can engage the world in a multisensory affective manner and still maintain a state of internal regulation and regular cyclic patterns. Other infants can only remain regulated or calm by shutting out the external world (e.g., by closing their eyes and sleeping). Still other infants, unable to regulate their internal processes, remain hyperexcitable and irritable, with only the slightest engagement with the external world.

Another illustration pertains to the capacity for forming a human attachment, one of the first and most important developmental tasks. Between two and four months, infants clearly begin to demonstrate a unique investment in the animate as opposed to the inanimate world. They exhibit a special interest in those caretakers who are relatively permanent in their environment, an interest expressed in the social smile (Spitz, Emde, and Metcalf, 1970; Emde, Gaensbauer, and Harmon, 1976). They also show individual differences in communication patterns and in the affect expressed and experienced in their special dyadic attachments (Brazelton, Koslowski, and Main, 1974; Stern, 1974a, 1974b). This capacity for attachment may also be viewed as a stage-specific structural achievement and considered in terms of the dimensions outlined earlier (e.g., range, depth, stability, and personal uniqueness of the organization of experience). Do we observe a warm, loving dyad, in which infant and mother both experience a range of affects from deep, rich pleasure to assertiveness and protest, or a shallow, mechanical attachment, devoid of affect, behavioral richness, and flexibility? What is the range of sensory modalities used by the infant and mother—are they visually, aurally, and tactilely connected, or are only one or two of these modalities used? What is the range of motoric involvement? Do these experiential organizations exist only intermittently or are they the usual mode of involvement? Can the dyad re-engage after a disruption? Are unique personal characteristics beginning to express themselves? That is, are there special games or preferred affects and sensorimotor patterns that characterize this relationship?

The degree to which an individual experiences the full range of stage- and age-appropriate experience in stable, stress-resilient personal configurations may be viewed as an indicator of his readiness to begin organizing the more complex experiential realms of the next developmental stage. In this sense, the optimally adaptive structure at each developmental stage facilitates further development. Thus an infant who begins warding off affectionate, intimate behavior is unlikely, unless there is a reversal of that trend, to learn those skills that involve personal intimacy. On the other hand, the infant who organizes experiences of physical closeness and interpersonal affection is likely to have an opportunity to learn the later forms of such intimate exchanges. Similarly, some adults can engage in a broad range of wishes, thoughts, feelings, and relationships, and deal with stress without compromising their capacity for human experience. Other adults, in contrast, must restrict major areas of engagement in order to contain anxiety. To the extent that they must avoid sexual or aggressive feelings, intimate relationships, success, assertion, etc., they are limited in their developmental progression. This is not to suggest that "catch-up" learning does not occur — it does. Such learning, however, may have a different developmental sequence and a different final configuration.

The developmental structuralist approach thus views each stage of development in terms of expected organizational characteristics. The level, range, stability, and personal uniqueness of the organization of experience expected at each developmental level provide the basis for a developmental structuralist diagnosis. Specific symptoms or behaviors in this approach are never viewed in isolation but in the context of the overall phase-specific experiential organization expected or achieved. Thus the eight-month-old who is calm, alert, and pleasant to be around, but who has no capacity for discrimination or reciprocal social interchanges may be of vastly more concern than an irritable, negativistic, food-refusing, night-awakening eight-month-old with age-appropriate capacities for differentiation and reciprocal social interchanges.

The developmental structuralist approach is consistent with, and partially derived from, current empirical research on early development. It is now well documented that the infant is capable, even at birth or shortly thereafter, of organizing experience in an adaptive fashion. He or she can respond to pleasure and displeasure (Lipsitt, 1966); change behavior as a function of its consequences (Gewirtz, 1965, 1969); form intimate bonds and make visual discriminations (Klaus and Kennell, 1976; Meltzoff and Moore, 1977); organize cycles and rhythms (e.g., sleep/wake, alertness states) (Sander, 1962); and demonstrate organized social responses in conjunction with increasing neurophysiological organization (Emde, Gaensbauer, and Harmon, 1976). It is interesting to note that this empirically documented view of the infant is, in a general sense, consistent with Freud's early hypotheses (1911) and Hartmann's postulation (1939) of an early undifferentiated organizational matrix. That the organization of experience broadens during the early months of life to reflect increases in the capacity to experience and tolerate a range of stimuli, and that this includes social interactional responses in stable personal configurations, is also consistent with recent empirical data (Sander, 1962; Escalona, 1968; Brazelton, Koslowski, and Main, 1974; Sroufe, Waters, and Matas, 1974; Emde, Gaensbauer, and Harmon, 1976; Murphy and Moriarty, 1976). Finally, there is evidence that these capacities to organize experience reflect individual differences in infants and their caretakers that are present early in life (Wolff, 1966; Thomas, Chess, and Birch, 1968; Parmelee, 1972).

The developmental structuralist approach presented here has been developed as part of an in-depth, longitudinal clinical study of mental health services for various groups of relatively high-risk and normal infants and young children, and their families, conducted at the Mental Health Study Center, Division of Mental Health Service Programs, NIMH. In this study, participation begins before birth, and participants are followed for five years (or longer) postnatally with a focus on assessing multiple lines of development in the context of family and community structures. Preventive and treatment services, when clinically appropriate, are tailored to the individual differences and requirements of each infant, young child, and family. Unique to this program, as will become apparent in the case illustrations, has been our work with those "multiproblem" families who usually do not avail themselves of traditional health and mental health services. The specifics of the clinical and service-system approaches to assessment and intervention that characterize this program will be presented in another work.

This monograph will present the preliminary conceptualizations of the principles of diagnosis and preventive intervention that have emerged from this intensive study. The range and variation in adaptive and disordered functioning, and the principles of preventive intervention appropriate to each age range or phase of infancy and early childhood, will be described. First, the core expected developmental capacities for each age range or phase of early development will be discussed, followed by descriptions of adaptive and disordered infant functioning, growth-promoting and growth-inhibiting environmental factors, and the principles of preventive intervention.

Finally, it should be emphasized that there are many ways in which the human organism can integrate experience. Some types of environmental events, or some types of biological proclivities, may challenge the organism's integrational capacities more than others. At times, these challenges foster not maladaptation, but unusually *adaptive* structures. Thus, when in the succeeding chapters, we present relatively more and relatively less optimal environments, these should not be understood as inevitably leading to maladaptation. Individual differences among human beings require us to recognize that the developmental structuralist approach is ultimately a construct, an approximation in the service of systematization. It should not be seen to suggest that one-to-one relationships between specific behaviors early in life and later in life can be established. But while the developmental structuralist approach cannot predict linear relationships between behaviors over time, it does provide a construct — the concept of levels of integration — that allows us to look at the overall relationship between levels of development under both stable and changing conditions.

Somatic Level of Organization: Phase I

Our first milestone occurs at the earliest stage in life. Internal and external experience are processed according to a system that relies predominantly on the use of the neurophysiological aspects of the human body. This step is consistent with Piaget's description of the sensorimotor period and with clinical observations of the way infants usually deal with internal and external affective stimulation.

At this stage of development a fundamental organizing principle is the capacity for basic rhythms. Piaget (1937) has highlighted this in terms of the rhythmical activity infants use to gain experience with their initial reflex patterns. Clinically, rhythmic patterns in infants, from rhythmic movements of their muscles to rhythmic alterations in their basic states, have been an area of important research interest (Sander, 1962). Basic somatic systems, even at this early

This material originally appeared in slightly different form in the author's *Intelligence and Adaptation: An Integration of Psychoanalytic and Piagetian Developmental Psychology* © 1979, International Universities Press, New York, New York. It should also be noted that a small portion of the introductory material of each chapter has been liberally adapted from that book.

age, are complex. Various researchers have demonstrated
individual differences among babies in terms of state regulation, habituation patterns, crying responses, the establishment of homeostatic cycles and rhythms, and broad measures
of temperament (Brackbill, 1958; Brazelton, 1973; Emde,
Gaensbauer, and Harmon, 1976; Parmelee, 1972; Thomas,
Chess, and Birch, 1968; Wolff, 1966).

Nevertheless, the flexibility of this early system for
dealing with internal and external experience (which, for
conceptual purposes, may be referred to as internal and external "stimuli" and which, in any case, may not be differentiated by the infant) is very limited. Sometimes we observe an infant deal with stress in terms of the interior of his
body; at other times we see him deal with it in an outward
fashion; and frequently we see him deal with it through repetitive action or rhythmic patterns.

Although during the first two to four months of life a
number of processes in neurological, cognitive, and affective development converge around acknowledged nodal
points, such as the social smile (Spitz, Emde, and Metcalf,
1970), it appears that this earliest phase of development still
does not have the quality of intentionality or "psychological
life" that later stages will have. As behavioral determinants,
somatic internal coordination and stimulation are relatively
more dominant than social interaction, which will become
more dominant later on. At this time sleep-wake, hunger,
and arousal cycles, for instance, play a large role in determining behaviors. Early distress is related to internal physical and neurophysiological events (Tennes, Emde, Kisley,
and Metcalf, 1972). It should not be overlooked, however,
that the infant may relate to and experience external environmental stimuli in ways that are not yet apparent. While
it is generally recognized that the harmony between the infant and the caretaking environment plays a vital role in establishing basic rhythms and homeostatic mechanisms, as
well as the character of early reciprocal interactions, there is

still a great deal to learn about the way in which the very young infant perceives and experiences the world (Lewis and Rosenblum, 1974; Sander, 1962; Stern, 1974a, 1974b; Yarrow and Goodwin, 1965; Yarrow, Rubenstein, Pederson, and Jankowski, 1972).

It appears that at this stage there are few, if any, detour or delay channels. At best the infant may possess some sensory thresholds. The infant's capacity to enter into rhythmic patterns both with important figures in the environment and within himself should not, however, be underestimated as an adaptive tool. This capacity provides the infant important protection during the earliest days, weeks, and months of life, and serves as a foundation for later adaptation. As we observe clinically, the basic somatic mechanisms of shutting out stimulation and of rhythmic patterning remain with us throughout life.

1
Homeostasis (0–3 Months)

The first task of the newborn infant is to achieve home-ostasis: the capacity for maintaining an equilibrium state in the face of internal and external stimulation. All infants exhibit some capacity to receive external stimulation soon after birth — by virtue of their sensory equipment, including their proprioceptive and position senses. Thus we notice, even in the first weeks of life, newborn infants making eye contact with their mothers or following attractive lights and colors. Some infants, of course, are born with severe deficits in one or another of these capacities, blindness or deafness being the most common. These gross deficits may be viewed as one end of a continuum on which the capacities of infants to receive and process stimulation can be ordered. That is to say, infants possess these capacities to varying degrees, or, what is the same thing, will exhibit them in more mature forms at different times. Although there are most likely differences between the ways sensations emanating from within the body and outside the body are perceived and processed, we postulate a similar continuum for internal stimulation (Greenspan, 1979). As maturation takes place, we can observe further differences in the degree to which stimulation, or, more broadly, experience is processed. The developmental structuralist approach explains these individual differences not merely in terms of constitutionally given factors. Rather, it attributes them to a complex interaction of factors, genetic and environmental, and, more particularly, to the ways in which constitutionally given primitive structures develop as a function of the individual's capacity to structure his experiences. More precisely still, the developmental structuralist approach, to the extent that it views development as a process of increasingly sophisticated structuralization, presumes that development cannot take place without experience, whether external or internal.

This presumption has important consequences for our study of maladaptive development in the homeostatic phase. For if the infant cannot maintain an equilibrium state in the face of internal and external stimulation, then he may not seek out further stimulation and indeed may shut out those stimuli that disrupt his equilibrium. Or, alternatively, he may become labile, hyperreactive, or unfocused in his attempt to maintain contact with his environment. In the language of this chapter, we will say that the infant cannot fully *engage* the world around him because the stimuli from that world cause him discomfort and/or tend to disorganize him. These stimuli, that is, cannot be organized in terms of the structures available to him. Critical, then, to development in the homeostatic phase is the infant's ability to regulate its states (Sander, 1962; Brazelton, Koslowski, and Main, 1974), including adequate states of alertness for exploration of the interesting sensations from the external world. This ability is related to the formation of basic cycles and rhythms (eating; sleep/wake; alertness); the ability to maintain a state of internal harmony by means of beginning capacities to regulate and organize experience (these beginning capacities conceptualized as stimulus thresholds); the ability to habituate to stimuli; the ability to organize initial response patterns, including sensorimotor coordination (e.g., turning to look at an interesting object); and the ability to integrate a number of modalities into complex patterns — for example, consoling oneself, receiving consolation from another, or coping with noxious stimuli.

But there is another perspective from which development in the homeostatic phase must be viewed. Given the central role of experience, the infant's capacity for self-regulation must be as much a function of his capacity for engaging the world as his capacity for engaging the world is a function of self-regulation. That is to say, increasing experience with the world (e.g., with soothing caretakers or comforting objects) will increase the infant's repertory of self-regulating capacities. Thus we can assess homeostatic capacity along two related dimensions: the infant's capacity to engage the world and the infant's capacity to regulate himself in response to stimulation. Adaptation in one dimension usually implies adaptation in the other.

Infant Capacities

Adaptive capacities in an infant must be discussed in relative terms. The more adaptive self-regulatory capacities are evidenced by those infants who carry out these tasks relatively effortlessly and across a larger range of experience. The most adaptive infant finds it easy to habituate to a broad range of stimuli, can console himself, and develops regular cycles of sleep/wake, alertness, eating, and elimination. He responds readily to the comforting intentions of his environment, and, when appropriate, uses rhythmic movement and soothing tactile, visual, or auditory stimuli in the service of comforting himself. Even when mother is tense, and when the environment is noisy and chaotic, he can maintain his own cyclical patterns, habituating to these distressing stimuli and establishing contact with the tense mother as he learns to adjust to her various moods.

In considering the self-regulating capacity of the newborn infant, we observe the specific ways in which the infant uses his available somatic equipment. Does the infant use or respond to rhythmic rocking as a way of calming down? Does the infant use vision to achieve a state of comfort, e.g., by looking at mother's soothing smile? Is there a listening response to pleasurable sounds as a means of finding relaxation? Is the infant able to use the voluntary muscles or motor system to seek a comfortable nuzzling position with his caretakers? Is the infant able to experience feeding from the breast or bottle as a way of finding comfort? Some infants, for example, can easily learn to tune out a noxious noise and return to sleep even after having been suddenly awakened. Other infants cannot do this for themselves, but can be readily soothed with rhythmic rocking and the calming sounds of a warm caretaker. Still other infants have difficulty being comforted, even by the soothing caretaker, and may cry for long periods of time before finally returning to a state of calm.

Similarly, in studying the infant's capacity to engage the world, we observe the specific modalities the infant employs. Does the infant seem visually engaged in what is about him — the mother's face, novel stimuli, etc.? Does he brighten up at certain sounds? Does he respond to soothing touch with increasing interest in what is about? Do certain positions, such as being held at a slight angle or in a relatively vertical position, increase the open-eyed, face-to-face contact of the infant with his caretaker, thereby demonstrating the use of his own proprioceptive and/or position sense as a way of supporting his interest in the world? Does the infant show his own *special capacities* for remaining alert when the world is interesting? Even further, does the infant show a capacity for self-motivated, alert periods during which the environment is not especially interesting? Can he carefully observe this environment until something interesting comes into sensory awareness?

Maladaptive or pathological homeostatic capacities are indicated by the relative inability to regulate internal states. Here we find the hyperexcitable infant who cannot habituate to stimulation, the infant with special sensitivities (auditory, tactile, visual), the infant with immature motor responses who cannot orient to or accept soothing from a caregiver, and the apathetic and withdrawn infant — in all of whom the capacity for self-regulation is compromised.

Gross physical and neurological defects, immaturity of the central nervous system, difficulties in early patterns of integration (Sander, 1962; Brazelton, 1973), organ sensitivities (gastrointestinal problems and allergies), and certain environmental conditions are a few of the factors that may contribute to a disorder of the capacity for self-regulation. A hyperstimulating caregiver may keep the infant too aroused, or the caregiver may miss those of the baby's cues that indicate a need for comforting. While gross deficits in perceptual apparatuses, such as blindness or deafness, will make an infant more prone to a homeostatic disorder, other integrative capacities may compensate, such that comparatively successful homeostatic experiences may still be possible, even with such major deficits (Fraiberg, 1977).

A disorder of the capacity for self-regulation can be specified in terms of the various modalities that contribute to the homeostatic capacity. It may be that these modalities not only cannot be used in the service of self-regulation, but, because of special sensory sensitivities, provide the basis for the infant's vulnerability to overstimulation. Similarly, the immature infant whose level of sensorimotor integration is insufficient to follow mother's comforting facial expressions, the infant who cannot organize his motor system to nuzzle in response to sensory input, or the infant who finds rhythmic rocking uncomfortable because of an imbalance in sensorimotor integration, all provide examples of the way in which the nature of the homeostatic disorder can be more specifically delineated.

At higher levels of integrative functions infants also demonstrate problems. Balanced cycles of sleepiness and alert responsiveness or regular eating and elimination cycles may not be evident even in the absence of any obvious chaos in the environment. One can also observe at these higher levels difficulties with the infant's overall capacity for self-consolation and interaction with primary caregivers. In addition to specific sensory sensitivities, one may find difficulty in habituating to and otherwise coping with noxious stimuli, e.g., the infant who cannot organize sensorimotor responses so as to turn away from an unpleasant noise, sight, or smell; or the infant who does not habituate to or otherwise "tune out" those same sensory experiences.

At the same time as it is essential to characterize the specific nature of the homeostatic disorder, it remains vital to consider this disorder in terms of the overall ability of the infant to achieve the goals of this first stage of development. Perhaps the most obvious example in this regard is that of the severely impaired infant cited above. Many blind or deaf infants can use compensatory sensory modalities to achieve self-regulation.

Just as the relative strengths and weaknesses of the infant's capacity for self-regulation must be studied, so must the relative strengths and weaknesses of the infant's capacity for becoming interested in the world. Here, too, specific pathological or maladaptive dimensions may be observed: the infant who cannot use vision to become interested in the world, and who demonstrates gaze aversion from the first weeks of life; the infant who does not brighten with auditory stimulation, or when held in the upright position, does not become more alert. And again, as important as it is to study each of these sensory and motor capacities specifically, it is the infant's overall ability to use these capacities to achieve a balanced interest in the world that remains critical. Some infants will show preferences for certain modalities. Some, with deficits in certain of these modalities, will compensate with others. The key to assessment is the degree to which the infant takes an interest in the world and makes use of available or intact modalities in this regard.

The degree to which the infant is able to integrate *across* modalities — hearing, vision, touch, and motion — must also be assessed. Can these modalities be used together for an alert, engaged involvement in the world, or do we find early fragmentation of such modalities? If two or three modalities are called on at one time, does the infant become apathetic, or withdrawn — or excessively irritable and disorganized; or show patterns of turning away, or gaze aversion?

One may observe *the degree* to which an infant organizes a homeostatic experience and thereby remains resilient to stress. For example, the infant who engages the animate and inanimate world in an organized manner in the context of established patterns of sleep/wake, eating, etc., may be contrasted with the infant who can remain calm only at the expense of an optimal state of alertness and engagement. For the former, mild stress (illness) may result in only a temporary change in sleep patterns, whereas for the latter, similar stress may result in intense apathy and lack of engagement in the animate world.

In sum, optimal homeostatic capacity permits the integration of life experiences in a way that facilitates further development. Stimuli taken in by the available sensory modalities are organized in developmentally appropriate cycles, rhythms, and states of alertness and relaxation. The experience that is organized will foster the initiation of human relationships and the elaboration of a differentiated interest in the world.

When viewing disordered functioning in the stage of homeostasis, we can look at the relative degree to which regulation and interest in the world is maintained; the degree to which stress can undermine otherwise intact homeostatic capacities; and the degree to which capacities for self-regulation and a balanced interest in the world are severely compromised even in the absence of stress. Excessive irritability, hypersensitivities, tendencies toward withdrawal, apathy, avoidance, gaze aversion, and turning away are some of the signs of disordered functioning in this first stage of development. Early maladaptive environmental accommodations may form the basis for later disorders, including autistic-like symptoms, and defects in such basic personality functions as perception, integration, regulation, and motility.

Finally, it should be pointed out that the homeostatic capacities for regulation and interest in the world should be considered not only from the perspective of postnatal development, but also prenatal development. The intrauterine environment is, of course, affected by maternal nutrition, medication, illness, and the mother's psychological states — her anxiety, depression, etc. The importance of appropriate prenatal medical care and self-care cannot be overestimated. Low birthweight babies or babies with malformations have been shown to be compromised with respect to regulation and interest in the world. Studies on fetal responses to sound and other stimuli (Brazelton, Koslowski, and Main, 1974) further emphasize the importance of intrauterine experience and the prenatal phase of development for the establishment of homeostatic capacities.

Environmental Characteristics

The growth-promoting environment is dedicated to learning about the individual differences of the infant, and to building on the infant's strengths in order to help him achieve harmony, regulation, and a balanced interest in the world. Thus the growth-promoting caretaker quickly learns the types and range of visual and auditory stimulation that will engage and, at the same time, comfort the infant. The picture of the caretaker holding the child in a comfortable, nuzzling position, rhythmically rocking or cooing with soft sounds, and then slowly engaging his attention with interesting and engaging smiles and sparkling eye contact is a frequent sight with a healthy infant and a healthy caretaker. The complexity of what is going on is taken for granted, as it should be, since much of this occurs quite naturally between the infant and the "fitting-in environment" (Winnicott, 1962).

The growth-promoting environment, however, may find itself challenged when the infant is difficult to comfort. In caring for a hyperexcitable infant, for example, the caretaker will explore special sensory or sensorimotor approaches and seek out experiences that may be comforting to the infant, such as special rhythmic rocking patterns, special ranges of vocalization, special types of lighting, and special types of soft clothing, if there is a tactile hypersensitivity. The caretaker will experiment to find those conditions and situations in which the infant achieves comfort and relaxation and in which it can feel protected and regulated. At times, intense rocking may be necessary to help an infant achieve a state of peaceful harmony. Stricter schedules for sleeping, eating, and other activities may be needed to help a disorganized infant achieve organization. Sometimes a sufficiently growth-promoting environment may follow the lead of the emerging organization of the infant, allowing the baby to set its own pace.

With the healthy, confident infant, simply being attentive to his preferred types of experiences, visual, auditory, etc., and helping him to integrate these, may be sufficient to foster his interest in the world. With others, however, such as the apathetic, withdrawn infant, the caretaker must find facial expressions, sounds, colors, and shapes that are interesting to him, and positions and rocking rhythms that help him to orient to and become interested in his world. In the case of a hyperexcitable infant, for example, the growth-promoting environment will attempt to find those low-key stimuli that can be both calming and engaging at the same time, such as rhythmical rocking, soothing sounds, and a soft, restrained smile.

To achieve the overall goals of regulation, organization, and engagement, the growth-promoting environment will work to strengthen less-than-optimal sensory or motor modalities. For the infant who has mild gaze aversion, for example, the caretaker might use the intact auditory sense to draw his or her attention to soothing sounds, and then present a comforting face so that the infant will slowly learn to tolerate visual stimulation for increasing periods of time. Thus, visual engagement is enhanced by using the already engaged auditory capacity. Similarly, if the infant responds to tactile stimulation or rhythmic rocking and avoids eye contact, visual engagement may be joined with these others in a gradual and sensitive manner. Soft clothing or low-pitched sounds may help the infant with a tactile or auditory hypersensitivity engage the world with his other sensory and motor modalities. Once the infant is engaged and soothed, the specific hypersensitivity can be worked on by slowly exposing the infant to stimuli at low ranges of intensity. Thus the infant may gradually learn to build higher stimulus thresholds and to habituate to stimuli in these immature modalities. In all instances, the purpose of the growth-promoting environment is to strengthen these sensorimotor modalities by which the world can be engaged.

In order for the environment to be able to facilitate regulation and interest in the world, the primary caretakers must be capable of experiencing, at a deeply emotional level, feelings of investment and dedication, and a desire to offer protection and comfort. They must find their own efforts pleasurable and interesting. Subtle emotional "fitting in" between the newborn and caretakers is an essential aspect of the adaptive milieu. Thus an unusual degree of ambivalence, hostility, indifference, unpredictability, etc., on their part, even if the behavior seems appropriate at the time, should signal that the environment may be less than adequate.

In a general sense, the growth-inhibiting environment does not support and can even undermine the homeostatic capacities of the infant. The unavailable caregiver cannot offer physical comfort or a sense of security. The chaotic caregiver cannot offer the predictability that would allow the new infant to stabilize his emerging cycles and patterns and permit him to develop a comforting, engaging interest in the world. The dangerous or abusive caretaker threatens the physical integrity of the infant. The hypo- or hyperstimulating, or dull caretaker may compromise the infant's own tendency to be interested in the world, leaving him apathetic, withdrawn, or hyperreactive.

It is a well-established clinical phenomenon that even during the first month of life one can observe increases in the capacities of infants to organize and regulate themselves, to console themselves, to habituate effectively, to find the world interesting, and to interact with it. On the other hand, one can also observe deterioration in these same capacities. Where primary caretakers are available, predictable, protective, and engaging in a soothing way, we often see dramatic improvements occur in homeostatic capacities.

At the grossest level, one can observe in the growth-inhibiting environment overt lack of physical care and protection, failure to respond to illness, pain, or distress, inadequate nutritional care, or physically abusive behavior. At another level, however, the growth-inhibiting environment must be assessed in terms of the basic soothing and comforting functions that are the foundation of human attachment. Are the primary caretakers available? Do they help the infant to build on his or her own capacities for comfort and regulation by means of touch, rhythmic rocking, vocalization, eye contact, etc.? The very depressed and withdrawn caretaker, or the very schizoid or narcissistic caretaker, may be able to care for the infant's basic physical needs, feeding him adequately and making sure that he receives adequate medical attention when ill. This same caretaker, however, may not provide the comforting functions so essential to human development.

There may also be a deficit in the caretaker's capacity to read the most fundamental cues of the baby with respect to pleasure and pain. Psychotic mothers responding to their own delusions or inner voices, or severely depressed and self-absorbed mothers, may not read the infant's distress signals so as to be able to respond to such physical needs as hunger. Similarly, they may not be able to observe when the infant is alert and ready to be engaged, and thus may not offer appropriate comforting, protecting, or engaging stimulation.

At an even more subtle level, the growth-inhibiting environment may be observed to lack the emotional attitudes appropriate to the first months of life, even while overt behaviors do seem appropriate. The caretaker who feels an unusual amount of anger or ambivalence, feels overwhelmed or unsupported by his or her own support system (spouse, own family, etc.) may communicate this to the infant through subtle compromises in the capacity to set up a regulating environment. While a mother holds and feeds the baby, her ambivalent emotional attitudes may be reflected in a wooden body posture, tense facial expressions, jerky rather than rhythmic handling, and noxious vocal or visual stimuli.

Common Fears in the Caretaker

There are a number of common fears that contribute to a less than optimal early environment for the infant. These include feelings of "hurting the baby," of "not having enough to give the baby," of "being a bad parent," of "losing one's independence," and of "being controlled by one's baby." Some caretakers may find that the relationship to the infant results in anxiety-provoking sexual feelings. These common fears can all interfere with the caretaker's capacity to offer a regulating and engaging environment for the infant.

Some caretakers, for example, may harbor resentment from having had to care for younger siblings, and may be fearful at an unconscious level of taking out this resentment on the new child. Others may actually feel competitive with their children, wishing that they were being taken care of themselves. This wish is then suppressed, so that resentment emerges as a fear of harming the child rather than a direct wish to hurt him. While periodic fears of this kind are not unnatural and need not interfere with the basic tasks of engaging the child's interest in the world, providing a regulating environment, and taking special pleasure in the new baby, persistent fears of this type can interfere with nurturing. Mrs. J., for example, became so frightened of hurting her daughter that she hardly ever picked her up. When she did, she changed and fed her quickly and put her right back in her crib. She was afraid even to hold and rock her and used a mechanical device to do so. In such a case, the mother's fear of hurting the baby compromises the infant's capacity to become interested in the human world, and compromises the quality of the regulating and calming experiences as well.

"Not having enough to give" is a frequent fear of breast-feeding mothers and is voiced in terms of a concrete concern, of not having enough milk to give. While this may sometimes be the case (and if so, it must be appreciated), it may at other times represent a growth-inhibiting trait, such that we can observe a similar concern in other areas of the mother's life. This fear, too, may have its roots in childhood. It is unnecessary to speculate about its source, but it should be pointed out that such a fear, even if ordinarily only an occasional part of one's life, may commonly intensify around a helpless, dependent, and demanding new baby. Sometimes "I don't have enough to give" can be related more to resentment based on the feeling that "I'm giving too much; I don't have any time for myself; I don't want to give any more."

Not uncommon with mothers, particularly those who have developed careers of their own, is the fear of losing independence. This, too, is a natural concern, particularly for a woman who has been on her own and enjoyed the satisfactions of living without the responsibility of a helpless baby. But when the interest and joy of caretaking are not present, and when, instead, the experience is dominated by fears of losing independence, one has to consider the defensive nature of the preoccupation. In one case it turned out that this preoccupation with losing independence was, in fact, related to the mother's deeper feeling that she could not be as close as she wanted to with her son; that she didn't know how "to get that close." Her son was not the kind of infant who cuddled easily or warmed easily to others. In fact, in some respects he was an unsatisfying infant, demanding that the caretaker "woo him." This mother was the kind of woman who had never "run after a man." She had frequently bowed out of relationships in which she had been required to pursue the other, thinking, "I'm not going to get dependent on that person; I'm an independent person myself; who needs that?"

Having sexual feelings toward their infants is another fear of parents. While there is ample evidence of sexual abuse of infants, this is, by and large, a comparatively rare phenomenon in the population as a whole. More common are uncomfortable "sexual feelings" that sometimes interfere with optimal tenderness, engagement, and relaxation in the relationship of parents with their children. One father found himself experiencing some sexual excitement with his one-month-old daughter. As a consequence, he stopped picking her up and told his wife to do all the holding and cuddling. In this case it was learned that the father was frightened of closeness and dependency and would frequently have sexual fantasies toward whomever he was concerned about being dependent on. For him, the sexual fantasy was a way of distancing himself from his more basic needs and fears concerning intimacy.

Principles of Preventive Intervention and Treatment

The primary focus of preventive intervention and/or remedial help is to transform a growth-inhibiting environment into a growth-promoting environment in the context of the individual needs of the infant. The first principle of treatment and preventive intervention is to assess the strengths and vulnerabilities of the newborn infant in terms of its capacity to achieve homeostasis. As reviewed earlier, one must assess the degree to which the infant is capable of organization and regulation on its own, and in response to appropriate environmental supports. Are there sensory hypersensitivities, immaturity in sensorimotor integration, difficulties in forming regular cycles of alertness and sleep, in eating, etc., that would compromise the infant's homeostatic potential? One must also observe the environment for potential growth-promoting and growth-inhibiting conditions. Is the environment unavailable, chaotic, dangerous, abusive, hypo- or hyperstimulating?

From the perspective of the infant's abilities, specific sensitivities or low stimulus thresholds should be identified so that protective measures may be taken. For example, a youngster with a tactile or auditory sensitivity should be protected from noxious stimulation. Eventually, normally occurring maturation may afford him appropriate protection. But where additional efforts are necessary to help the youngster with a particular sensitivity, the fundamental principle is to pair gradual exposure to the noxious stimulation with a pleasurable experience. For example, the youngster who is sensitive to sound in almost all ranges may be spoken to at the same time as he is soothingly and rhythmically rocked. Here the upsetting experience of hearing noise is combined with the soothing experience of being rocked so as to permit the youngster to receive some auditory stimulation while achieving some regulation by a soothing, complementary experience. Of course, this approach can be used with other modalities as well. Over time, maturation usually helps the youngster develop appropriate stimulus thresholds in these areas.

For the youngster who has a more generalized difficulty in achieving regulation, a careful assessment of his individual differences must be made to find an experience that is soothing and regulating for him. Sometimes this requires rocking the youngster to a certain rhythm, such as his own heart rate, his mother's heart rate, or his mother's respiratory rate. Other youngsters may need to be held in a special position. For example, a youngster may find the relatively vertical position too stimulating and may need to spend more time being held close to the body in a relatively horizontal position. We have seen a few such infants who are eventually able to begin enjoying the more alerting vertical positions.

The other primary goal during the stage of homeostasis is, of course, to facilitate the infant's engagement in the world. Obviously, the withdrawn infant who sleeps all day does not have an opportunity to become interested in the events around him. The infant with poor muscle tone or severe muscle rigidity will find it difficult to accomodate his body to his mother's, and thus to use his body optimally as a vehicle for exploring the world around him, animate or inanimate.

Again, the basic principle is to make a careful assessment of individual differences. Which of the youngster's sensory and motor modalities are not being used fully to explore and gain interest in the world? The infant who does not look at the maternal face or follow interesting stimuli may be helped by the presentation of stimuli which he does find interesting. Ordinarily, a bright light or a bright light paired with certain types of movement patterns will generate interest for infants. Such stimuli may help to catch the youngster's attention so that he begins to turn his head to follow the moving stimulus. This practice may then permit him to follow other stimuli which do not pair the two features, but present only light or movement.

Initially, the stimulus configuration may have to be made especially interesting for the youngster. If, for example, an infant with intact hearing does not react to sound, he may first require a range of sounds in combination with other sensory experiences, such as touch or visual stimulation. This may eventually enable him to respond when he hears an interesting sound alone. The youngster whose body becomes rigid and who turns away when held may require exposure to especially comforting and pleasurable physical experiences. These might include being held in certain positions, or a combination of being talked to, looked at, held, and rocked in special ways until he can relax and enjoy physical comfort and closeness. The infant who has muscular rigidity may require a wide range of motion exercises in which his arms and legs are gently moved for him until they are relaxed, these combined with experiences which tend to soothe and relax his whole body. The especially "floppy" youngster with poor muscle tone may enhance his control over his motor system by means of the extra exercise he gets in moving his limbs in response to pleasurable experiences. While the movements infants make to auditory or visual stimuli may seem random, they are often semi-purposeful. Presenting rhythmic vocalization, for example, offers the infant the opportunity to do the best he can in trying to move his arms and limbs in a responsive way, thus enhancing his capacity for control. Combining this with a series of motion exercises may allow him to catch up in this area.

In each of these areas of sensory and motor functioning, the careful assessment of the youngster's individual differences, and the patient presentation of interesting experiences in a repetitive manner offers the infant the opportunity to strengthen existing functions, thereby strengthening homeostatic capacity.

It is pivotal to help the parents or other primary caretakers deal with any personality limitations and family or other social difficulties that may interfere with providing the optimal environment for the infant. At times, reading and responding to the infant's individual differences may exceed the environment's capacities. Traditional psychiatric care for major emotional difficulties is one aspect of the preventive intervention program for the caretaking environment. At the same time, however, the therapeutic program for the caretakers and family must take into account the special impact of a new baby on the individuals and family members. New emotional requirements are placed on the family to the extent that the infant offers intimacy and requires care. If he is hard to console or regulate, he may make great demands on the caretakers. These emotional requirements may activate existing conflicts and/or personality patterns that are not usually evident under other circumstances.

Thus, it becomes especially important to understand not only the parents' overall personality organizations, strengths, and vulnerabilities, but also how the members of the caretaking environment function as individuals and as a group in response to the special characteristics of their new infant. The therapeutic work with the family must help them understand not only their more general limitations and strengths, but also how certain limitations or strengths have been activated by the infant's development. For example, the depressed mother may respond to the withdrawn infant as though the infant is rejecting her. It may be especially useful to help this mother understand that her infant's tendency to withdraw accentuates her already existing tendency to feel rejected and depressed. She may then be able to exempt the infant from her typical response of anger at those who reject her, and discover a constitutional ability in the infant to respond, not to her anger, but to her warmth and engagement. Similarly, caretakers who tend to be suspicious may feel they are being attacked by a labile or hyperreactive baby. They may need to understand not only their tendencies toward suspiciousness, but that their misperception of the infant as an "enemy" is being accentuated by the infant's very real individual differences. Thus they can be helped to see that a more appropriate pattern of care for their infant would be to respond protectively to the infant's lability. Many more examples like this could be given. The basic principle, however, is to offer appropriate clinical care to individual caretakers as well as the family as a unit, and to focus on the issues activated by both the presence of an infant and his special individual differences.

It should go without saying that the functioning of the entire family as a unit should also be viewed in terms of its capacity to support or undermine the infant's development. In some families, for example, the caretakers may be able to tune in to the needs of the baby as individuals but not as a unit, so that communication patterns break down and the infant is relatively ignored or misread when they are together. Siblings may compete with the new baby for the parents' attention. A jealous husband may distract mother from the baby. To all of this, the mother herself may respond by misinterpreting the baby's signals.

Attention, therefore, must always be paid to the family as a system, and work at this level, if necessary, must be pursued. There will be further discussion of the complex issues involved in working with the family later in this monograph.

In studying the infant and his or her environment, special emphasis should also be placed on the degree to which infant and environment fit together. A relatively depressed caretaker, who can be somewhat responsive, may be able to comfort and engage a highly competent infant who is already capable of self-quieting and self-consolation and who can reach out to the mother in search of further opportunities for engagement. As one watches such a dyad interact it seems as if the infant is taking the lead in the patterns of comforting and engagement. But a dyad consisting of this same depressed mother and a more subdued infant may require a great deal of active intervention. Similarly, the hyperstimulating, somewhat chaotic mother with an infant who is only mildly subdued and has an unusual capacity for habituating to a variety of noxious stimuli may not constitute a worrisome situation, whereas this same mother with a hyperreactive baby may create a growth-inhibiting environment.

Specific approaches in the phase of homeostasis are thus based on the special characteristics of individual family dyads. This involves not only helping the environment to read the individual differences of the infant in order to engage it appropriately. It also implies helping the environment to cope with issues that may be contributing to its own growth-inhibiting tendencies, including such concrete issues as stress, poverty, and the provision of medical and nutritional supplies. While programs of care for the parents are designed to help them deal with their own difficulties, such programs must, at the same time, help them set up an adequate environment for their infant as quickly as possible. Where the assets and strengths of the parents are such that their growth-promoting capacities cannot be mobilized quickly, additional supports may need to be enlisted in the form of surrogate caretakers. Where possible, the temporary use of other family members such as siblings or extended family members may provide the nurturing the infant requires. This will be commented on further at a later point.

Clinical Illustrations

CASE 1

Mrs. A. and her son, Ted, illustrate what can occur in the phase of homeostasis when both mother and infant tend to be withdrawn and relatively unavailable to each other. Mrs. A. had a history of severe learning problems and a diagnosis of minimal brain dysfunction during childhood. Around the time of her son's birth she was generally depressed and withdrawn. At best, she functioned at a marginal level intellectually, and tended to use withdrawal and avoidance whenever emotions became intense.

Even before Ted's birth, we were concerned that she would be unable to reach out and engage her infant; she had already demonstrated this problem with her first chld. We also thought that if her new infant tended to be withdrawn, the difficulties would be compounded. When Ted was born he was a flaccid infant, with little muscle tone. He could alert for short periods of time visually and respond to sounds. Generally, however, he tended to tune out rather quickly. During his first month, he tended to sleep more than 18 hours a day and this pattern increased rather than decreased. Mrs. A. seemed only too content to leave little Ted sleeping comfortably, often saying, "He can't get hurt if he is sleeping." Interestingly enough, they both seemed to enjoy rhythmically rocking and relaxing with each other when Ted was briefly awake for his feedings. Neither Ted nor Mrs. A. was able to proffer the interesting engagement needed to lengthen the periods of alertness.

A program was begun in which Mrs. A. was taught how to offer Ted interesting and novel experiences. For example, high rhythmic sounds, certain facial gestures, rubbing his hands gently, and holding him in certain positions were experimented with and found to help him tune in and stay alert. As her baby became more alert, Mrs. A. became anxious, began to have nightmares with destructive themes, and wanted to "let him sleep again." She was able, however, to begin dealing with her fears of hurting him and "doing things wrong," which permitted her to engage her infant more spontaneously. Homeostasis and healthy attachment subsequently formed.

CASE 2

Hilda was a robust-looking, sizeable infant who alerted quickly and easily. She was the kind of baby, her mother said, "we've always dreamed about having." Mother was a confident, slightly hypomanic woman, organized around hysterical lines, with no evidence of ego defects or borderline personality features. She talked at a rapid pace and in an enthusiastic high-pitched voice. Father was a subdued, conservative, observant man.

As Hilda began spending more time with her mother in the hospital, it was noticed that she became extremely rigid and cried most of the time. Mother continually tried to comfort her by rocking and talking but the rigidity and crying only seemed to continue. In the hands of the nurses, or when alone in the nursery, Hilda habituated very well to all but auditory stimuli. When presented with auditory stimuli, particularly high-pitched sounds, she showed the same rigidity and ceaseless crying that she evidenced with mother. Repeated presentations of a rattle, for example, kept Hilda upset, whereas another infant would normally habituate to such a stimulus after a few trials.

The initial impression, therefore, was that Hilda's sensitivity to auditory stimulation was responsible for her rigidity and intense crying. Mother's high-pitched, hypomanic vocal quality appeared to be especially difficult for her to handle.

A program was begun in which mother, after being instructed about Hilda's special sensitivity to sound, was taught to speak in a low-pitched, rhythmic voice, which still led to some rigidity, but not of the previous severity. Father was particularly good with Hilda because of his slower speaking patterns and lower tones. At the same time, mother was taught to soothe Hilda with rhythmic rocking movements and the presentation of interesting visual stimuli which helped distract her from the upsetting sounds. The exercise would begin with quiet rocking, and proceed to an occasional attempt to catch her attention with an interesting visual stimulus. After she seemed to be engaged, the gradual presentation of the noxious auditory stimulus was presented in its least distressing form. Hilda slowly learned to integrate an increasing range of auditory stimuli. She became a comfortable, relaxed, and alert infant with both her parents.

In this case, time was on the side of the intervention approach. In many such instances the infant's own maturation will help him overcome such sensitivities. It is only when the sensitivities go unrecognized that the early noxious experiences can set up a growth-inhibiting pattern of relating whereby mother may feel rejected and the infant may come to experience the world as disturbing and painful.

CASE 3

Mrs. C. was a chronically depressed, withdrawn, very large woman with large, disproportional facial features, who lived in a rural area under fairly primitive conditions. While she was willing to work with us, it was only in a suspicious, guarded fashion. She adamantly avoided anyone's intrusion into her or her family's life. At times she would permit us to visit, perhaps once out of three scheduled visits. Often, after our arrival, she would look away from us, or sit silently, glaring in angry suspicion. However, she would soon respond to slow and patient talking, and about half an hour later would warm up and begin sharing some of her concerns about being pregnant and expecting another baby. She mentioned briefly that she had already encountered severe difficulties with the emotional and cognitive development of two older children. She was very worried that her baby would "not be okay." Her elaboration on this theme was her fantasy of giving birth to a "monster," and associations with deformity and worries as to whether the baby would be responsive to her. It was almost as though she were afraid that her infant would be like her both physically and emotionally and would not provide the kind of reaching out that was necessary for her to be responsive (as we had learned through our earlier contacts with her).

Her baby was a large, physically healthy infant, but lethargic and, in his first months, tending to be unresponsive to various environmental stimulations. His muscle tone was not good. When in an alert state (which he found difficult to maintain), little Jim tended to get irritable very easily. It was as though the range within which Jim could be engaged was limited. He was usually withdrawn or asleep, and when alert, irritable or crying. Needless to say, Mrs. C. was quite tense and confused about how to relate to her baby, and became even more apprehensive, suspicious, and guarded toward us.

Attempts to help her deal with her feelings of having

created a "deformed baby" were not successful (though, in fact, her baby was physically quite healthy and neurologically competent within the usual variations in normality), nor were attempts to teach her ways of maintaining her baby in a relaxed and engaged state for reasonably longer periods of time. It had been found, for example, that Jim enjoyed certain low-pitched sounds and would alert and brighten up on hearing them. Mrs. C., however, would persist in trying to engage him with intrusive high-pitched sounds and/or pushing her finger in Jim's mouth, while staring apprehensively at the baby, as if to say "How dare you not respond to me?" Although Mrs. C. tolerated our visits and even seemed able to begin dealing with her own feelings and to recognize some of the individual differences in her infant, she moved out of the area suddenly, and the programs developed for her and her baby were not able to be continued.

Her parents who lived in the area told us that she had gone to live with relatives in another state and was not interested in hearing from us, but might be willing to see us again if she "returned in the future."

CASE 4

Mrs. D., an extraordinarily narcissistic, self-absorbed, borderline woman, dealt with her pregnancy by continuing her experimentation with various drugs, including marijuana and cocaine. She focused almost entirely on her intermittently satisfying relationships with a number of boyfriends, including the father of the anticipated offspring. Little conscious emotional attention was focused on pregnancy or the expected baby. When Laura was born she was a very healthy, average-sized little girl who was capable of being both alert and engaged with the world, and at the same time of relaxing comfortably. She showed unusually good muscle tone, good capacities for orientation, habituation, self-consolation, and other attributes associated with good homeostatic potential. However, Mrs. D. dealt with her new baby much in the same manner as she had during pregnancy. She was preoccupied with her personal life, and would often stare off into space as she breastfed her baby, holding Laura's body as far as she could from her own. It was a rather dramatic picture, to see this rigid person with a preoccupied, faraway stare on her face, engaging in the physical intimacy of breastfeeding. Still, little Laura had a good capacity for sucking in spite of mother's wooden posture and distant emotionality.

Soon, however, mother's inability to offer engagement with the animate world and/or soothing nurturing experiences undermined Laura's solid constitutional capacities. Her capacity for being alert diminished during the first month, and by one-and-a-half months she was vacillating between periods of alertness and withdrawn and apathetic facial expressions. It was hard for her to orient visually to any animate objects, and she would go into uncontrollable crying fits in which it was hard to soothe her. When she cried this way, mother became even more aloof and refused to consider the relationship between herself and her baby except to talk about what a nuisance she was and how her crying had interfered with mother's lovemaking with a new boyfriend the evening before.

Laura began to lose weight and her developmental progress also began to lag, so that we became concerned over her failure to thrive. At this point Mrs. D. and her infant moved a two-hour drive away from the intervention program and concern over Laura's continued loss of weight and developmental lags became much greater. Through coordinated efforts with the departments of health and social services in Mrs. D.'s new area, and visits by one of our staff members, sufficient nutrition was made available to Mrs. D. at her new location, where she was employed as a housekeeper for a single male. But while she did not lose further weight, Laura barely maintained her present level, and continued to have a withdrawn, apathetic appearance with little engagement with the animate or inanimate world. During our periodic visits and through work with the health and social services departments, attempts were made to encourage Mrs. D. to engage her infant more and to deal with her own underlying preoccupations. These efforts were not successful.

Through continued personal contact and occasional telephone calls, a relationship was maintained between Mrs. D. and her clinical worker. When her new job did not work out because of personal difficulties in her relationship with her employer, Mrs. D. returned to our area. She accepted our suggestion that she and her baby come into the Infant Center where both could work with staff on a daily basis.

In a brief two-month period, during which Laura was able to work with a social worker trainee and Mrs. D. was able to meet with her clinical worker on a daily basis, there was a dramatic turnaround in this dyad's developmental pattern. Laura began to gain weight and to become interested in the inanimate world. She caught up developmentally to the extent that she was within the average range in her eight-month Bayley exam and showed an interested, if somewhat uneven, affective curiosity about the animate world. Laura did show a mildly promiscuous quality in her relationships, in contrast to the typical eight-month-old's cautiousness. She sought out any human contact. Nevertheless, the two to three hours per day of warm personal engagement, holding and cuddling, and interesting engagement via the various sensory modalities, focused on a combination of animate and inanimate experiences, and, in particular, on face-to-face interaction, served to reduce for the most part Laura's pattern of developmental and physical retardation.

Work with Mrs. D. was slower, but she did begin to see that anger and withdrawal from her infant was her way of dealing with her own feelings of frustration. She also became somewhat aware that she saw her infant as competing with her for "life's goodies." This permitted at least islands of affective interchange between mother and daughter. By the time Laura was nine months old, Mrs. D. was able to provide adequate physical care in terms of food, nurturance, and visits to medical clinics, etc., and enough affective interchange to maintain Laura's interest in the world and the process of differentiation she had begun. However, the depth and intensity of this beginning human attachment was not at age- or stage-expected levels and we were concerned that Laura would have a promiscuous orientation toward the human world. Work continues with Mrs. D. and with Laura to see if this affective developmental issue cannot also be successfully resolved.

CASE 5

Mrs. E. was a chronic schizophrenic who, during the prenatal period, had concerns about having a dead baby. After giving birth to a very robust infant, she became worried every time the baby slept and would ask, "Is the baby dead?" Islands of delusional thinking would focus at times on not being sure whether she was herself dead, whether ghosts existed, whether baby was dead. We reassured mother frequently that this robust, alert, engaging infant was quite alive. We were, of course, concerned that Mrs. E. would not be capable of fostering homeostasis in her son. Would her delusional processes involve the baby? Would she misread fundamental needs for physical care or physical protection? Her capacity for engagement seemed adequate as we watched her hold her son, rhythmically rock him, and appear to enjoy his extraordinary capacity for engaging her.

Initial therapeutic work focused on trying to help Mrs. E. contain her islands of delusional thinking (she did have a reality orientation in some areas of her life). She was able, in the first few months after the birth of the child, to understand that when he slept, it meant that he was resting and did not mean that he was dead. Similarly, when her child occasionally pushed her away—he was an active and almost feisty baby at times — she could understand that this did not mean that he was trying to kill her. On the few instances when he threw up and she thought at first that she had poisoned him with the formula, she was able to see that this was simply an upset stomach. Over the first two months, through constant reality orientation and feedback, it was pointed out to her that her delusional thinking was misapplied to the baby. While her concerns with death, poison, murder, etc., remained with respect to her husband and with respect to her relationship with her therapist, she was able on her own (as observed by visits at the Infant Center and in home visits) to correct her tendency toward delusional thinking with respect to her baby. For example, she would begin by saying, "Oh, oh, he is sleeping, he is *not* dead like I used to think."

Mrs. E. was also on phenothiazines (major tranquillizers), which, while helping her achieve some reality orientation, had not totally solved her chronic delusional thinking. Her son, however, was progressing reasonably well, and Mrs. E. was making remarkable progress in keeping him out of her delusional pattern. A warm, empathic relationship with her clinician was an important factor in her progress, as was the constant feedback given to her. It was anticipated that, even though Mrs. E. was developing a very deep attachment to the child, her problem would become even more severe when he reached the stage of somatic-psychological differentiation and she was called on to read more subtle cues. In the therapeutic program, then, the worker anticipated this stage and began to help Mrs. E. to learn to read her child's signals more accurately. When Mrs. E. was hungry, for example, she would frequently feel that her *baby* felt hungry and try to overfeed him. She was able to see that she was projecting her own hunger onto the infant, and to learn, although somewhat mechanically, to pay attention to his signals.

CASE 6

Another chronic schizophrenic mother, Mrs. F., while

using a great deal of her own drugs, including marijuana, was reluctant to use any of the medications, such as phenothiazine, that had been prescribed for her when she was in the state mental hospital. She evidenced early difficulties not only in reading her child's basic signals for protection, but also in providing such comforting experiences as rocking or cuddling. Mrs. F. was deeply concerned about issues of murder and "shooting people" and claimed to have a gun hidden somewhere in the house. Yet, paradoxically, and not surprisingly, she was extremely worried that she would harm her child. As a consequence, she held her baby rigidly, and somewhat at a distance from her body, to make sure that she didn't "smother it and keep it from breathing." There was an immense amount of tension evident when she was holding and feeding the infant, who began a pattern of regurgitating his feedings. (It is interesting to note that during demonstrations, when our clinician would show Mrs. F. how to feed her son, he was able to keep his food down without regurgitating. It was only when Mrs. F. fed him that he regurgitated.) In spite of the regurgitations, however, he was gaining weight on an appropriate timetable and it was apparent that he was able to hold down enough food for nutritional purposes. Needless to say, there was concern about Mrs. F.'s capacity to offer the most fundamental elements of physical care—protection for her son and maintaining adequate nutrition. Although the infant was an alert and engaging youngster, he did at times become hyperreactive and did have a hard time consoling himself and allowing others to console him. He was, however, a youngster who gave good, clear, loud signals when he was hungry or uncomfortable. This made it somewhat easier for Mrs. F. to read him and to try out the suggestions that our staff clinician made to her regarding holding the child more tenderly and rocking him more rhythmically than she had been able to do on her own.

The provision of structure and support, with daily visits either at home or at the Infant Center, proved pivotal in diminishing Mrs. F.'s anxiety about hurting her son. As she gradually became able to relax, her son could also relax, and slowly the intensity and frequency of his regurgitations decreased, although they did not stop altogether. To date, he has continued to gain weight and she has become somewhat less anxious about hurting him. The staff is still quite concerned about Mrs. F.'s capacity for providing the necessary protective environment, given her concern with her own impulses and her claims to have a gun hidden in the house. An increasingly open relationship is developing, however, between Mrs. F. and the staff clinician, and she occasionally talks about "sharing where the gun is." At the same time, she is talking rather more openly about her aggressive fantasies and her relationships with other people. Our strategy is to maintain sufficient daily contact with her to monitor the balance between her delusional capacities and her reality orientation, particularly as it relates to her infant, while at the same time continuing to build on the already existing positive relationship to help Mrs. F. become more secure.

CASE 7

Mrs. G. was another schizophrenic mother. Her husband was deaf, and appeared to be a borderline psychotic. The two had a history of giving up their children to foster care. (The children are impaired psychologically and cognitively.) But when Mrs. G.'s pregnancy began while she was in the state hospital, she adamantly insisted that she would keep the child. During the first few months after delivery of a rather large, somewhat lethargic and "floppy" infant, concern over dehydration was expressed by the public health nurse after a routine visit. The baby was taken to the hospital, where he was rehydrated and then given up to foster care until Mrs. G. could assure an appropriate environment. The clinical team already involved with Mrs. G. helped her deal with her sense of loss, and began a process of mediation between Mrs. G., the attorney she had hired to sue for the return of her child, the public health and foster care people in the county, and the relevant social service agencies. Her clinician was able to help Mrs. G. go back on the medication she had recently stopped taking, and, by encouraging her to practice with those of her older children who were still with her, helped her to prepare for the return of her infant to her own home.

Independent legal opinion was that Mrs. G. could easily win back her child with appropriate legal counsel. It was felt that she was not sufficiently impaired for Protective Services to keep the child in foster care. Thus, it was important to help her learn to take care of her child once he was returned to her. By joining our own efforts with those of the public health nurses, we were able to set up a program of daily visits either to the home or the Infant Center, so as to provide Mrs. G. with structure and support in the daily care of the youngster. When it finally became possible for the youngster to return home permanently, he received appropriate nutrition and formed a rich emotional attachment to his mother. With assistance, Mrs. G. has learned to reach out to her son and not to take his tendency for withdrawal and apathy as a sign of rejection. Mother and father have been worked with as a couple, and father, who is more outgoing and less preoccupied than mother, has been able to help establish a pattern of engagement with their new baby. While the work on this case is still in the early phases, the infant has, at four months, made normal cognitive progress. While he still has some tendency toward withdrawal from the inanimate world, and some mild gaze aversion, he is fairly interested in the human world and taking more and more pleasure in his parents. With the continuation of a structured support system, the earlier concerns about physical protection and adequate nutrition have disappeared.

SUMMARY

The above cases illustrate a number of characteristics

of clinical work and preventive intervention during the stage of homeostasis. We have found generally that if we can succeed in developing a regular and predictable structure with the mother and/or father, they can begin to set up a regular and predictable structure for their infant. Where, however, a chronic schizophrenic mother skips appointments, shuns her medication, and makes herself hard for us to reach, we almost invariably find a characteristic pattern of deterioration in the child, resulting from poor nutrition and/or lack of physical care, as in the case of Jim and Mrs. C. (case 3). With such mothers and their families, considerable therapeutic work must take place before their delusions and patterns of behavior no longer interfere with the development of a regular and predictable relationship.

In discussing preventive intervention and therapeutic approaches during the stage of homeostasis, it is also important to emphasize the importance of having all the relevant community service agencies and organizations working in harmony. Often, protective service, social service, and public health and clinical service programs may work in isolation from each other, or even worse, at cross purposes (often unknowingly). Where fragmentation of personality already exists, it is imperative to offer a clinical relationship and an integrated system of support services which can provide the structure for more effective functioning.

Somatic Level of Organization: Phase II

The second step in development is characterized by learning by consequences. As the human organism develops, it begins to show a response to consequences: The infant is able to repeat action patterns that bring satisfaction. Eventually the infant can distinguish patterns that lead to certain ends, distinguish means from ends, and can even use intermediary devices to achieve a desired end. The differentiation of means from ends and learning by feedback, as described by Piaget, might be conceptualized more broadly as the capacity for learning by consequences. Our formulation here encompasses differentiation not only of means from ends in the impersonal or inanimate world, but also of self from nonself, because in order to observe one's impact on the environment, one must be able to differentiate oneself from another and from the environment, and experience the differential impact of consequences.

During this early stage of development the young in-

This material originally appeared in slightly different form in the author's *Intelligence and Adaptation: An Integration of Psychoanalytic and Piagetian Developmental Psychology* © 1979, International Universities Press, New York, New York.

fant still explores his world by using his somatic system. He learns about internal feeling states through experiences inside the body, and he explores the external personal and impersonal world through his actions on it and its actions on him. We observe a growing capacity to use intermediary devices to gain ends in both the animate and inanimate worlds — for example, through the use of imitation in the interpersonal world or the use of a carpet to pull something closer.

That these experiences are at the level of somatic intelligence, rather than the later level of psychological representational intelligence, is evidenced by the fact that later on, when the capacity for mental representation has been established, there is a regression at the representational level to magical thinking, a dedifferentiation of means-ends relationships. While a certain amount of logic or causality has been established at the somatic level, the youngster is not able to transfer it to the representational level right away. This observation supports Piaget's hypothesis that learning in terms of the internal world is also primarily a somatic kind of learning. During this stage, schemes are probably internalized in terms of beginning mental structures, but these schemes are of the action patterns used to deal with the environment, with interpersonal relationships, and with the beginning differentiation of internal states. They are not yet representations of either whole objects, animate or inanimate, or the whole self.

As the infant develops through the second half of the first year, behavior at all levels — cognitive, affective, and social — becomes more differentiated and organized. Although the conceptualization of stranger anxiety (Spitz, Emde, and Metcalf, 1970) as an indicator of a certain level of psychological organization may be an oversimplification, this reaction — or, more important, the appearance of different responses to the nonprimary caregiver — does signal the capacity at this time to organize perceptions into more complex units and make discriminations between the primary caregiver and others. The capacity for these discriminations, by inference, leads to the impression that the infant has a greater capacity for differentiating various organizations of internal experience, including both memory and present perceptions. The complex behaviors of surprise and anticipation, for example, appear between nine and ten months (Charlesworth, 1969). In general, affect and cognition appear more connected (Brody and Axelrad, 1966, 1970).

Behavior during the second year of life gradually becomes more organized, original, and intentional. Ainsworth (1973) and Waters, Matas, and Sroufe (1975), among others, have highlighted the existence of more organized behavior patterns through the study of complex patterns of behavior such as attachment. Whether attachment in itself is the most useful paradigm for the organization of infant behavior is perhaps less important than the fact that investigators have developed high-order behavioral constructs indicating (though perhaps not intentionally) their respect for the infant's greater organizational capacities. Studies of the vicissitudes of attachment and separation have increased our understanding of later behavior and even made some limited predictions possible.

As development proceeds, the capacity for new levels of organization becomes identifiable, e.g., imitative and identificatory behavior, the beginnings of a sense of self, person and object permanence (Décarie, 1962; Mahler, Pine and Bergman, 1975; Piaget, 1936). While we should not lose sight of the adaptive value of basic rhythms, which continue, the infant now has some capacity both for delay and detour (intermediary devices) and for originality and initiative (Piaget's tertiary circular reactions). This capacity affords greater flexibility in dealing with and, to some degree, determining internal and external experience. Earlier we illustrated this advance in terms of the young child's ability to woo mother's attention in a variety of ways, rather than just being frustrated and crying as in the first month of life. The youngster's use of imitation to satisfy himself for a short time or his actively leading mother to a desired play object are other illustrations.

The toddler's capacity for behavioral organization, initiative, and internalizations (as illustrated by increased imitative behavior) actually represents a transitional stage between somatic and representational levels of organization. The organization, originality, and initiative we see in tertiary circular reactions in the interpersonal and emotional sphere set the foundation for the next level of integration.

2
Attachment (2–7 Months)

While in the first few months of life we can observe the infant's efforts to achieve homeostasis, by two to seven months we should see a higher level of organization indicative of the evolving capacity for human attachment (Spitz, 1965; Emde, Gaensbauer, and Harmon, 1976). Now that the infant has achieved some capacity for self-regulation and for engaging the world, he becomes selectively interested in the human world, more attuned to interpersonal interaction and better able to form a special relationship with the primary caregivers, as evidenced by the social smile and by his beginning capacity to engage in complicated, clearly affective human communications (Charlesworth, 1969; Tennes, Emde, Kisley, and Metcalf, 1972; Brazelton, Koslowski, and Main, 1974; Stern, 1974a). The nature of these communications parallels the gradual development in the cognitive sphere of basic schemes of causality — means-ends relationships (Piaget, 1962; Greenspan, 1979). The capacity for human attachment is thus both the basis for and a precursor of the later differentiation of self from nonself.

Infant Capacities

The capacity for attachment originates in the homeostatic experience achieved between the infant and primary caretaker(s), that is, in the quality of the feelings and reciprocal interactions characterizing their relationship. The use of multiple sensory modalities (holding, touching, sucking; proprioceptive, visual, auditory) is a primary indicator of the infant's capacity for attachment. The adaptive infant is able to mobilize and integrate all his available sensory and motor equipment to engage his caretakers in varied and increasingly complex interactions. Just as in the homeostatic phase, specific defects in sensory and motor modalities may not lead to an overall compromise in the quality of attachment — the blind or deaf infant, for example, may compensate by means of other modalities.

The most severe attachment disorder appears in the autistic youngster who, because of genetic or consititutional difficulties or severe early environmental trauma, never fully achieves homeostasis and therefore does not move on to the task of human attachment. The infant whose constitutional differences make physical touch or other kinds of human stimulation painful may also have a proclivity for a disorder of attachment. Anaclitic depression, psychophysiological difficulties (vomiting, rumination), failure to thrive (metabolic depression, marasmus), feeding and sleep disturbances may all be related to attachment disorders.

A second indicator of the capacity for attachment is the degree of relatedness and synchrony in the dyadic interactions — how the infant and caretaker respond to each other (Stern, 1974a, 1974b). The adaptive infant is able to use and to read and respond to a wide range of cues, and is able to recover from a momentary disappointment when his signals are not met. Thus when his mother is preoccupied or depressed, he is able to recapture her attention by smiling or reaching out, while making appealing sounds until she is finally able to respond.

In contrast, the maladaptive infant may misread the caretaker's signals, or withdraw at the slightest hint that his own signals are not being met. In some instances, infant and mother may by physically intact, and may even have a range of stable affects available to them, yet somehow each member of the dyad appears to be out of sync with the other. When they do come together, each one seems preoccupied, as though they do not belong together. Here we may find that their lack of attachment stems not from a paucity of modalities, or from an inability to invest themselves in each other, but rather from the way in which they misread each other's signals and continue to respond in terms of their mismatched communication patterns.

A third indicator of attachment capacity is the range, depth, and phase-appropriateness of the feelings expressed and experienced by the dyad. The adaptive infant experiences deep, rich pleasure in his attachment with his caregivers. We see a wide range of affect, and often a buildup of low-level excitement to extreme pleasure and joy, followed by relaxation. On anticipating breast feeding, for example, the infant may smile with extreme delight, without becoming disorganized. The attachment pattern also accommodates negative affects such as protest, early forms of rage, and assertiveness. To carry the above example a bit further, if on occasion the mother prematurely stops breast feeding, the infant's desire for more sucking, physical contact, and milk will be expressed in easily understood affective facial expressions and body postures rather than in disorganized motor responses. In short, the infant seems comfortable when involved with mother across the whole spectrum of human emotional possibilities.

The maladaptive infant, in contrast, may evidence only mechanical or intermittent excitation. Gradations of pleasure do not seem to be evident. The affect pattern may be representative of only one type of affect — mild, compliant pleasure, for example, with no capacity for protest or expression of frustration. Or it may involve only protest, with little pleasure and only occasional rest and relaxation.

The final indicator of attachment capacity is resilience to stress. The adaptive infant retains the fundamental capacity to become involved with the primary caretakers even when stressed by his own discomforts, though perhaps at a more subdued level. Even when compromised altogether (by illness, for example, or separation for a brief time), the capacity for attachment is recovered. It is never entirely disrupted. While the infant may show protest and even temporary gaze aversion, there is, with some wooing, re-engagement in the attachment patterns. The maladaptive infant, in contrast, shows relatively less capacity to resist stress, and the degree to which his hunger or his mother's tension disrupts his attachment ability provides a picture of the lack of integrity of his early attachment patterns.

It cannot be emphasized too strongly that these four indicators of attachment capacity must be viewed in relation to one another, and that each contributes to what we have called the final common pathway by which the individual organizes his experience of the world. Even at this early stage of development, the individual's unique personal signature begins to emerge.

Environmental Characteristics

The growth-promoting environment offers an affectively and physically rich, pleasurable, stable involvement to the infant. At the same time as it is "in love" with the infant, it woos him to "fall in love." With an infant who is subdued or unresponsive, for example, the growth-promoting environment experiments until it finds those experiences that are pleasurable and will engage the infant in the human world. Perhaps colored lights turned on the caretaker's face may draw the infant's interest, thereby diminishing gaze aversion. Or with the infant who vacillates between hyperreactivity and withdrawal, smiling, cooing, or using inanimate objects as a transition to the human world may be used to engage the infant in his momentary states of alert attention. Slowly, these small islands of affective interchange can be enlarged and built upon by the caretaker. Obviously, it requires a great deal of confidence, patience, and emotional stability to work with each of the sensory and motor modalities and their various combinations to find just the right pleasurable experience. The growth-promoting mother is not easily disappointed when the infant turns away from her gaze or the sound of her voice.

The environment can be assessed along the same four dimensions we have noted above. Does it make use of multiple sensory and motor modalities? Does it combine these modalities in an effort to broaden the range of the infant's experience? Does it read and respond to the infant's cues? What is the range and depth of affect experienced by the caretaker? Can the caretaker express unpleasant feelings as well as pleasant ones? Are its affects shallow? Are they limited to angry and controlling emotions? Do protest, disappointment, despair, or depression disrupt the dyad? Are attachment patterns stable enough that they can recover from such disruption?

Like the adaptive infant, the growth-promoting environment will begin to exhibit preferred modes of establishing attachment. A particular type of smile or a certain kind of rhythmic interaction will mark the beginning of the development of a personal style of parent-infant attachment.

While the growth-promoting environment is capable of a wide range of affects, those of pleasurable and loving experiences outweigh unpleasant feelings. The feeling of being in love with and enjoying the infant is not one that can be mechanically evoked. There are times when the growth-promoting environment quite naturally, spontaneously, and *relatively* unambivalently wishes to entice and engage the infant. But when ambivalence is great, or when anger, depression, or the feeling of being overwhelmed begin to dominate the emotions and undermine loving engagement, the growth-promoting environment takes notice and attempts either to alter those external circumstances that may be causing stress or to gain insight into those internal conflicts that may compromise pleasurable emotional engagement with the infant.

Even the most frustrating infant — the excessively irritable and colicky child, for example — has moments when he or she is capable of joyful interaction. No matter how temporarily distressed, overwhelmed, or depressed, the optimally adaptive caretaker maintains a fundamental optimism as he or she waits for the child to at last sleep through the night. Certainly, fleeting wishes to "give the infant away" or wishes that he were never born are present, but the growth-promoting environment is aware of these wishes and attempts to understand them.

The growth-inhibiting environment, in contrast, is emotionally distant and highly ambivalent. Schizoid or autistic-like caretakers, or very depressed and preoccupied caretakers — those caretakers, in other words, who are often devoid of emotional interest — mark the extreme end of the continuum on which we measure the environment. Less severely inhibiting caretakers may be capable only of shallow, mechanical, or narrowly circumscribed affects. The smile that should accompany pleasure, for example, is not the deep, rich smile we observe in the growth-promoting caretaker, nor do we observe affective gradations of interest and curiosity. Even with respect to negative experiences, we do not find an appropriate depth of emotional expression. Sometimes these caretakers show deep affects only along a single avenue of care — scheduling, for example. Perhaps they are involved in a continual power struggle, determined not to allow the protest behaviors of the infant to "control" them.

The growth-inhibiting environment may show severe inhibition in the use of available sensory and motor modalities. Some caretakers, for example, will only relate to the infant from afar. Conflicted about experiencing pleasure through tactile sensations, they may hold the infant in a wooden posture, avoiding gentle touching and nuzzling even while they are cooing or rhythmically rocking their infant. On a more subtle level, we may observe the use of vision, holding, touching, and rhythmic movements in engaging the infant, but little vocalization and appeal to the learning potential that auditory stimulation can have for the child. Or there may be a nearly exclusive use of sound, with little or no comforting visual or tactile involvement. The mother may hold the infant at an angle that prohibits eye contact such that he cannot experience the joy of the human smile.

The growth-inhibiting environment continually misreads the infant's cues. The primary caretaker may project his or her own needs onto the infant, interpreting the infant's smile as a demand, his reaching out as a threat. Or the infant's irritability may be viewed as anger directed toward the caretakers rather than as an expression of his desire for comforting. Such misreading of cues, even when the caretaker's range of affects and sensorimotor engagement is appropriate, may undermine the integrity of early attachment patterns and may prevent the development of preferred modes of affective engagement.

The growth-inhibiting environment shows little capacity for maintaining the stability and integrity of early attachment patterns in the face of stress. The infant's crying or apathy as it results from illness may cause the parent to withdraw, and perhaps to feel rejected, just when he or she is most interested in engaging the infant. Instead of attempting to re-engage the infant, the caretaker then becomes preoccupied in other areas—family relationships, for example. This preoccupation then further undermines the process of re-engagement. Compare this with the growth-promoting parent's ability to lose him or herself in the relationship with the infant and thereby escape the harsher realities of the outside world.

Finally, we must carefully examine the emotional integrity of the caretakers themselves. Conditions ranging from severe depression to psychosis to narcissistic self-absorption will of course play a part in any failure of attachment, as will family stress, whether owing to financial pressures or interpersonal conflict.

Common Fears in the Caretaker

A number of typical fears may interfere with the development of appropriate attachment patterns. Many of these are quite common and occur in mild form in all normal mothers, fathers, or other caretakers. In exaggerated form, however, they can begin to disrupt the environment's efforts to foster attachment with the infant.

One is the fear of merging with the infant and losing the sense of oneself. In one case, a mother responded to her healthy, competent, robust baby and his affectionate longings for her by trying prematurely to teach him independence. Thus, when he reached out for her and tried to nuzzle, she would move away, feeling that he should learn to fend for himself. Underneath, of course, she was afraid of the intimacy the infant offered.

Fear of rejection is another frequently expressed concern, especially with regard to infants who are excessively irritable and have trouble focusing attention on their caretakers, or who are apathetic and withdrawn. These youngsters require a caretaker secure enough to woo them until they respond. The parent who is sensitive to rejection may find it extremely difficult to woo such children, or, instead, may "overwoo" them and become intrusive and controlling.

As the infant begins to become a person and to show his capacity for social interaction, he will often exhibit great joy and contentment. Some parents may secretly envy the baby his calm and dependent states. One basically competent mother, very uncomfortable with her envious feelings, dealt with them by trying to overcontrol and overprotect her infant. Another mother, less mature than the one just described, vacillated from one day to the next between a responsive interest in her infant and a view of him as selfish, greedy, and spoiled. The fear of one's own envy, then, can be as growth-inhibiting as the fear of rejection or merger.

Fears of damaging or hurting the infant can lead to overprotection and overintrusiveness, or, just the opposite, withdrawal. These are often related to the caretaker's own hostile feelings, just as the fear of sexual intimacy may be the source of physical avoidance.

Principles of Preventive Intervention and Treatment

Just as in the phase of homeostasis, the primary focus of preventive intervention and/or remedial help is to transform a growth-inhibiting environment into a growth-promoting environment in the context of the individual needs of the infant. Once again, we examine the infant's sensorimotor modalities, the relative strength of his sending power, and the range of his affect. We also study the range of sensory modalities available to the caretakers, the range and stability of the affect they express, and their capacity in general to woo the infant and fall in love. We then assess the way in which the infant and parent interact with each other, read each other's signals, and respond to those signals in appropriate ways.

Thus, where an infant does not seem able to use all his sensory modalities, where, for example, he is not using vision or is avoiding gaze contact, we work with the parents to teach them how to use novel stimuli gradually to engage the infant visually — various facial expressions, perhaps, that would increase the infant's response to them as human beings. Where the infant is hypersensitive to one or another form of sensory stimuli, we may instruct the caretaker to avoid such stimuli in the early attachment. Then, as individual patterns of comforting engagement are found with respect to other modalities, the caretaker may gradually, in benign increments, expose the infant to increasing stimulation in the hypersensitive area, comforting him all the while in the more pleasurable modalities.

Where the infant shows only shallow emotions — weak, transitory smiles, for example — the parents can be taught to find more intense experiences of pleasure for the child, certain soft vocalizations or visual stimuli, that can be built on systematically to deepen the infant's capacity for joy.

If the infant's initial attachment patterns lack stability, if they are easily disrupted by his own discomfort or by the environment's inability to read his cues, the parents can be taught actively to seek re-engagement with the child so that he does not experience long periods of non-attachment and, indeed, can recover from such periods quickly. The environment can also be encouraged to help the infant achieve a sense of personal uniqueness by fostering favorite modes of interaction.

In all these areas, educative modes may suffice so long as the caretakers are emotionally competent. Education may help these parents interpret the infant's cues and expand and integrate sensory modalities so as to broaden the infant's range of affects. But where parents are emotionally incompetent and where intrapersonal or interpersonal problems interfere with the development of age-appropriate attachment patterns, a more integrated program involving emotional support and exploration in addition to education may be necessary. A depressed or narcissistically self-absorbed parent may require emotional exploration in order to experience loving feelings for his or her infant. The borderline or psychotic caretaker who perceives the infant as an enemy may need such exploration and support in order to perceive the infant more appropriately and shield him from distortions of reality. Obsessive caretakers with conflicts over pleasure may need brief emotional support in order to engage their physical and sensory capacities. Or, alternatively, they may require more extensive therapeutic approaches so as to resolve underlying conflicts.

To help parents and caretakers understand and work

through their difficulties in the phase of attachment, the clinician must recognize the unique way a particular infant, or phase of infant development, contributes to maladaptive parental patterns. The overly intense, clinging infant, the withdrawn infant, the labile and excessively irritable infant, the very calm, alert infant may each evoke different aspects of earlier parental patterns of behavior, unresolved conflicts, and typical modes of identification. Similarly, the family or extended family may reveal characteristic group patterns that undermine optimal attachment. Again, the caretakers must be helped to recognize the disruptive influence of patterns of sibling or spousal jealousy or disorganized communications as they result from the infant's entry into the family circle.

Where severe stress, poverty, or other socioeconomic factors interfere with adaptation in this phase, cooperation among health, mental health, social service, and legal service agencies is critical in providing needed supports. These can range from relief such as that provided by homemakers and surrogate caretakers to psychological relief from unusual financial or legal pressures.

Finally, it should be noted that external, interpersonal, and intrapersonal factors rarely exist in isolation from one another. Programs designed to address maladaptive patterns in this phase of development must be able to draw on a wide system of supports in helping the infant and his family.

Clinical Illustrations

CASE 8

Mrs. H., a borderline psychotic mother with paranoid and depressive features, gave birth to a good-sized, healthy-looking infant. In an initial examination, however, the infant showed a tendency toward slight irritability and tense musculature. During his first few months, when irritated or otherwise frustrated, he showed a tendency to arch his back, push and turn away from his rigid mother, who would look at him as if to determine whether he was going to behave himself. Mrs. H. had short periods in which she could relax and hold Richard softly and tenderly, nuzzle him, and occasionally seduce him into joyful visual exchanges in which the two gazed at each other and smiled. More often, however, she would relate to him much as she related to her therapist and other adults, with a somewhat suspicious and aloof stare, holding him rigidly, somewhat away from her body. When afterward she tried to cuddle him, Richard, now in his fourth month, systematically turned away to look at anything other than his mother, arching his back in a fashion even more pronounced than before and pushing her away from him, leaving her, in turn, free to reestablish her distant relationship with him. At these times, she could verbalize her feeling of rejection and her sense that "something bad was going on."

Her own early history revealed that she had been given up by her parents when she was only a few months old to be brought up by friends in the neighborhood, having apparently been fathered by someone other than her mother's husband. Beatings by her foster mother and the early death of this woman were followed by episodes of depression, severe suspiciousness, and withdrawal. These symptoms, and a brief period of hospitalization in a state facility, characterized her early and late adolescence. Relationships with others had been intermittent and had the same characteristic as the relationship with little Richard. Treatment in the past had been irregular, with Mrs. H. stopping after a few weeks as soon as an acute crisis subsided.

By four months of age, Richard showed a capacity to become interested in the world and to manipulate inanimate objects. He was also able to maintain an alert attention span, and though he did have a tendency to become irritable, with tense musculature, his overall homeostatic capacities for engagement and relaxation were reasonably good.

His lack of engagement with the animate world was quite worrisome, however. When he was held by the clinician or infant specialist, he would arch his back and look away, just as he did with his mother. Because the fundamental capacity for human involvement seemed to be compromised, an intervention program was developed in which we tried to help each member of the dyad be more available to the other. We found, for example, that Richard would look at a picture of a human face if it was painted on a piece of cardboard. He would become interested in the various facial shapes, following them from left to right and up and down. At the Infant Center our infant worker developed a game in which she would first show Richard the cardboard face, then quickly drop it to expose her own bright, smiling face. Richard enjoyed the game and would smile gleefully at the infant worker when she exposed her face in this surprising way. After three weeks of playing the game, Richard would brighten up at once when the infant worker appeared, and was able to respond not only to her face but also to the sound of her voice. He began to show some capacity to attach himself to the infant worker through these multisensory systems and through non-specific emotional communications. When unhappy, hungry, tired, or frustrated with mother, he would still arch his back, look away, and withdraw. But over time he began to show increasing flexibility and ease in being wooed out of this state and an ability to become involved in a rich, multisensory, affectively deep involvement. As the treatment progressed, he became capable of pursuing our infant specialist even when she was attending to another youngster at the Infant Center, showing a capacity himself to initiate a rich emotional attachment.

He was soon able to do this with his mother as well. If mother was in a withdrawn, detached state, Richard would make sounds to her and reach out to touch her. If he were on the floor, he would adjust his body so that he could fall in her direction. He would smile at her to gain her attention.

Occasionally, this succeeded in bringing her out of her pre-occupation and detachment, so that she would smile at him in return and engage him affectively.

By the eight-month assessment, Richard was actively seeking out a depressed, withdrawn, somewhat angry-look-ing, still largely unresponsive mother. He continually reached out toward her leg, smiling and cooing at her, looking in her direction, while she stared off into space, impervious to her interested youngster. When asked what she thought he was trying to do, she said, "He is trying to control me." Contrast this with our four-month assessment in which it was Mrs. H. who had been trying, mostly for our benefit, to engage her infant while he arched his back and looked away from her.

As work with Richard progressed, he gradually became better able to woo his mother. Mother, meanwhile, began to develop a relationship with the clinician and to gain some understanding of those fears of being controlled, that had led her so often to become suspicious and distant in her rela-tionships and finally to flee them. The relationship with the clinician had gone through several crises around these themes, sometimes culminating in her flight from treatment. The clinician's constant availability now enabled her to discuss those feelings that had led her to flee. During a crisis over her housing, the clinician, working with appropriate agen-cies, helped her find a new place to live. Her chronic para-noid and depressive stance lifted somewhat, and she could enter into a more open, verbally expressive relationship with the clinician. She was able to talk about her feelings, about some of her early background, including the sense of rejection she had felt, her preoccupation with killing, death, and dying, and how she often felt lost within herself while she was in the detached, preoccupied state we have described. She was subsequently able to keep her appointments regu-larly, and evidence islands of warm feelings toward the clin-ician. The primary clinician would take her for long automobile rides, providing a special setting for discussions. She began to show some capacity for forming a fairly consistent, affectively rich relationship with the primary clinician as long as she was not too anxious or depressed. Other factors in her life, such as her relationship with Richard's father, of course played a role in her feelings from day to day and week to week.

As the relationship with the clinician took on a more consistent pattern, with aspects of attachment, Mrs. H. began to show a similar capacity with Richard. Her affective availability increased and took on qualities of consistency and regularity. This occurred in spite of crises in her life situation which, in the past, would have put her right back in the totally withdrawn, preoccupied state that we have described.

At the 12-month assessment, it was striking to watch Mrs. H. pick up a toy telephone during the free play session and say, "Richard, are you there?" and to see Richard walk over to her with a bright smile in response to her call. Their play together was varied and interactive, and for the first time we saw them maintain an affective engagement by means of complexly organized reciprocal play that reflected mutual initiative. It was dramatic to watch them woo each other.

By the 18-month assessment, the two had developed some complicated games. In one, they took turns chasing each other around the room in a playful and imaginative manner. In another game, Richard went out of the room and when his mother pretended to pout, he came back and surprised her. They then reversed roles. Subsequently, they chased each other under the tables, using the dolls, etc., to dramatize the theme of "I'm going to chase you and you are going to run away from me and then you chase me and I'll run away from you." They would joyfully meet in the middle of the room where Mrs. H. would pick her infant up. Together they would look in a mirror and engage each other with deep, rich smiles. It was particularly interesting for us to observe how they had incorporated the themes of abandonment and rejection of the four- and eight-month assessments but now in the context of an organized game. These earlier themes were no longer ignored but integrated in the play activity itself, suggesting an active effort to work them through. At 18 months Richard's development was emotionally and cognitively phase-appropriate.

CASE 9

Mrs. I. was a somewhat manipulative and sociopathic woman with a history of criminal behavior. She was very concerned about being exploited, and had aggressive fantasies of "being cut off" after her new baby, a healthy, robust, 7-½ pound boy, was born. She had been reared in a foster home, and had been seduced as a teenager by a Lesbian foster mother, an incident which she claimed had made it impossible for her to experience pleasure.

She was able to attend to her baby's medical and physical needs, making sure that he was clean and well-fed. But whenever Jeffrey was close to her, or nuzzling against her body, she became anxious. She wanted to enjoy physical intimacy with him but invariably tensed up. A markedly impersonal quality characterized their relationship as the infant began to exhibit withdrawn and apathetic patterns of behavior, even while he was developing at an appropriate pace cognitively. Associations in her therapy sessions often led to aggressive themes of "knifing people," and to talk of people who had exploited and seduced her. At the same time, it was clear that not only was she involved with a number of individuals whom she permitted to exploit her, but she was herself adept at exploiting others.

Initially, her treatment went slowly. Whenever a session aroused any sense of interpersonal pleasure, she would skip a session or two thereafter. As the clinician began to point out her tendency to flee the experience of enjoyment in their relationship, she began to tolerate the relationship even when she "didn't feel like it." She could then talk about her anxiety or depression, or her feeling that the clinician was going to exploit her, or that she was going to exploit the clinician. Consistent with the more regular relationship she formed with the clinician, she was able to begin to tolerate physical intimacy with her infant.

At six months Mrs. I. seemed to be more available to her infant and better motivated to form a deeper attachment with him. For the first time she was able to verbalize her own concern that he would have problems with pleasure himself. We demonstrated several games she could play with him involving smiling, vocalization, various tactile experiences, and rhythmic interaction. Since he was a constitutionally sound youngster and had not developed avoidance responses, he readily responded to this new engagement when it was offered.

By eight months the dyad showed some capacity for reciprocal smiling, though still at a subdued level. By ten months both members were capable of enjoying each other, again at a subdued level. Work with Mrs. I. continues, directed toward helping her tolerate her anxiety and further explore her difficulties with intimacy.

SUMMARY

Just as in the homeostatic phase, there appears to be a parallel in this developmental phase between the therapeutic work with the parent and the capacity of the parent to support a relationship of attachment with his or her infant. That is, when the parent becomes capable of an attachment to a clinical worker, a similar capacity for attachment becomes possible between the parent and child. If the relationship between parent and clinical worker is characterized by pleasure and satisfaction and is stable over time, these same qualities generally characterize the relationship of caretaker and infant. In a number of instances we were able to predict a satisfactory attachment with the infant on the basis of the relationship between caretaker and clinical worker. The practical value of reliable predictions is greatest of course in planning treatments and marshalling resources. Such predictions often allowed us to withdraw those supports (surrogate caretakers and the like) that had been necessary for the infant previously and that were now urgently needed elsewhere.

Just as it is essential for service agencies to work together in coordinated fashion in the homeostatic phase, so too is it essential here. Even where mother can take care of the infant's basic homeostatic needs, other support systems may still be necessary to provide attachment experiences for the youngster while work with the mother is going on. Intensive outreach work can take place at the home or at the Infant Center, on a daily basis, if necessary. In the case of Mrs. H., the ability to work intensively with Richard eventually helped him respond to the human face and not only to the inanimate environment. Our success was based in part on having continued access to him, and in part on our ability to work with mother on a regular basis. This is not possible to achieve through routine office visits or similar non-intensive methods of counseling. Where difficulties with forming human attachments are at the most fundamental level, intervention approaches must involve intensive work, best carried out at an infant center.

3
Somatic-Psychological Differentiation
(3–10 Months)

Once a secure human attachment is achieved through the mutual cueing and reciprocal responses of infant and primary caregiver, a process of differentiation occurs in the affective, behavioral, and somatic realms of experience (Piaget, 1962; Brazelton, Koslowski, and Main, 1974; Sroufe, Waters, and Matas, 1974; Stern, 1974a, b; Emde, Gaensbauer, and Harmon, 1976). Through this process, basic schemes of causality are established that form the basis for reality testing. We use the term "somatic-psychological differentiation" to indicate that, although the infant experiences internal "emotional" sensations, these do not yet exist at an organized psychological or mental representational level.

Infant Capacities

Means-ends differentiation may be observed in the somatic-psychological sphere as the infant begins to differentiate one person from another (this reaches a noticeable level at eight months, with the appearance of what has been called stranger anxiety [Spitz, 1965]). We also see the beginning differentiation of somatic-psychological states; hunger, for instance, is distinguished by means of different communications from other need states such as affection or dependency. The infant is also able to decipher distinct communications, such as anger, from the primary caregiver. The infant is now less dependent on internal states; he is not just a victim of his own hunger or weariness, but is more of a social, interactive being (Emde, Gaensbauer, and Harmon, 1976; Sroufe and Waters, 1976).

Through social interaction, as well as interaction with the inanimate world, differentiation is facilitated. Contingent responses help the infant to appreciate his role as a causal agent and thereby to distinguish means from ends in interpersonal relationships. When, for example, the infant smiles and the mother smiles as a consequence, the infant in some rudimentary way relates his smile to that of his mother. Not only obvious patterns of cognition and interaction, but subtle emotional and empathic interactive patterns undergo their own differentiation, and at their own rate. It is therefore possible for an infant to be able to differentiate in the areas of gross motor responses and general interpersonal causality, and yet remain unable to differentiate at a subtle empathic emotional level. If, for example, an empathic interaction between caregiver and infant is lacking because mother responds in a mechanical and remote manner or projects her own feelings onto her baby, the infant may not learn to appreciate basic causal relationships between people at the level of feelings as compared to acts — to see that feeling angry can cause another to feel bad. Or, because of undifferentiated (noncontingent) or inappropriate (misreading the infant's communication) reactions, the infant may learn to respond somatically to situations in which it would be more adaptive to respond socially. For instance, the infant may show gastric distress rather than use motor activity to communicate emotional hunger or frustration. We have observed infants who differentiate adequately in the impersonal assertive domain of human relationships but not in the intimate pleasurable domain of such relationships.

During this stage we also observe the shift from magical causality (the infant pulls a string to ring a bell which is no longer there) to the consolidation of simple causal links (the infant pulls the string only when the bell is there) to more complicated means-ends differentiation (use of substitutes, detours, intermediary devices). Instead of simply crying out and expecting the caretaker to be aware of its hunger or its need for comforting, the infant learns to interpose certain noises, gestures, and/or affects that increase the likelihood that it will get picked up, cuddled, or fed. The foundation for flexibility of coping style has thus been laid.

In essence, then, this phase sees the development of complex interactive responses at the prerepresentational level. Just as in the phase of attachment, we assess the infant's capacity for differentiated responses along the four dimensions of range and depth, degree of contingency, resilience to stress, and personal uniqueness. Is the infant capable of differentiated responses in all the relevant sensory and motor modalities? Is he able to integrate such responses across modalities? Is he able to coordinate differentiated sensory responses with appropriate motor responses? Are differentiated affects seen across a wide spectrum of emotion? Are they appropriate to the caretaker's signals? Are they resilient to stress? Do we observe cause-and-effect type interactions across the affective domains of dependency, pleasure, assertiveness, protest, etc., or are these limited to only one affective domain, with the others marked by relatively undifferentiated interactions? Do we see these types of interactions with respect to interpersonal as well as impersonal events? It is not infrequent that we see infants who can clearly communicate their wishes for milk or food with a cause-and-effect type signal, become disorganized or withdrawn when their wish appears to be for physical contact.

An example of an extreme defect in differentiation is

the infant who fails to develop age-appropriate contingent behavioral and emotional responses (a basic sense of causality as the foundation for reality testing), either because of his own constitutional factors or failures of earlier development, or because of a withdrawn or overly intrusive (projecting) primary caretaker. The eight-month-old infant who smiles and looks happy but has no capacity to signal purposefully, who responds to his caretaker's signals with random or chaotic gestures is an often overlooked but quite typical illustration. A less severe problem exists when only one aspect of emotional differentiation is compromised; for example, anger may be ignored or lead to withdrawal. Symptoms such as sensorimotor developmental delays, apathy or intense chronic fear (stranger anxiety), clinging, lack of exploratory activity and curiosity, flat or nonresponsive emotional reactions to significant caregivers, as well as specific maladaptive patterns of relatedness such as biting, chronic crying, and irritability, may all be related to disorders of somatic-psychological differentiation.

Defects in this phase may result from constitutional factors or from difficulties in the previous stages of homeostasis or attachment. They may also result from the environment's lack of response or inappropriate response to the infant's signals. If the emerging capacities of the infant are not encouraged to develop, lack of practice may lead to secondary apathy, withdrawal, or disorganization. Or, alternatively, the environment's failure adequately to respond to the infant may result in a pattern of negativistic responses. Instead of reaching out, the infant may cry and refuse to respond, generating, in turn, a further inappropriate response from the caretaker. Negativistic patterns may extend to such basic functions as eating and sleeping, or, in less severe form, may result in the lack of practice to which we have referred. In this sense, then, the adaptive aspects of negativism — as an experiment in individuation (Reginald Lourie, personal communication) are outweighed by its aggressive and maladaptive consequences.

It should finally be noted that where, as here, the infant's new capacities for contingent interaction are ignored or misread, the earlier-achieved capacities for homeostasis and attachment may be compromised as well. And, of course, uncorrected disorders of the capacity for differentiation will result in later defects in reality testing, the organization of thought, the perception of communication, the regulation and perception of affects, and the integration of affects, action, and thought.

Environmental Characteristics

A growth-promoting environment at this stage of development is one that, in the context of a secure attachment and a supportive regulatory relationship, reads and responds to the infant's communications at the behavioral, somatic, and affective levels. While the growth-inhibiting environment may either not respond at all or may respond only to certain of the infant's signals — his protest or anger — and not to others — his love, joy, or curiosity — the growth-promoting environment can read a wide range of even weak signals and respond to them differentially. The growth-promoting environment will create opportunities for the infant to use new signals and will seek to foster resilience to stress by teaching the infant how to recover from frustration (e.g., by offering alternatives to unmet needs). Finally, the growth-promoting environment will reinforce the infant's emerging personal signature.

The growth-inhibiting environment can be measured in terms of its inability to read the infant's signals or its inability to respond differentially to them. The depressed or unavailable mother may not read the weak signals of her infant (a "weak sender" in the language of this chapter), or the schizophrenic mother may project her own needs onto the infant. Obviously, no environment is perfectly responsive, nor should this be expected. Infants must learn to accept delay and frustration in the normal course of development. What is essential is that this learning take place in the context of a comforting and supportive overall environment.

Common Fears in the Caretaker

At this stage of development the infant is becoming a better communicator. He is able to read, respond to, and produce a wider range of more complex signals. Instead of simply holding, cuddling, or rocking him, the parent should now be able to carry out a complicated and purposeful interaction with the child.

Naturally enough, the typical fears of this stage revolve around communication. One of the caretaker's prominent fears is that the infant does not find him or her "interesting enough." One mother, for example, did not read her infant's signals well largely because he was a weak sender. Because he did not brighten up for her, she assumed that it was she who was uninteresting and unappealing, when she should, instead, have focused on how to read his signals better. This led her to feel despondent and to withdraw further. Many of the fears of the attachment stage become more prominent now as the infant's growing capacity for complex communication makes greater demands on the caretakers. In many cases, the fear of not being interesting enough, of not responding correctly, of merging with the infant, or losing one's independence is the parents' response to the child's implicit demand that they respond more selectively and intensely.

Another common fear has to do with the fear of assertion. As the infant asserts his needs more forcefully, parents are often required to reply with assertiveness of their own. But sometimes an adult's assertiveness is tied to frightening angry feelings, as in the case of the father who felt the wish to slap his child whenever he began any sort of assertive protest. As a result of his own fear of these angry feelings, he remained passive and unresponsive to the infant. Conversely, the fear of passivity may cause some parents to overread their infant's signals and overintrude in their lives. Patience, for example, may be equated with inadequacy.

Principles of Preventive Intervention and Treatment

Assessment of the infant at this stage should minimally

be conducted at two levels. First, each sensory modality and motor system should carefully be assessed to see if it is available for optimal use in reciprocal interaction patterns. Are there treatable and reversible organic factors at work — chronic ear infection or poor vision? Or, as is more usually the case, are the infant's problems related to individual developmental differences? Second, each sensory modality and motor system should be assessed with respect to the degree to which they are coordinated with one another. That is to say, when an infant hears an interesting sound, and when we know that his auditory capacity is intact, does the infant alert visually and look toward the sound? When the parent dangles an interesting object in front of the infant, and we know that the infant's visual capacity is intact, can he reach out with his hand and smile at the same time? In each of these instances, sensorimotor coordination is obviously required. Some infants may appear to receive stimuli but to respond only minimally. If this is the case with several modalities, it may appear to the parent that the infant is not interested in reaching out and communicating. To a mildly depressed parent, sensitive to rejection, it may be easy to tune the infant out.

In treating the infant's less than optimal capacities, the basic principle is to offer repetitive, pleasurable, gradually more interesting and wider-ranging stimuli to the particular underused capacity. The youngster who appears unresponsive to auditory stimuli should be presented with a range of auditory stimuli until he or she responds to a particularly interesting one. This should then be used to help the infant alert and interact with the parent. The parent will typically shake the rattle or coo in the special interesting tone until the infant alerts and looks at him or her, at which point the parent will repeat the interesting sound. The parent is then instructed to use this sound as a base, adding variations — going up an octave, going down an octave — all the while trying to maintain the infant's attention. If the parent begins to lose the infant's interest because the range is too high or low,

the parent is instructed to return to the basic sound and begin again. The entire technique is designed to give the youngster practice in the underused modality in the context of a
pleasurable interactive experience. Of course, the parent
must be careful not to use only the first interesting sound,
since most infants will habituate to the same stimulus presented repetitively.

Where sensorimotor coordination is vulnerable, the
same principle applies: Increase the range and complexity
of stimulation presented to the underused capacity while
holding the youngster's attention. The infant who looks but
rarely reaches out his hand can be offered a novel stimulus
as part of the social interchange. A brightly smiling mother
or father presents a bright red block while facing the youngster so that he or she is sufficiently interested to grab for it.
The object may then be placed on the floor and moved progressively further and further away to encourage further
reaching. Slowly but surely the infant will become more
vigorous in his reaching activity. Or where auditory-motor
coordination needs further support, the sound of a bell or
whistle off to the side of the infant can be used to draw his
attention so that he begins actively to seek out the interesting object. Initially, the stimulus must be close enough to
encourage the infant's pursuit. Gradually, it can be moved
further away. It need hardly be emphasized that with each
successive accomplishment the congratulations and social
comforting of the parents are essential to reinforcing the infant's sense of mastery. And, of course, the ingenuity of the
clinician in suggesting a range of stimuli — fingers, smiles, a
flashlight focused on the mother's brightly smiling face, a
combination of smiling and interesting noises — is critical to
this approach.

Where a range of ordinarily expectable affects is not
present, the principle of intervention is again the same.
With the infant who cannot show pleasure, different combinations of novel stimuli may evoke a brief smile, if only for a
fleeting second or two. That brief smile may then become

the basis for further affective elaboration. By presenting the experience that drew it out in the first place, and slightly varying the experience so as to maintain the youngster's interest, a range of expressions may emerge. If a soft bell in conjunction with a smiling adult face brought a responsive smile, perhaps the next time one would present another sound with the smiling face. Similarly, with the compliant, superficially smiling youngster who cannot show intense curiosity, an interesting object can be presented in the context of a social interchange in a way that encourages the infant to come forward and assert himself. Such infants often have parents who tend to bring everything to them, who are extraordinarily active in social exchanges. The youngster then learns to be a passive recipient. The clinician must work toward achieving a more balanced arrangement in which the infant will assert himself more freely. Again, the parent must be encouraged to respond contingently to the youngster's achievement. The youngster will then come to see his success as leading to, or causing, the parent's response. A basic sense of causality thereby becomes established.

Easily disorganized infants present another kind of challenge. For these youngsters, a parent's smile may lead to such intense excitement and pleasure that their patterns of communication become disorganized, frenetic, and random rather than contingent and causal. The first step in such cases is to diagnose whether a particular type of affect or sensory modality is involved. If, for example, auditory stimuli disorganize the infant, the parents should be taught to present such stimuli first in a non-noxious range and then, slowly increasing the range, in conjunction with pleasurable stimuli. Gradually, the infant will begin to integrate a greater range of auditory stimuli and use them as part of a contingent interaction pattern. Disorganizing affects should be dealt with similarly.

But some infants become disorganized with *any* social engagement. In such instances, the goal of the clinician is to identify experiences that can help the youngster focus his attention for successively longer periods of time without becoming disorganized. A sufficiently interesting visual or auditory stimulus may help some such youngsters calm down, while more severely hyperexcitable infants may need to be held tightly or even swaddled. Operating, so to speak, as an auxiliary ego, the parent can help the infant regain his sense of equilibrium. Once the sufficiently calming experience has been identified, other stimuli can be presented — at first in a fairly circumscribed range, restricted perhaps to one or another sensory modality — in the context of a reciprocal interaction. As soon as the youngster becomes disorganized, the activity is terminated and the calming experience is re-introduced. When the infant is soothed, the activity is started again so that gradually the infant's periods of concentration and his capacity to tolerate more complex stimuli increase. The youngster will experience the cessation of the hyperexcited state as causally related to a social interaction. In other words, rather than forming the (prerepresentational) impression that disorganization leads to further disorganization (e.g., as the frustrated parent shouts at him), the infant learns that he can be soothed by social interaction.

Of course, the diagnostician must also carefully assess conflicts, character limitations, and gross personality disturbances in the primary caretakers. A mother with a defect in reality testing may grossly misread the infant's communications and not be able to respond contingently. A caretaker with conflicts about experiencing pleasure may be willing to engage the youngster around assertive behaviors, but not around pleasure. Even very circumscribed limitations on the parents' part can come into play around specific affective interchanges. Parents who have conflicts about sexuality, for example, may not be able to interact contingently when they see the infant touch his or her genitals. Such conflicts become more apparent now that the infant's complex behavior makes more specific demands of the caretaker.

In all such instances, the diagnostician must judge how pervasive the parental limitation is and the degree to which educative approaches need to be supplemented by varying forms of psychotherapeutic support. The grossly psychotic parent may require a complete program of therapeutic care, including concrete supports, medication, structure, and education in order to respond to the most fundamental communications of the infant. On the other hand, parents with only very mild, encapsulated conflicts over their infant's behavior may benefit from an educative approach and some reassurance. That is to say, such parents may be able to overcome their conflicts with respect to the infant even while these same conflicts continue to affect their relationships with other important figures in their lives.

Finally, it should be noted that the now greater autonomy of the infant and the greater demands implied by his clearer communications all place a special burden on the family as a unit. The clinician's understanding of the family's collective affective response in dealing with the infant at this level of development may be a very important component of a successful treatment strategy.

Clinical Illustrations

CASE 10

Mrs. J., a depressed, slightly paranoid borderline woman, reacted to the birth of her daughter Evelyn with mixed feelings. On the one hand, she showed some delight and excitement and a desire to be protective of Evelyn and close to her. On the other hand, there were fears of Evelyn rejecting her, or, conversely, not being as good as her. Mrs. J. tended to manhandle Evelyn, tickling her to the point of overexcitement and tossing her around much too vigorously. When, with this mishandling, her daughter became irritable and cried uncontrollably, Mrs. J. would either feel rejected or claim that her daughter was spoiled.

Mrs. J. appeared to be genuinely interested in her daughter, and able to supply appropriate nutritional and medical care and an overall protective environment. She was also emotionally involved with her daughter and able to engage her affectively. But from the beginning, Mrs. J. had tremendous difficulty reading Evelyn's signals. Unable to see that Evelyn was overstimulated or exhausted, Mrs. J. would continue to overstimulate her or feel rejected when Evelyn protested.

It was discovered that Evelyn was particularly sensitive to touch around the torso so that even minimal stimulation would make her cry; she was otherwise able to calm herself reasonably well. When Mrs. J. was told of this individual difference in her otherwise constitutionally sound and engaging two-month-old, she claimed that Evelyn was faking it and refused to be especially careful while bathing or handling her. She would not, for example, wrap Evelyn in a soft garment so as to avoid irritation from physical touch in the trunk area. Even when, finally, with the insistence of the clinical team, Mrs. J. recognized her daughter's particular oversensitivity, her tendency to misread Evelyn's signals continued.

Her relationship with the therapist was quickly characterized by a reliable attachment, much as she had been able to form with Evelyn. Here too, however, she would misread the ordinary social cues of everyday life and overreact at any hint of rejection. Anything less than smiling satisfaction on the therapist's part would lead Mrs. J. to say "I know you don't like me." If, during a session, the therapist was tired or preoccupied with something else, she would begin a verbal assault on him that sometimes seemed to threaten physical attack.

Our suspicion that she would have further difficulty in reading the more subtle cues of four to eight months was subsequently confirmed. Her interactions with Evelyn still consisted of throwing her around, shaking her, and other haphazard forms of stimulation. She rarely smiled in response to Evelyn's smile, did not return her looks, and did not vocalize in response to Evelyn's own vocalizations. Thus our work with Mrs. J. focused on helping her to read signals, first in the therapeutic situation and then in her relationship with her cognitively quite competent infant.

By nine months of age Evelyn was beginning to show a number of developmental lags. Early sensorimotor schemes of associating cause and effect had not developed. Language development had begun to show a pattern of regression, as had, to some extent, overall gross motor development. Certain sounds that Evelyn had been using were no longer apparent. And where previously Evelyn had pulled herself up and cooed, only to be picked up by her mother and tossed around, now she had begun to crawl away from her mother. Gradually, Evelyn became more apathetic and simply sat still rather than invite further inappropriate responses by her mother.

We worked intensively with Evelyn and Mrs. J. at the Infant Center. By now, Mrs. J. had developed some understanding of her tendency to overreact and misread the therapist's signals and to interpret his ambiguity as a sign of rejection. Playing with Evelyn under the guidance of the infant specialist now allowed Mrs. J. the opportunity to correct her distortions of Evelyn's signals. She was beginning to learn what her infant was capable of doing, and the multiple ways her infant communicated with her, visually, vocally, and motorically. With the support of the infant specialist, Mrs. J. was able to learn to react contingently in each area of her infant's development. At home, however, she continued to regress to her earlier patterns. Her therapist, who felt that she was now aware of some of these tendencies, even while she had already learned to correct her distortions with him, wondered aloud how it was that she went back to her old ways while alone; to which Mrs. J. replied, "Evelyn is the only person I can pick on." With her boyfriend and with the therapist, she said, she couldn't "get away with what she liked to do." When this theme was focused on, and when it became apparent that there were feelings she was afraid to express with the therapist, she slowly began to carry her careful reading of Evelyn's signals at the Infant Center back to the home environment.

In her therapy sessions, she expressed uncomfortable envious feelings with respect to other people and, eventually, with respect to the therapist. It seemed that some of these envious feelings were also behind her earlier difficulties with Evelyn. Gradually, she became increasingly able to express these embarrassing aggressive feelings in the therapy hours. It then became possible for her to contain some of these same disruptive feelings when she was with her infant. As a result, she was able to read Evelyn's signals correctly even when she was upset or frustrated.

With this shift, together with work at the Infant Center, Evelyn's development rapidly progressed. By the 12-month assessment, she was capable of rich reciprocal interactions in both the affective and cognitive spheres. Overall, her developmental status was in the average range. Most important, however, except for minor regressions, Mrs. J. was for the most part able to support Evelyn's development and contain her own desires to manhandle her. The work with Mrs. J. continues so that we can help her further understand what she now finally recognizes as her disruptive feelings.

It is important to note with respect to this case that when work with mother progressed to the point that she could maintain a constant relationship with the therapist and develop some capacity for observing her own feelings, it became possible for her to read her baby's signals without the intrusion of her own needs. The development of an observing ego in the therapeutic sessions thus enabled her to control her feelings of envy toward her infant and toward others in general. This, in turn, allowed her to respond contingently to her infant in a relationship now free of her own conflicts.

CASE 11

Mrs. K. was an obese, quite depressed, borderline woman who gave birth to a healthy, competent infant somewhat on the sluggish and passive side. Jill was an adorable little girl, smiling, alert, and easily soothed. Initially, Mrs. K. sought to care for Jill in every possible way, anticipating her every need, interpreting her every cry as a signal of hunger, and overfeeding her to the point of regurgitation. A rich attachment had developed, and overall physical care seemed to be adequate. Nevertheless, Jill began to lag developmentally. Expected capacities for crawling, vocalizing, and for initiating reciprocal affective interchanges (by smiling and so on) had not appeared. While Mrs. K. seemed quite capable of rhythmically rocking her infant and looking at her with a broad smile, we noticed that every time Jill pushed herself away so as to get a better view of her mother, perhaps to begin a pattern of reciprocal communication, Mrs. K. forcefully brought Jill back to her shoulder, saying, "She needs to be comforted." Discussions with Mrs. K. often revealed her need to "fill her baby up." References to eating and feeding dominated her view of how she must care for her infant. Attempts to point out to her that Jill was trying to communicate with her through smiles, glances, and sounds, and that it was important for Jill to begin developing her motor capacities, met with general agreement, always qualified by Mrs. K.'s assertion that Jill was "a little bit slow" and needed "more taking care of." While Mrs. K. had formed a solid relationship with her clinician, she could take little distance from her own picture of her infant and her own feelings toward the world.

Mrs. K. had experienced a number of separations early in life, but, at least on an intermittent basis, seems to have been satisfied — "filled up" as she once again put it. She was married to an alcoholic, a man whom now she felt she took care of. As she became more involved with her therapist, she attempted to dominate the sessions and would frequently interrupt him. When he pointed out the parallel between her interference with his own attempts at communication and her interference with her baby's attempts, she was at first quite annoyed. Associations then led her to say that the therapist only wanted to talk in order to hurt her. The idea that people might hurt her if they were permitted to communicate on their own, if they were not controlled by her, then became the focus of her treatment. As she became able to confront this fear and to see that overfeeding Jill was an attempt on her part to ward off her own anticipation of being hurt, she began to be able to permit her daughter to initiate communications, to which she responded contingently. By 12 months of age Jill was functioning phase-appropriately in the cognitive as well as affective spheres.

This case, as well, illustrates the relationship between therapeutic work with mother and her ability to deal with a new stage of development in her infant. While Mrs. K. was quite capable of establishing an early nurturing relationship with Jill, characterized by adequate homeostatic patterns and adequate attachment, her own conflicts made it hard for her to facilitate her daughter's differentiation. Once again, the development of an observing ego permitted the caretaker to perceive and respond to her infant's needs in an appropriate way.

4
Behavioral Organization, Initiative, and Internalization (9–24 Months)

As the infant becomes able to differentiate clearly and subtly means from ends, aspects of self from nonself, and significant others in his interpersonal sphere, there develops a capacity for enhanced learning, as evidenced perhaps most strikingly by increased, highly organized imitative behavior. It is as though the infant-toddler is now "internalizing" what he experiences (i.e., sees, hears, feels, etc.) in large, organized, interrelated units. As this capacity becomes more developed, we see the organization of certain emotional systems, such as affiliation, separation, fear and wariness, curiosity and exploration (Bowlby, 1969; Ainsworth, Bell, and Stayton, 1974; Sroufe and Waters, 1977). By 18 months we observe toddlers integrating in an organized manner a number of affective themes, e.g., aggression and "taking care," into their play.

Initiative and exploration are enhanced at this stage by the capacity for combining schemes into *new* goal-directed behavioral organizations, with further use of detours, substitutes, delays, and intermediary devices. The infant's capacity to take initiative is enriched by, and in part further facilitates, his capacity to internalize. After eight to ten months of age we see progressively more imitative behavior which, in turn, facilitates organized exploratory behavior from the secure base of the primary caregivers. The gradual individuation that occurs is perhaps best depicted in Mahler's descripton of the practicing subphase of the separation-individuation process (Mahler, Pine, and Bergman, 1975).

The capacity for original or new behavior is enhanced by combining known schemes, complex behavioral patterns (tertiary circular reactions [Piaget, 1962]), trial-and-error exploration, increased memory, and the gradual shift from imitation to identification. We have a much greater sense of the toddler as an organized, initiating human being; for example, the child will now actually pull his parent somewhere to show him something. There is also evidence for a beginning psychological sense of self (Lewis and Rosenblum, 1974).

Infant Capacities

At this stage the toddler is able to enter into complex interpersonal communications. He and his parent can share a complicated exploratory game in which the toddler tells the parent to "chase me around the room," which the parent does. The toddler then ducks into another room, then into a closet, and later doubles back to sneak up on the parent, laughing joyfully and jumping into the parent's arms with a hug and a kiss. Obviously, this is a complex activity involving exploration, anticipation, pleasure, etc. The angry toddler, similarly, can be mischievous in a complex, organized manner. He may leave his toys scattered around, arrange for himself or his parents to trip over them, and pretend to be upset. Thus, whereas in the phase of somatic-psychological differentiation we might see one or two behaviors tied together in causal links (the child smiling, the parent smiling, the child returning the smile), we now see the stringing together of several related behaviors. It should also be noted that around 16 to 20 months we have observed many toddlers begin to explore their genital areas in a purposeful, deliberate manner, in contrast to the reflex-like mouthing and sucking of the young infant.

The toddler also begins to integrate polarities of feeling. The adaptive toddler at this stage of development is limited neither to obsequious, unassertive, seemingly passive states, nor to states of chronic anger or irritability (biting, poking, kicking things over). Rather, he has the ability to organize both these polarities in a range of complex behaviors. He also shows the ability to respond to the organization of the environment — its limit-setting function, for example.

Finally, the adaptive toddler is developing distal communication capacities. His use of looks, vocalizations, and other affective signals permits the infant to distance himself from mother and explore his surroundings without giving up the security of affective contact with her. The integration of these distal modes with proximal modes (holding, touching, rhythmic movement) provides a transition to the level of development at which the human affective object can be conserved over space and time (e.g., via affective memory) as part of an organized mental representation.

Disorders at this stage may compromise the beginning of internal "psychological" life. Behavior remains fragmented, related to somatic or external cues, or stereotyped (the child does not develop original schemes). Intentionality and a sense of self are nipped in the bud, so to speak.

Specific disorders of this phase involve compromises in the internalization, organization, and originality of behavior. These disturbances range from a complete lack of imitation, intentionality, and organized emotional and behavioral systems to circumscribed limitations in certain emotional or behavioral systems (e.g., no assertive or affiliative behavior). Symptoms may include chronic temper tantrums, inability to initiate even some self-control, lack of motor or sensorimotor coordination, extreme chronic negativism, de-

layed language development, and relationships characterized by chronic aggressive behavior and/or fragmentation
and disorganization.

A severe disorder at this stage affects the basic capacity
for organizing behavior and for forming what are still only
the precursors of organized mental representations. We can
see the results of such a structural defect in adult patients
who evidence states of fragmentation (whose internal representations are disorganized) or who exhibit an inability to
tolerate affects and/or the rudimentary repercussions of internal imagery as these are related to the interpersonal world
(e.g., certain borderline and psychotic patients, severe substance abusers, patients with psychosomatic and impulse
disorders). A less severe disorder at this stage will be reflected
in the narrowness of the range of experience organized, as
evidenced by extreme character rigidities. An example is a
child who can only organize and experience very limited
ranges of affects and behaviors and a rudimentary level of
internal imagery. Such individuals are tied to concrete, immediate states of need fulfillment and are often locked into
rigid and narrow behavior patterns reflecting extreme affective and behavioral polarities (e.g., passive-compliant, ag-
gressive-negativistic). They may never form the intermediary warning and delay capacities afforded by internal affects and imagery as these are used for satisfaction and planning. Such individuals, we often observe, may later exhibit
a variety of difficulties, including psychosomatic syndromes,
substance abuse, borderline or more severe behavior disorders. The stability of their personality organizations may also be limited, as evidenced by their sensitivity to a variety of
stresses.

Symptoms at this stage are related to an inability to
form organized behavioral patterns and can be clearly differentiated from the symptoms of earlier stages of development in which different basic issues are implicated. A youngster who has successfully negotiated the stage of somatic-

psychological differentiation and is now capable of stringing together an organized pattern of contingent responses, for example, will become immensely frustrated with an overcontrolling or intrusive caretaker who does not permit him to practice his new abilities. Sleep disturbances, negativism, chronic aggression, or excessive irritability and/or withdrawal may emerge as reactions to this frustration. Such a youngster can be contrasted to the child who has not accomplished the tasks of homeostasis, attachment, and differentiation and, consequently, is not now ready for more organized social and emotional responses. Successful diagnosis, then, depends on a knowledge of the resolution of earlier developmental stages *and* a knowledge of current influences on the youngster's development. It is important also to note that attachment patterns and homeostatic capacity may be secondarily disrupted as a result of disorders at this stage. For example, we have observed some toddlers who pull away from the human world and turn toward the more easily controllable inanimate world when their capacity for initiative has been undermined.

Environmental Characteristics

The growth-promoting environment at this stage of development admires the toddler's new abilities, greater initiative, and greater originality, and is available, tolerant, and firm when necessary. It follows the youngster's lead, supporting his initiatives and helping him to organize one step further than he is able to on his own. The optimal caretaker not only admiringly enters into a game with the happily smiling toddler, but permits him to shift the game, and will help him reorganize if it becomes necessary. Parent and child, for example, may begin looking at pictures together. The toddler then initiates a game in which they chase each other around. As the youngster becomes somewhat disorganized around the running, the caregiver will bring the youngster back to the point from which they started — looking at pictures in a book, helping the youngster name objects. The optimal caretaker helps the youngster complete the circle.

The growth-promoting environment is not threatened by the child's range of affective expression, but rather helps the youngster integrate affective polarities into meaningful, organized, interpersonal responses. When the optimal environment observes that the youngster is maintaining an organized negativistic or chronically aggressive pattern, it will try to identify those events or experiences that may be heightening the child's sense of frustration. Parents may notice, for example, that their own work-related stresses have made them emotionally unavailable to the child. This awareness can then allow them to respond to the child's negativism and chronic aggression not with scolding and punishment, but with efforts to shift the youngster's attention to more intimate, pleasurable activities. The youngster's realization that he can escape an unpleasurable state and re-enter a more emotionally satisfying relationship with his parents helps him tie together his angry feelings with satisfying experiences.

Simple notions that the youngster's chronic anger will be reinforced if followed by relaxing experiences ignores the importance of providing integrating links for the youngster. At the same time, limit-setting is quite important during this stage of development when youngsters are experimenting with aggressive behavior. If there does not appear to be a good reason for the youngster's upset state, firm limits in the context of a stable relationship pattern are quite appropriate. In dealing with aggressive behavior, the key issue is parental involvement and engagement with the child rather than withdrawal or embarrassment.

In the disordered environment the primary caretakers tend to be disorganized or may be conflicted about the toddler's new independence and originality, and embarrassed by, or ashamed of, his initiatives. They may be able to engage the infant only in fragmented units of interpersonal involvement as compared to complexly organized chains. Mother may be capable only of relatively brief causal exchanges, a smile in response to the toddler's smile. But when the toddler tries to develop the reciprocal smiling exchange into a more complex pleasurable game by showing her some toys to arouse her interest in him, she becomes distracted because of her own depression, preoccupation with other issues, or basic personality limitations. For example, she may become disorganized or panicky because the youngster's capacity for complex social interaction exceeds her own capabilities for social interaction. Thus the toddler's desire to develop and consolidate these more organized patterns never receives reinforcement from the animate environment.

Some overprotective caretakers may attempt to control the child. Instead of developing initiative and autonomy in the context of organized patterns, the toddler finds that these qualities of his behavior are discouraged. Some youngsters become apathetic and passive as a result. Others try to retain the initiative, but organize their behavior in negative and aggressive ways. Still others surrender their investment in the human animate world for complicated relationships with the more easily manipulated inanimate world. Relative overinvestment in the inanimate world may form the basis of an inabiity for internal experience (fantasies) with respect to the human object world.

Common Fears in the Caretaker

Unacknowledged fears of the toddler's increased independence may interfere with his development at this stage of childhood. Many of these are common even in optimal settings. When they exist in an environment that is already admiring, supportive, and secure, they pose no great threat to the child's development, provided that the caretaker is aware of them.

One of the most common fears is that of being abandoned. Let us say that a mother has enjoyed being close to her infant and has consistently provided love, support, and security. She has often said that she and her baby are "as one." Being "as one" may have been extremely useful during the first year of life. But with the child's development the mother may begin to feel rejected because the toddler now does not stay with her, nuzzle, or cuddle as much as she would like. As the mother often puts it, the toddler now "has a mind of his own." As he begins to move around the house, exploring by himself and showing greater initiative, mother may no longer make herself available or, conversely, may attempt to overcontrol him. It is true that at this stage her toddler does not need her in quite the same way. The toddler, however, does need her in an important but different way. He needs her for some of those warm, although now intermittent, loving exchanges they had shared together previously, and he needs her to take pride in his newly developed skills.

Jane was a needy, depressed woman who did very well as a mother until her infant began to walk at 13 months. Gradually, Jane became depressed, sleeping all day and having suicidal thoughts, finally deciding that "my child hates me, and I hate him." Treatment revealed a deep sense of loss and rage which, when dealt with, permitted her slowly to admire her toddler and again to establish a secure relationship.

Another common fear, but one which does not manifest itself quite so openly, is the fear of the toddler's "taking control." Here the parents perceive the toddler's new sense of initiative as willfulness. If this fear becomes too strong and outweighs the parents' admiration for and pride in the toddler's new abilities, it can set the stage for a power struggle of many years duration, one which sometimes lasts until the youngster goes off to college and, sometimes, even beyond that. Again, withdrawal by the parents, or intrusiveness on their part, may cause the child to shift his interest to the inanimate world.

Another set of fears has to do with the meaning that parents attach to the youngster's newly emerging abilities, some of which may frighten them. Some parents, for example, mistake their youngster's originality for aggressiveness. One energetic youngster loved to explore, learned to walk early, and by 14½ months could not only run with good coordination but was even beginning to jump a little. His motor skills were so advanced that he could throw a ball fairly accurately, could scribble with crayons, and so on. He could say "da da" and "ma ma," and a few other words, and was essentially a loving, happy child. But he was also a high-energy child, frequently racing around the house or pushing a little truck along the floor with such exuberance that he occasionally banged it up against a chair.

His father, a passive man, was just the opposite of his little son, uncomfortable with his own assertive or aggressive activities. Mother seemed to take her cue from father so that when he was worried about his toddler breaking something, she would worry about it too. Every time their industrious and rather well-controlled toddler pushed his little truck, father became concerned that he was going to have a hyperactive and aggressive child. Every avenue for assertive behavior was then quickly intercepted and blocked. Not surprisingly, this very competent, industrious youngster began to do the only thing, perhaps, that he could do. He became negativistic, belligerent, and disorganized in his aggression. He began crying and throwing objects. When his parents would scold him, he would cry even harder and cling to them. He alternated between disorganized play and clinging behavior, clutching their legs aggressively.

Soon father felt that his prediction had come true. He had an aggressive, hyperactive youngster. In talking to the father about this, it was interesting to note that he had had a very aggressive younger brother and had been afraid that his own son would turn out like him. In fact, his younger brother had been labeled hyperactive and had had learning problems in school. When father saw that he was misperceiving his youngster's industry, he was slowly able to give his confident toddler the support and admiration he needed.

Parents can give many meanings to their children's behaviors at this stage of development. A newborn infant's behavior is comparatively simple — crying for food or wanting to be rocked — so that parents do not so often distort the message into something other than what it is. In contrast, as the toddler's behaviors become more complicated, the parents are more likely to misinterpret them in different ways, particularly if they have a tendency to misread the infant's signals to begin with.

Another situation in which many parents' special conflicts may lead them to react in a less than adaptive way to the child's initiative relates to the child's interest in his or other people's bodies — what might be called the beginnings of his or her interest in sex. Between 15 and 20 months, children often begin to show interest in the differences between boys and girls and men and women. They begin to show a special curiosity in their own bodies and in their parents' bodies, all at a nonverbal level. They will follow father or mother to the bathroom and watch them as they shower. They may point to the different body parts with wondrous looks on their faces. They are frequently observed looking at or playing with their own genitals.

In one family, whenever the toddler touched herself or tried to follow her parents into the bathroom, they scolded her, hit her hands, closed the door in her face, and generally made this phase of development very upsetting for her. When they found their daughter tearing up the genital area of a doll with her fingers, they became frightened and sought help from their pediatrican. The pediatrician advised them to look at this in terms of their youngster's overall curiosity. He suggested that they take pride in their child's interest in this area, just as they would take pride in any of her other interests, while also trying to convey a sense of modesty and privacy in dealing with sexuality.

We should add here that there is no right or wrong way to deal with a youngster's sexual interests and curiosities, which are present even before he or she is able to talk. Each family has its own cultural values and special traditions it wishes to communicate to its children. It is important to respect each family's values in the broader context of recognizing the child's natural curiosity about sexuality, a curiosity that is part of his wider-ranging interests at this point in development.

Another common fear of parents involves the issue of setting limits. Some parents, feeling that they have to "tame" their children, undermine initiative and curiosity and eventually the child's ability to set limits for himself by overcontrolling the child. Other parents, however, have the opposite problem, and set no limits at all. In either instance, fear of aggression and loss of control are often prominent.

Some youngsters at this stage of development do not display the kind of industry, curiosity, and initiative expected for their age. They cling to their parents and seem to fear taking initiative. Although these children can walk and say a few words, they generally do not use these abilities. It is almost as if they were fearful of taking the next step in development. Instead of offering comforting encouragement, however, their parents often become frightened by their child's dependency. A common reaction to this fear is to try to separate from the youngster too abruptly for fear that he or she will never become independent.

Principles of Preventive Intervention and Treatment

Intervention at this stage seeks primarily to encourage organization and integration. Whereas in the somatic-psychological stage, it was essential from a structural point of view to locate interferences with contingent interaction patterns, here it is important to understand those limitations of the youngster and the environment that prevent him from operating in a more complex, organized, and integrated way. From the youngster's point of view, he must now integrate complicated sensory and motor schemes, affective polarities, a wider range of social relationships (including his relationships with mother and father as different individuals rather than simply as replacements for one another), and the various tasks of earlier developmental stages.

It is essential, then, first to diagnose any pre-existing difficulties from an earlier stage of development. A youngster, for example, who never had a secure attachment or never formed differentiated causal relationships is unlikely to be able to organize his behavior into longer chains of contingent responses. The therapeutic plan must then be based on the principles outlined earlier, strengthening capacities that have developed inadequately. But whether these are capacities for homeostasis, attachment, or differentiation, therapeutic work with them should be done in the context of the current level of maturation of the central nervous system and the child's current level of cognitive development. If a youngster is able, for example, to play in a complex, organized way with a puzzle, but is unable to interact warmly and contingently with another person, intervention should not merely involve holding and cuddling and infantile games that would have been appropriate at seven or eight months. Rather, one should engage the child's more complexly organized cognitive capacities in the context of a contingent affective interchange. That is, the parent can interact warmly and intimately with the child while the two of them play with the puzzle at one and the same time. The child's emerging capacities must, in other words, be acknowledged.

In assessing possible interferences with the youngster's capacity for integration at this stage of development, the diagnostician must take into account the great variations in the rate of children's maturation. Some 11-month-old youngsters, for example, will not only interact contingently with a caretaker, but develop a chain of such interactions, moving from a peek-a-boo game to a more complicated game, back to the peek-a-boo game, finally to end with parent and child looking at pictures together. Other 11-month-olds will not develop such patterns until three or four months later. The important issue is not so much the rate of maturation of such behaviors — which will vary as much as gross motor maturation, language, and so on — but whether or not forward movement is occurring at all and, indeed, whether or not the *basic* elements of these new capacities seem more or less to be present.

Where integrative capacities do not seem to be developing, the fundamental principle of intervention is to create a setting that will encourage such development. In looking at a picture book, for example, mother and child can silently look at pictures while mother turns the pages. All that is required from the toddler is to look. But mother could also combine the child's visual stimulation with verbal descriptions of the pictures. She could further increase the range of stimulation involved by periodically looking at the youngster and explaining what is in the picture. The youngster's sensory capacities are far greater than his language capacities at this point and so one might see the eager youngster looking from the picture to mother and back again, hanging on her every word. At the same time, instead of turning the pages herself, mother can have the youngster turn the pages, offering a little help, thus enhancing the youngster's fine motor coordination. As part of this exercise, mother may also be instructed to have the youngster point out the different parts of the picture after she does, thus increasing imitative activity and perceptual-motor coordination. Obviously, this sort of approach will help the youngster integrate across a range of modalities.

With respect to the child who exhibits only a narrow range of affects, the caretaker can be taught at times to follow the youngster's lead while waiting for opportunities for new affects and behaviors to appear, and at times actively to create occasions for the natural emergence of such affects and behaviors. The mother who tends to intrude on her child's attempts at mastery and assertion, and leaves little opportunity for the spontaneous pleasure of discovery, may need to allow the child to explore on his own. The discovery of the inner workings of a toy or of the warm and pleasurable feeling of his fingers in his mother's mouth may lead the child to the sought-after spontaneous smile. Mother can then be helped to respond with alert excitement of her own.

But with other youngsters, more firmly entrenched in a pattern devoid of joyous spontaneity, the parent may have to experiment actively to create opportunities for new emotion. Thus, as parent and child look at pictures together or explore a new toy, the parent might present the toy in a new position or try to get it to do something it would not ordinarily do, or bring in a new toy as a novel experience. Or a parent who always sits in a chair might get down on the floor to make him or herself available for the youngster to crawl over and explore. Once the youngster shows the first spark of enthusiasm, the parent should be encouraged to show admiration for the new affect. As assertive exploratory behavior is enlarged to include pleasure, integration across affects can begin.

The clinician must be prepared to work with the caretaker and child to encourage experimentation until situations are created in which new affects and behavior can appear. One youngster, for example, fretful and negativistic in general, was noticeably comforted when certain rhythmic music was played. As mother took him by the hand in a modified dance, he showed spontaneous joy and relaxation. Mother was not a musical person and so it had never occurred to her that music could soothe her toddler now that he no longer responded to rocking. Indeed, the music appeared to provide the same kind of rhythmic experience for him. The youngster then began to see that it was possible to escape his irritable, negativistic mood.

Where initiative and originality also require support—

where, for example, the youngster has a cautious style and seems to wait for the parent to come to him — the parent can learn to wait for the youngster to take the initiative and, at the same time, can try to create new opportunities for him to do so. With supportive advice, for example, one father was helped to find that his daughter loved to play with water. She especially enjoyed turning on and off the faucet in the kitchen or bathroom and, at times, spraying water around with the little hose attachment. Father hated the mess that resulted and avoided for many weeks acknowledging that his seemingly passive and unoriginal daughter indeed had interests. Needless to say, with father's support and admiration, this little girl was able to develop many original water games. She and father were, as he eventually put it, "wetter but wiser." Soon her originality and initiative spread to other areas. This issue helped father and daughter work through a more general problem they were evidencing around curiosity and pleasure.

Another important strategy central to encouraging greater behavioral organization and initiative is to teach and/or encourage the use of distal communication modes, particularly with regard to affective interchanges. While the youngster explores a room, a prideful glance from mother will often result in a reciprocal show of pleasure by the youngster. Vocalizations as signals (prior to clear words) can keep the toddler and caretaker in an affective field despite spatial distance. Interestingly, new research shows that toddlers are sensitive to the interests of their parents and show greater capacity to confront new objects when the parent is looking at them alertly rather than reading a newspaper (Emde, 1979).

With the youngster who at 14 or 15 months is evidencing impulsive behavior (biting, for example) or negativism, and is showing little initiative and originality, the basic principle of intervention is to provide the youngster with an opportunity for alternative, more sophisticated behavior. In these circumstances, a balance must be struck between encouraging the child to take the initiative and setting limits for him. At the same time as the environment affords the child opportunities for pleasure (e.g., new activities, more "quality" parental time) and seeks to understand its own covert contributions to the child's behavior (overcontrolling him or prematurely separating from him), it must also set limits in a highly systematic way. By engaging the youngster directly around his impulsivity — holding him, or engaging him in a serious affective interchange — the parent offers not only structure, but intimacy. The structure will help the youngster organize what he cannot organize himself and convince him of the caretaker's interest. At the same time, of course, the limit-setting activity and the new opportunities for intimacy and play with parents offer him an opportunity to experience those pleasurable emotions he had not been experiencing before. Simple limit-setting, then, is not enough. Rather, each time one wishes to take away one mode of behavior, one should also be prepared to offer the youngster an opportunity for a more sophisticated means of engaging.

At this stage of development some caretakers may have difficulties following the youngster through a chain of contingent interactions. Some may become disorganized because of the complexity of the activity. They may be unable to shift from one game to another and back again without becoming upset. In effect, their youngster's capacity to organize complicated behavior exceeds their own. Some such parents may have a thought disorder and may require comprehensive psychiatric care, including medication, structure, and education. Modeling approaches may be particularly useful in teaching such parents how to enter into organized behavioral patterns with their children.

Other parents may become selectively disorganized around specific emotions or conflicts. They may be comfortable in one emotional realm and not in another, becoming anxious when the child asserts himself by shifting shared play activities. Or they may be made anxious by the child's shifting patterns themselves, his desire at one moment for "emotional refueling" (Mahler, Pine, and Bergman, 1975) and his desire at another moment for independence. Caretakers who can only engage in concrete contact (only physical holding) or caretakers who withdraw emotionally as soon as the toddler moves off on his own must be encouraged to develop their own distal communication skills in order to support the youngster's exploration and initiative in the context of an affectively secure relationship.

In these cases, parental limitations can be worked with at a number of levels. An educative approach may help the parents gain an awareness of the youngster's needs, an awareness that sometimes will allow them to respond in more appropriate ways. But where character limitations make certain types of affects frightening, or where affects in general are frightening, psychotherapy may be necessary. The parents must be made aware that the same emotions they find frightening in the therapeutic relationship and in life are those emotions they find frightening in their relationships with the child. While psychotherapeutic efforts to increase the range of tolerated affects ordinarily take a great deal of time, a focused, time-limited therapeutic effort may be quite as effective under these circumstances. The parents' special motivation to facilitate their toddler's development, along with the therapist's clarification and support, may allow them to tolerate affects in the toddler which remain frightening to them in another context. That is to say, normal working through is not quite so necessary.

Where it is not possible to work with the primary caretaker, working with other family members with a greater range of available affects and a greater tolerance for the youngster's developmentally emerging capacities may be appropriate. Father (if he is not the primary caretaker), siblings, grandparents, or day-care centers may all be mobilized. While other adults may be used in supportive roles, however, the primary role of the main caretaker should never be ignored.

Just as in the other phases of development, attention must be given to the family's concrete needs and to the family as a unit. Problems with housing, finances, or health may all play a crucial role in undermining the child's emerging capacities. And as discussed earlier, individuals may function one way while alone with a youngster and quite another way as part of the family unit. These issues will be dealt with in more detail later in this work.

Clinical Illustrations

CASE 12

Mrs. L., superficially competent on presentation, evidenced underlying chronic thought disorder on further clinical investigation. When not under stress, she was able to function reasonably well. She responded positively to Helen's birth, although her initial involvement had a quality of play-acting. She was nevertheless able to attend to the physical needs of her constitutionally sound infant, providing adequately for her physical needs and engaging in a somewhat satisfying attachment. When not under pressure (and, fortunately, her life circumstances were such that she was not generally under acute pressure), she was able to read her baby's signals and support her through the stage of differentiation. Her relationship with her therapist was consistent and appropriate, and her occasional lapses in reality testing or disorientation in thinking responded well to support and structure. Emerging themes in the therapeutic work focused on Mrs. L.'s concerns about her own body and her fears and fantasies that her growing infant would develop some kind of defect. Mrs. L.'s associations to this defect usually referred to bone cancer, leukemia, or assorted vague injuries. The image that usually emerged was one of an amorphous cancer distorting the rather distinctive features of her pretty little girl.

As long as the discussions stayed fairly simple, Mrs. L.'s reality orientation and capacity to organize her thinking was not disrupted. It was only with respect to her complex and ambivalent feelings toward her husband or her older daughter (who was already having considerable cognitive and behavioral difficulties) that her thinking became disorganized.

Mrs. L. seemed to enjoy her intimacy with Helen and, indeed, Helen's ability to respond contingently to her signals helped Mrs. L. organize herself. But when Helen began to enter the stage that we have called "behavioral organization, initiative, and internalization," she began to demonstrate a wider range of emotions, a deeper sense of affiliation and love, and more organized anger, protest, and jealousy of her older sibling and her mother. She was also beginning to organize her behavior and to imitate complex interaction patterns, sometimes patterns she had observed in Mrs. L.'s relationship with her husband, sometimes patterns of Mrs. L.'s relationship with the older sibling (e.g., pretending to comfort her mother or teasingly ignoring her). Mrs. L. became particularly disturbed when Helen began doing new, unfamiliar things (a hiding game, in particular). At these times, Mrs. L.'s underlying thought disorder began to emerge at home, something that had not been in evidence until now.

By this time, Helen was also able to walk around and to enjoy her autonomy, coming to and going from mother as she wished. While, intellectually, Mrs. L. verbalized her pleasure in these new abilities and the greater autonomy of her confident toddler, at the emotional level, she became disorganized whenever she talked about it. Somatic delusional-type thinking began to emerge (e.g., "I think there is a hole in my chest. My blood is running out."). During a home visit, we noted that when communication was simple, when daughter sat on her lap and just let mother hold her, or said a word to which she would respond, Mrs. L. remained organized. But when her daughter demanded that she take part in a complicated game, or when she demonstrated organized feelings either of jealousy or affiliation and love (when she ran to father and hugged him, for example), we noticed that Mrs. L. became diffuse in her thinking and then tangential, going off on themes related to physical illness. Particularly difficult for mother to handle was Helen's age-appropriate ability to relate to mother and father and older sister all at once, in an integrated pattern. She could walk around and communicate with each figure in the room, bringing a block first to father, then to the clinical worker, then going over and trying to engage her older sister, and finally affectionately returning to her mother. This degree of complexity seemed to upset mother and she would become further disorganized. If, for example, she were talking about how Helen had said a new word, and at the same time watching Helen negotiate one of her new complex patterns, she would suddenly begin to talk about a person she had read about who had cancer. Her affect then became flattened and she became more impersonal. We reasoned that Helen was reaching a stage of emotional behavioral organization that was in some ways more complicated than Mrs. L. could handle. Just as Mrs. L. had previously demonstrated the tendency to become disorganized in her therapy sessions if the themes became too complicated, here, too, when her daughter offered her more complex and rich themes, she seemed to be overwhelmed by them. The therapy sessions then focused on the general issue of Mrs. L.'s disorganization and the types of experiences that were associated with it, especially as they related to her daughter. At first, even the very subject of disorganization was disorganizing.

As Mrs. L.'s disorganization continued, we noticed that her imaginative, curious, and innovative daughter had begun to regress. By 15 months she began vacillating between extreme negativistic behavior and fragmented aggressive behavior (she would run up to her older sister, for example, and bite and kick her). There was still some organized innovative and imaginative behavior, but it occurred less and less frequently.

Father, who *was* able to engage Helen, came home too late to be available to help. The older sister was having too many emotional and cognitive problems of her own to be supportive. Thus, we began seeing Mrs. L. and Helen at our Infant Center, where other adults were available to help Mrs. L. support the child's emerging behavioral organization, initiative, and capacity for innovative behaviors. Within two weeks, with the help of our clinical workers, and with her mother present, Helen's regressive patterns reversed themselves. We watched mother and daughter interacting with each other for longer periods of time, and observed at which point Mrs. L. became disorganized. Gradually, a program was developed that helped Mrs. L. focus on exactly what had occurred. At the point when Mrs. L. became disorganized, we would immediately intercede. Generally, these points involved misperceptions on her part of her daughter's behavior. She would interpret something assertive as aggressive, or something independent as abandoning. With our feedback, however, Mrs. L. slowly began to understand some of the more complicated behaviors of her daughter. At the same time, in her own therapy sessions, she became able to grasp more fully the implications of her disorganized states: that they were her response to emotional complexity.

While work with Mrs. L. continues, she is now able to support her daughter's continued development at home and, indeed, Helen has resumed an optimal developmental course. It is interesting to note that Mrs. L. still tends to disorganize with complex emotion. Still, she has learned enough about her daughter's behavior that what was once so unfamiliar has now become familiar; what was formerly too complex for her is now more clearly understood. It is expected that her difficulties will continue as her daughter further develops. Now, however, she realizes that she can learn from her daughter's developing behavior.

CASE 13

Mrs. M. was a rather attractive woman with paranoid tendencies. She was socially sophisticated and could engage others verbally around a variety of themes and issues. She gave an overall appearance of assertiveness and competence. She tended, however, to be suspicious and distrustful, and struggled with underlying feelings of envy. Occasionally, she lashed out violently at her boyfriend, the father of her son Dennis, once going so far as to attack him with a knife. Her son was constitutionally sound, with some lability in response to stress. Mrs. M. had cared for his physical needs adequately and had engaged him in a loving relationship. She seemed to identify with his "manly traits," which were similar to certain traits of her boyfriend; she seemed to enjoy talking about how "assertive and manly he would be." The tendency at times for her thinking to become disorganized or for her behavior to be overly suspicious did not interfere with the early attachment. A supportive psychotherapeutic relationship seemed to help Mrs. M. at those times when she felt that Dennis was interfering with her life or manipulating her.

She negotiated the stage of differentiation quite well, using her sophisticated cognitive capacities to read Dennis's signals, and with support and encouragement from her clinician, took pride in encouraging his cognitive and motor development. She was able to tune into his assertive and more aggressively oriented communications, such as banging his fist on the table, hitting a block against another block, and also to his longing smiles or intense looks. She tended to get somewhat confused, however, by Dennis's more affectionate, dependent communications, much as she was confused by her dependent relationship with her female therapist and her dependent relationships with men in general. Here, work with the therapist helped her to read her son's signals correctly.

Dennis began to walk and to show assertiveness and initiative at the beginning of his second year. At first Mrs. M. took pride in his accomplishments but slowly her initial admiration began to give way to envy. She talked about Dennis in terms more appropriate to describe her relationship with her boyfriend. She was angry that he had more freedom in the relationship than she did, and that she had responsibilities that he did not have. She began to express envious feelings toward the therapist, saying that she had nicer clothes. Unfortunately, the therapist did not pick up on these general concerns quickly enough to link them with the possibility that her envious feelings would interfere with the admiration that Dennis needed at this point to support his development.

We noticed that Mrs. M. began to overcontrol and criticize Dennis. Her attitude toward her son had shifted from admiration to a fear of his interference with her life. She felt compelled to set limits. Even more disruptive than this, she had begun to pull away from him emotionally. We saw Dennis gradually change from an expressive, assertive, satisfied youngster who enjoyed his new motor abilities and his capacity to explore his house, to a sober-looking, withdrawn, almost depressed youngster. He was lethargic, and showed little curiosity or interest in the world around him. He no longer evidenced original behavioral schemes. His relationship with his mother became more clinging and dependent, and his sense of autonomy and satisfaction decreased markedly.

When her clinician spoke about her envy and competitive feelings in the therapeutic relationship, Mrs. M. began to skip her sessions. She also began returning home later than usual, leaving Dennis with the baby-sitter for much longer periods. She talked very little about him now, except to say that "others could take care of him, he was off to a good start." She began to talk about terminating the therapeutic relationship. When she was questioned about this, her associations were to a woman in her office who had made homosexual overtures to her. Hints of homosexual feelings toward her therapist began to emerge. Here again the therapist did not confront these issues directly. Nor did she deal with them as part of the larger theme of envy and competition which existed in all of Mrs. M.'s relationships. Mrs. M. gradually increased her working hours, leaving the care of her son to the baby-sitter. Dennis continued his cognitive development, but now as a much more subdued child than he had been before, a child without spontaneity. Mrs. M. subsequently terminated her relationship with the therapist, stating that she might return if a crisis arose.

The above case illustrates the way in which a cognitively competent mother without a basic personality disturbance can inhibit her child's development by failing to recognize the way in which her own negative feelings have come to dominate their relationship. Indeed, Mrs. M.'s problems with her son may have been a direct consequence of his newly emerging capacities. Unwilling to acknowledge her own envious feelings toward him, and her envious feelings toward the therapist, she chose to flee both relationships, possibly to her own detriment and certainly to her son's. The therapist's early disinclination to deal with these issues may have further supported her flight. It is our hope that there will be another opportunity to work with Mrs. M. to help her resolve these issues. Dennis, currently going through a stage of premature separation from his mother with some sadness and a tendency to withdraw, had fortunately developed a solid enough early foundation to be able to recover with an appropriate therapeutic program.

During the stage of behavioral organization, initiative, and internalization, the child's increased behavioral capacities permit relatively more sophisticated treatment approaches than we have seen before. In a case similar to that of Dennis, a youngster whose mother abruptly withdrew from him between 13 and 15 months became lethargic and subdued, with occasional dramatic temper tantrums and negativistic postures. By having him and mother come to the Center, it was possible for this cognitively precocious youngster to play out scenes of separation. He would run, crawl, and jump away from the therapist working with him, doing to the other as had been done to him. As he got a little older, he began to play out this scene with dolls. The therapist then began introducing different possible outcomes. For instance, the abandoned doll was not left to simply lie there helplessly, but made to seek out other dolls, or to look assertively for the doll that had gone away. These scenes were repeatedly presented as useful alternatives. In this particular case, even though mother had been unable to adapt to her youngster's greater abilities, the youngster himself was gradually freed from his withdrawn, negativistic postures as he played out these scenes with an empathic adult. In fact, he was then able to be of help to mother by asserting his own right to her when she tried to separate from him. He could, that is, woo her back into a relationship with him. Mother, somewhat surprised at his ability to find her, reported that "he is nicer now, he shows me that he loves me."

Representational Capacity: Phase I

The capacity for psychological representation indicates the potential for a new order of functioning. The child can now mentally represent aspects of impersonal external objects, as well as external emotion- or affect-laden human objects, in whole or in part. In addition, the child is able to represent internal psychological events. These beginning organizations of the self call on various sensory experiences — proprioceptive, visual, auditory, olfactory, etc.

In its unstable form, the capacity for representation may be lost with the absence of the object, particularly the human object, or under the pressure of strong internal experiences (drive derivatives or affects). In optimal development the capacity for human object constancy becomes stabilized only around age three (Mahler, Pine, and Bergman, 1975). This stabilization is gradual. The capacity for object permanence has a developmental sequence similar to that of object constancy, but it reaches relative stability much earlier (Dé-

This material originally appeared in slightly different form in the author's *Intelligence and Adaptation: An Integration of Psychoanalytic and Piagetian Developmental Psychology* © 1979, International Universities Press, New York, New York.

carie, 1962). This difference in timing is most likely related to the greater variability and unpredictability of human objects (changing moods, behaviors, etc.). In any case, the capacity to maintain representations of the self and of both animate and inanimate objects, as well as to maintain the differentiation of self-representations and object representations, probably begins early in the first year and continues to develop throughout life.

In this regard, it is interesting to note that the capacity for symbolic elaboration in the inanimate sphere was postulated by Piaget (1962) to progress through a series of invariant steps, from the toddler's functional understanding of objects (e.g., picking up a telephone receiver), to the precursor of symbolic capacity proper (the child evidencing through a grin that he knows he is pretending to eat from a toy spoon), to the further distancing of the symbolic act from this initial sensorimotor scheme (Werner and Kaplan, 1963), finally to the emergence of symbolic capacities proper where the "pretend" characteristics are clear and where objects clearly represent others or the child is clearly pretending to be an object (human or otherwise) other than himself or herself. Further elaborations into more complex dramas, first in a seemingly random manner and then in a more realistic manner (e.g., undressing the doll and bringing it upstairs and tucking it into bed), mark the entry into an early form of games.

Psychoanalytic observers and Piaget agree that there is a kind of regression in thinking after the capacity for internal representation becomes established. Piaget refers to a vertical *décalage*, and psychoanalytic clinicians point to an increase in magical thinking. In line with this, Mahler, Pine, and Bergman (1975) describe a regression in the interpersonal dimension as characteristic of the rapprochement subphase of the separation-individuation process. At this time the child has the capacity for constructing mental representations of internal and external objects. He is, however, not yet able to organize them in any logical relationship to each other or to the external world; rather, he uses magical thinking.

Piaget notes that at the sensorimotor level the young infant begins with magical thinking. For example, we observe the young infant pull in the area of his crib where there once was a string, or pull on a string repeatedly even though there no longer is a bell at the other end. Only later, when learning by consequences occurs, does the infant differentiate between pulling on a string and hearing a sound, and pulling on a string when there is no sound. Thus, at the prerepresentational, or somatic level, the young infant begins to differentiate means from ends. The same process, Piaget posits, is repeated at a new level with the beginning of the capacity for psychological representations. While somatic intelligence continues, the capacity for representational intelligence begins again with magical thinking — hence his term *vertical décalage*.

Psychoanalytic observers describe this type of thinking as primary process, in which the mechanisms of condensation, displacement, incorporation, and projection, among others, are at work. They also describe it in terms of freely mobile cathexes, as opposed to the more stable, fixed cathexes that become invested in secondary-process thinking.

Mahler beautifully describes a regression similar to Piaget's vertical *décalage* crisis (Mahler, Pine, and Bergman, 1975). According to her, the youngster, at 18 to 24 months, after seeming to be "king or queen of his or her universe," undergoes regression in terms of becoming much more dependent. She hypothesizes that this rapprochement crisis occurs in part because the youngster becomes capable of seeing his own true size in relation to the universe; with the greater capacity for psychological representation, he can represent himself and others more accurately and see himself more separately from the "omnipotent" parental objects. Visualizing oneself as small in relation to the universe,

Mahler posits, leads to much greater dependence on the maternal object in that the toddler no longer shares an "omnipotent umbrella" with her.

At this point it is important to distinguish two components of the capacity for psychological representation. Representational capacity: phase I does not involve learning by consequences or means-ends differentiation to any significant degree. It is nevertheless a great leap in intelligent functioning. Now the child can represent stimuli from the inside and the outside; he is not limited simply to dealing with stimulation through patterns using the body. Also, there is now a capacity for organized psychological experience. A representation of the maternal object, for instance, can be held in the child's mind and the youngster can call on this representation even when the mother is absent. If there is stimulation from the interior in terms of yearning for physical contact with the mothering person, memories of the mother's sound, visual image, touch, smell, etc., can be organized through mental representation, and some sense of satisfaction of the need for physical closeness with the mother can be gained. Thus, stimulation from within can be dealt with by a new route. Earlier in life, the best the infant could do was to use imitative activity; before that he could only cry in protest and perhaps begin to quiet himself with rhythmic rocking.

As another indication of beginning representational capacities, it should be mentioned that during the first year many youngsters begin to comfort themselves with a transitional object associated with the nurturing experience, such as a piece of cloth or an old blanket. (See Winnicott's [1953] discussion of the "first not-me possession" and Greenacre [1969].)

At first, when representations are just beginning to be organized, they are susceptible to regression under the pressure of internal affect states. Feelings of displeasure, loss, or anger may bring forth a loss of the capacity for representation and a state of panic in the youngster. Later on, when there is greater stability in the representational system, the child can experience more differentiated affect states and psychological events without the danger of loss of the internalized object. Thus, the flexibility of the internal system increases in terms of being able to tolerate a wider variety of wishes and affect states.

It is important to emphasize that phase I of representational capacity is simply the capacity for representation. As we have noted, it is not reinforced by additional stabilizing influences and is vulnerable to regression. In addition, during the early phase of representational capacity, there is not full differentiation between self and nonself representations.

5
Capacity for Organizing
Internal Representations (18–30 Months)

With the development of representational capacity at around 18 to 30 months, the youngster gradually becomes capable of an internal sense of self and object and an initial ability to conserve internal representations of animate and inanimate objects, as evidenced by an increased behavioral, emotional, cognitive, and interpersonal repertoire. At this age, we observe the ability to say "No" and the development of personal pronouns. The child can now organize mental images to search for inanimate and animate objects, and has the ability to recall events, as well as memory, for emotional experience. We see the beginning of cognitive insight (combining internalized schemes). A beginning distinction is made between experiences pertaining to the self and the nonself, and the child is now able to identify the various parts of self. He relates to others in a less need-fulfilling manner and shows the beginnings of cooperation and concern for others.

The Child's Capacities

The most adaptive child at this stage of development

has an ability to form and arrange mental representations into organized units of increasing range and depth. For this child, "out of sight" no longer means "out of mind." Experience becomes the basis whereby one segment of reality or fantasy can be integrated with another. The manipulation of symbols gradually becomes possible.

At the earliest stage of representational capacity we can assess adaptive capacities in terms of the range of experience that can be represented. We can look, for example, at the degree to which not only pleasurable experience but also assertive and exploratory experience can be represented at a symbolic level (now the toddler is able to look for something hidden in a drawer; he can ask for a favorite cookie which he knows is in the jar). We can also observe the degree to which angry protest and negative behavior become organized at a symbolic level as the growing toddler not only uses "No" more frequently, but begins to show a *selective* capacity to "know" what he wants; that is, the toddler can say "No" to eating chicken and "Yes" to ice cream and candy by stating "want candy; want ice cream." While it is unusual for the toddler just past his second birthday to be able to use complex sentences, the juxtaposition of "No" with the demand for something else will make his intent quite clear.

We observe the adaptive capacity of the toddler not only in the breadth of experience represented but in its depth and richness as well. The adaptive toddler might play a complex game with dolls in which the mommy doll bathes and kisses the baby doll and then puts the baby doll to sleep. His delight in this play suggests that he can experience the pleasure of interaction with another in the symbolic realm. Just as we can assess the depth and richness of this pleasure in the actual interaction, so can we assess its depth and richness in the child's symbolic play. Indeed, the child who is capable of such actual interactions is generally capable of representing them symbolically. And the same will be true with respect to his imaginative behavior: The story line of his play will be elaborated upon rather than ceasing abruptly or shifting from one subject to another. Other dimensions of experience and their accompanying affects will have similar depth and richness where representational capacity has developed appropriately: assertion and demand, exploration and curiosity, negativism and anger.

The adaptive youngster begins to show an increasing capacity to elaborate on his or her symbolic modes in each of these ranges of experience. As the youngster first begins to use words, an experience is described in its most basic terms, "doll," or "cake." When, a few months later, modifying words have been mastered, the toddler may be able to say "eat cake — happy," as he or she pretends to hold a tea party. Yet a few months later on, the toddler may be able to communicate in a full sentence — "I gave her cake; she's happy." Thus, with the child's growing vocabulary more and more experiences can be described — happy experiences, upsetting experiences, demands, etc. This is clearly seen in relationship to the inanimate world where the toddler evidences a deep interest in describing what is seen. Bright, curious, alert toddlers will be naming everything they see. It is amazing how quickly their vocabulary increases as they learn not only to imitate what the parent has said, but to do so in the appropriate context. This kind of contextual, imitative learning should, perhaps, more aptly be described as identificatory learning. The alert observer will notice similar complexity in the adaptive toddler's descriptions of the animate world. He might describe a scene in which two dolls are holding each other such that the dolls are clearly enjoying the experience.

As symbolic elaboration occurs, we look for the adaptive toddler to go beyond mere description of the animate and inanimate world. That is, the child will begin to represent personal *interactions* as well. For example, the toddler might embellish "This is a house; this is a car; this is a doll; this is a smiling doll," with "This doll is smiling because the mommy doll is holding it." Or he might say, "Pick me up. I like to be held." The shift from description to the representation of personal interactions occurs not only in the child's overt verbalizations and symbolic play, but also, implicitly, in these personal interactions themselves. The toddler who begins to use personal pronouns and verbs in an action-oriented sense—"I want you to do this; please get me that," etc., — is using language instrumentally, and, in a broader sense, is using symbolic capacities instrumentally in the interaction. At a nonverbal level, the toddler who plays a trick on mother (e.g., hides her pocketbook when she is about to go shopping and then laughs as mother looks confused) obviously has an excellent capacity for the symbolic elaboration of interactions, as evidenced by the planning and anticipation involved in his complex strategem, even though he has not used a single word. It should be highlighted that words are only one way the child evidences the symbolic or representational mode. Symbolic play and/or interactions which involve complex planning and obvious manipulation of "thoughts" are other ways the child evidences the existence and complexity of his representational capacity.

As the youngster becomes able to use the symbolic mode in representing interactions, he begins to emerge as a person. Parents begin to converse without the use of baby talk. The interactional dramas that are elaborated, whether in reality or in play, encompass multiple themes involving various behavioral and affective domains. Here, too, one must carefully observe the range of affective themes to which the youngster can apply his or her new ability. There is a great deal of difference between the youngster who can interact symbolically only in aggressive ways and the youngster who can use this ability across all the age-expected thematic and affective domains.

It must be emphasized that we are talking here about the elaboration of the symbolic mode during the earliest period of representational capacity. Initially, these representations of experience exist as isolated islands, unrelated to other islands of experience. The youngster may make reference to a birthday party as though it had happened yesterday, when it had actually taken place two weeks earlier, and then quickly talk about an experience that had happened three weeks before as though it were about to happen tomorrow. The youngster who one day goes to a park and another day goes to a birthday party might represent each of these experiences verbally as though they had occurred together when in fact they had occurred a week apart. This type of primary process thinking is usual in the early stages of representational capacity when a capacity to organize symbols into small cohesive islands has already developed but these islands cannot as yet be connected by logical or reality-oriented linkages.

It is interesting to note that before primary process thinking can become evident, and before the mechanisms of condensation, displacement, etc. (Freud, 1900) can be used to explain the juxtaposition of seemingly unrelated experiences, the youngster must first seek to connect symbols that represent temporally non-successive or spatially non-proximate experiences. When a youngster is still at a descriptive level, naming one object and then another, his "thinking" may appear quite logical. It is only when he attempts the developmentally more advanced task of connecting representations of non-successive or non-proximate experiences that his connections will seem illogical.

We also look specifically at whether the youngster is using his adaptive capacity in the service of developing more effective coping mechanisms. Now that the youngster can represent experience in terms of symbols, can he manipulate these symbols in order to make his needs known? Is he able to communicate more effectively with parents and peers? Is he able to deal with frustration more effectively than was true earlier in development? Do his new capacities help him become more explorative and independent? Does he master

new situations more easily? Or are these new capacities simply being used to make the youngster more skillful in a negative way? Are they being used manipulatively to have his
needs met immediately? In other words, has frustration tolerance not increased at all? Generally, if the symbolic mode
is used across the whole range of human experience in an
age-expected balance—if it reflects life's polarities of love
and hate, passivity and activity, etc. —it will be used to help
the child cope in a constructive way. But if it is loaded toward one end of the experiential world—toward negativistic and angry experiences only, or superficially pleasurable,
passive, compliant experiences—then one may see maladaptive trends. Similarly, if the symbolic mode is used predominantly in relation to the inanimate world, causing the child
to turn away from people, maladaptation will result.

The most adaptive youngster will exhibit some stability
in his capacity to represent experience. Under stress—a brief
separation from his parents, for example—the youngster
may feel angry and frustrated, but will lose representational
capacity only temporarily, if at all. Chronic regression to
disorganized behavior or loss of ability to use the symbolic
mode will not occur. Even physical illness will lead to only
temporary regression in the symbolic mode. Compare this
youngster with the child who may regress in representational capacity for days on end following even the slightest stress
—a separation of a few hours from his mother or some minimal frustration of a desire. Where representational capacity
is not stable, even more dramatic regressions may occur
from which the youngster will find it difficult to recover.
The less adaptive youngster with a mild fever and a cold
may begin to crawl again and give up the use of language
and symbolic play. He or she may want only to be held and
fed with a bottle like his baby brother and sister, and may
even refuse to relinquish this behavior from an earlier time
several days after his fever has gone.

Finally, we can assess the personal character of the

child's representations. Are individual characteristics or patterns beginning to emerge? Does the youngster show a personal style? Are there certain repetitive and characteristic symbolic games organized around pleasure or assertiveness? Or is there a random quality to the child's behavior? Has the youngster begun to put his own personal stamp on experience, even as he continues to imitate and identify with others? Or does the youngster seem to be more like the adult "as if" personality who imitates in random and chaotic fashion?

In summary, then, one studies the emergence of the symbolic or representational mode first in its descriptive phase (e.g., naming objects) and then in its interactional or instrumental phase (e.g., action and interaction sequences). At each level the range, depth, richness, stability, and personal uniqueness of expression must be assessed.

Disordered children at this stage of development exhibit a relative inability to form mental representations. Their imagery will not coalesce into organized experiential units. Whatever language capacity is evidenced will remain at the descriptive level, and will not be applied to the representation of complex interactions. They often demonstrate such symptoms as disorganized emotional and motor responses, chronic unrelenting clinging with complete disruption of exploratory behavior, chronic primitive aggressive behavior (biting, scratching, throwing things), chronic fearfulness, and either interpersonal promiscuity or withdrawal. Disorders in the organization of internal mental representations have a profound influence on all areas of basic ego functioning, as we see in adult psychotic and borderline patients.

At the most extreme level, severely regressive behavior may begin to surface. The effort to relate to others is given up as autistic-like patterns and/or other inappropriate affective responses appear. Integrated sensorimotor patterns, affective patterns, and already acquired interpersonal patterns can all become fragmented as maladaptation in this phase disrupts earlier development. Indeed, the ability to form mental representations and thereby to organize psychological life can be conceptualized as a means of stabilizing the behavioral organization and initiative of the prior stage of development. The adaptive child consolidates his earlier gains. The maladaptive child, faced with the task of organizing the greater variety of more complex experiences now made available to him by his increased motor capacities, the increased discriminatory capacities of his sensory equipment, and his increased awareness at the concrete impersonal level, may well regress without an accompanying capacity to organize the broader range of experience he now confronts.

Mental representations *structure* experience, as the adaptive toddler shows us. While his initial attempts to portray the interaction of experience may be isolated from one another, they are at least internally consistent. His quasi sentences, however short, make sense. In contrast, the youngster whose cognitive development has reached a level of verbal imitation, but who lacks the capacity to represent human interactional experience mentally, may either speak nonsense syllables or recognizable words that bear little relationship to one another. Instead of saying "Come here . . . candy" to indicate a wish for candy, the maladaptive youngster may say the word "eat" as a signal that he is hungry, followed by "dog" or "horse" as he points to play objects around the room. In other words, even the most rudimentary form of purposefulness at a representational level is not mastered.

At a less severe level, some youngsters may attain representational capacity but with serious limitations in one or another area. Some of these youngsters may be able to represent the inanimate world but not the animate world. They can describe inanimate objects, talk in sentences, and recall the inanimate world — a game seen the day before, for example. These same youngsters, however, are withdrawn from the animate world and uninvolved in human relationships. When they are involved, they behave more like one-year-olds, unable to demonstrate the organized interpersonal behavior that we see under optimal circumstances. Not infrequently we see a youngster who can do complicated puzzles and use words in short sentences shy away from any relationship to parents or siblings, preferring to play by himself. Involvement in his weekly play group consists of going off to a corner in a withdrawn state. When coaxed into interpersonal activity, he or she becomes aggressive toward the other children, or begins throwing games, crawling, and uttering nonsense sounds rather than using language in an interpersonal context.

At a somewhat higher level, we see youngsters who have developed a representational capacity in both the inanimate and animate spheres, but show severe limitations with respect to certain areas of human experience. They may be able to use symbolic modes only around negativism, dominance, and aggression, always saying "No" or "I want that." These children seem always to look solemn, stubborn, and angry, and show little range of symbolic expression in the domain of pleasure. Their relationships with their parents or siblings are characterized by demands and temper tantrums. On the same level are the youngsters who use symbolic modes only in a passive, compliant, and superficially pleasurable way. They may seem overly dependent, wanting to sit in mother or father's lap. They may lack exploratory capacity and an ability to be firm or assertive. It is rare for them to be negativistic, angry, or to say "No" adamantly.

Other youngsters may vacillate between compliant states of superficial pleasure and temper tantrums. They show little ability to elaborate symbolically along either of these dimensions, or to bring to a consecutive set of experiences both sides of their nature. They are incapable of experiencing hearty laughter and joyous compliance at one point during a game with a loved parent, and assertive demandingness shortly thereafter.

Some children may show severe limitations in their capacity for exploration, a trait that is usually combined with excessive dependency needs. A youngster, for example, may play a complicated game with dolls as long as he or she is sitting in mothers lap. In the game, one doll may always be doing for another — feeding it, holding it, etc. When separated from the mother even briefly, this child will take to crawling or playing nonsymbolic games such as rolling a ball back and forth aimlessly or throwing toys on the floor. He or she may walk around without purpose or look for infantile interactions which do not require symbolic activity, a patty-cake game perhaps.

Further maladaptive trends are illustrated by youngsters whose representational capacities are easily disrupted by stress, or whose representational capacities lack a personal signature.

In the former instance, even the slightest stress, such as a brief separation, frustration, a slight illness, etc., will lead to profound regressions and the loss of the representational capacity. When frustrated, the child will cry and cling, stop talking, and will for days on end not be able to play symbolically.

In the latter instance, the youngster may initially seem charming and impressive to relatives and family friends. But because there is little cohesion in his evolving representational organization of himself and his world, his personality is shallow and has a make-believe quality. Eventually, the charm he has had for others is eroded as he changes personalities almost daily. One child, for example, was so unpredictable that his mother described him as "a great actor." One day he was like a television character, the next like a friend, and the third like his father. While this imitative pattern may be typical during the early representational phase, and may even remain an important tendency during later development, with this child it tended to dominate his daily life.

Finally, it should be mentioned that during this stage of development one normally sees certain regressive phenomena, described so well by Mahler (Mahler, Pine, and Bergman, 1975) in her rapprochement subphase of the separation-individuation process. Because the youngster begins to have a more realistic picture of himself in relatiôn to the world, i.e., can represent the world more realistically, an earlier sense of omnipotence may be undermined. As this takes place, it is appropriate for fearfulness, anxiety, demandingness, and clinging to result. Such regressive phenomena, however, are usually temporary and intermittent and respond well to supportive and empathetic measures. In itself, this regression does not undermine the child's overall forward momentum. Under optimal circumstances, the development and elaboration of the representational modes of organizing experience continue with spurts forward and small slips back. Generally, in looking at disordered functioning during this phase, we need only become concerned if the regressive pattern in question is chronic rather than vacillating and does not respond to empathetic and supportive measures.

Environmental Characteristics

At this stage of development, the growth-promoting environment reads, responds to, and encourages symbolic elaboration across a range of behavioral and emotional communications and is, at the same time, available for age-expected dependency needs and regressions. The goal of the environment is to facilitate representational or symbolic modes in deep, stable, and individually unique configurations. Whereas in earlier developmental stages, the parent related to the youngster in concrete fashion (feeding in response to hunger, holding and cuddling in response to dependency needs), now the parent must engage the child symbolically.

Thus, we look at whether the parent is able to engage the youngster at the level of language. Does the parent encourage the descriptive use of language, the youngster's identification of his inanimate and animate worlds (e.g., that's a car; that's a truck; that's Daddy; that's Mommy; that's my friend David, etc.)? The parent who engages the youngster in such a symbolic mode will respond "Yes, that is so and so." And the same parent will try to take the conversation a step further by saying, "There is Joanne" and then adding "Say hello to her" and so on. The environment encourages the use of new verbal skills.

The optimal environment encourages the use of language to represent personal interactions. When the youngster says "I want my cake" or "I want this toy" or "Please pick me up, Mommy," the parent will respond "Yes, I'll come pick you up" or "Sorry, I can't pick you up now. I'm cooking. But I'll pick you up in a minute."

To take this example a step further, the mother might suggest "I can't pick you up now, I'm cooking. Stay next to me and I will tell you what I am doing." The mother then proceeds to describe the pot and pan, the rice, etc., and what she is doing with them. The youngster, in such a situation, may smile happily, point, and begin to imitate mother, naming some of the foods and other items that perhaps he or she had not had a chance to have seen or learned about before.

What is the mother doing here? Not only is she responding to the youngster's use of the symbolic mode, she is also offering a substitute for direct physical satisfaction of his dependency needs. Rather than picking him up, she soothes the youngster with words. She responds symbolically rather than concretely. Her warm and friendly description of her activity is a way of symbolically holding the youngster in her lap. We all experience this mode of comforting when we are in a warm and supportive discussion with a close friend. The youngster in this situation learns that this most basic form of comforting can be achieved in representational form. He feels respected in a way that facilitates his movement toward a higher level of development.

Use of the symbolic mode is not dependent on language and can also be encouraged in play activities as youngsters begin to show, through their play with dolls, cars, guns, or other objects, the ability to develop themes or dramas that symbolically express aspects of themselves (e.g., their ideas, feelings, wishes, etc.). The 25-month-old toddler may hug a doll and say, or otherwise indicate, that the doll is Mommy, or that he or she is Mommy, holding baby sister. As the youngster gets a little older, there may be a tea party, with all the dolls involved in a complex drama wherein the dolls serve as symbols, as representations for certain already internalized configurations of experience. The youngster, in playing out the game, demonstrates that he or she already has a drama, a configuration, in mind. Parents can enter into these games and help to make them more complex. Father may sit down and participate in the tea party along with the dolls, and when his daughter either motions instrumentally or asks, "Do you want some more coffee?" father can respond either with gestures or words, or with both, "Of course I want more coffee, it is very good." He then takes the cup to his mouth and pretends to drink. By his warmth and interest, he is encouraging the use of this symbolic mode of involvement. When, in contrast, the bored father withdraws behind his newspaper, his daughter may throw her tea set to the floor and begin grabbing at father's knee as she tries to crawl up into his lap, giving up the symbolic mode for the concrete.

While the use of verbal communication and symbolic play are the most obvious examples of representational capacity, there are more subtle forms that can also be described. The child, for example, may indicate that he or she is hungry by walking into the kitchen and pointing to the refrigerator. Mother, by a facial expression and/or hand gesture, implies, "Not yet." The youngster understands this and goes to cuddle next to father reading the newspaper. Or begins to play patty-cake with father or some other more complex game. While in this sequence we can only speculate that symbolic modes are being utilized, it is noteworthy that the hungry youngster does not cry in frustration like a three-month-old child. Instead, he understands that he must wait and substitutes another form of interaction about which he may already have a preconceived configuration. He sits next to father or initiates the more complex game as a substitute satisfaction of his needs. The representational mode is enlisted in the service of delay.

Many such complex interactions have symbolic or representational properties, and are already in evidence in the phase of development we have called "behavioral organization, initiative, and internalization." The behavior of the youngster who takes the parent by the hand and shows him the food in the refrigerator suggests that there is some kind of internal scheme associated with his hunger. His subsequent patience in the face of his needs, his persistence in addressing them (but now by means of substitutive activity), and the very fact that there is a delay between what the youngster does and the concrete bodily satisfaction he receives suggests that symbolic modes are at work. And just as in the phase of behavioral organization, initiative, and internalization the growth-promoting parent encourages the child's use of these complex communications, so must the parent encourage their use in the phase of representational capacity.

Once representational capacity has been established, the growth-promoting environment seeks to support its elaboration across a range of animate and inanimate experience. With respect to the inanimate world, the parent can supply the youngster with material that can be described, manipulated, and creatively transformed — a puzzle, for example. Such material should have qualities that appeal to the child's various senses. Textured, brightly colored toys, for example, will engage the child's sense of touch and vision and encourage the use of the symbolic mode.

With respect to the animate world, the growth-promoting environment tries to encourage the elaboration of representational modes around pleasure, assertiveness, curiosity, protest, and the like. If the parent shows little or no interest in the youngster's assertiveness and curiosity, the child may gradually conclude that exploration does not elicit human interaction. Representational modes organized around exploratory behavior may then suffer for lack of parental support. The parent who responds to the aggressive, demanding, or angry youngster by giving up an opportunity for symbolic interaction in favor of dealing with him concretely by physical means or, what is worse, figuratively abandons the youngster by refusing to interact or talk to him, will only discourage the use of the child's representational capacity with respect to these affects. This is not to suggest that limit-setting isn't vital. As we will see, limit-setting with "meaning" enhances the youngster's symbolic capacity.

But the parent must also attempt to deepen the child's capacity for representation. Let us suppose that parent and child are engaged in a chasing game. The youngster suddenly pulls out a toy gun and pretends to shoot at father. Father could pretend to falter, shoot back, or engage in a variety of other sequences, then pick up the child and hug him and they could end by laughing together. But if the parent feels threatened, and abruptly switches to some other game that he is more comfortable with, the youngster may never develop a capacity to use symbolic modes around aggression. As another example, let us suppose that the parent is so conflicted around sexual and pleasurable issues that when the youngster diapers the baby-sister doll and asks about the doll's "bottom," the parent immediately shifts the symbolic game to a doctor game of fixing the doll. Here, again, the youngster may never develop an appropriate representational capacity in the pleasurable domain. Or if he does, it may be filled with expectations of injury and/or other conflicts.

The growth-promoting environment fosters stability of representational capacity and a capacity to deal with stress by helping the youngster re-engage in the symbolic mode

after disruption. We have seen that during a temporary separation, or when the youngster is frustrated, angry, or physically ill, a disruption in the use of the symbolic mode may
occur, with regression to earlier, more concrete forms of interacting and behaving. Parents at this stage must be aware
of the stage-appropriate regressions discussed earlier in this
chapter. The regressive dependency and clinging of Mahler's
rapprochement subphase, with its clear suggestion of the
vulnerability of representational capacity, may require that
the parent respond, at least initially, in concrete ways. The
youngster who, when slightly ill, needs to be held and cuddled, should be held and cuddled. The adaptive environment tries to help the youngster feel calm and secure before
it attempts to re-engage the child in the effort to represent
his dependency needs symbolically. At times this may call
for limit-setting, i.e., when the youngster is involved in disorganized aggressive activity. The parent, however, always
tries to re-engage the child in the symbolic mode of relating.
For example, should the youngster throw a temper tantrum, the parent does not withdraw, or, what is the same
thing, punish the youngster by sending him to his room. If
punishment is necessary, it should be brief and clear. The
youngster should then be re-engaged at a higher level of expression and organization of experience. Alternatives can be
offered to the frustrated youngster. At times, for example,
the youngster's development and needs can best be satisfied
by offering concrete support at the same time as he is encouraged to use his representational capacity in an area apart
from the source of conflict. The child who is misbehaving
because father just went on a business trip is cuddled while
he and mother look at and describe pictures in a book and
together describe the places father may visit.

The adaptive environment supports the child's unique
sense of self. The use of personal pronouns and the youngster's name or nickname, if accompanied by a warm emotional tone, will foster differentiation and inherent respect
for the self of the youngster as he or she acts in the context of

the family environment. Contrast, for instance, "Johnny, you must not do that," with the vaguer generalization, "We don't behave that way." Even more important is the emotional sense of individuality and respect a youngster develops when the family attributes to him or her a sense of responsibility. A parent may say, "Sally, that made me very happy." Or through emotional interaction with the child make clear to Sally that something she did made the parent happy. Compare this with those family settings in which the youngster's impact remains obscure because of parental noninvolvement. Or those parents whose emotions are so entangled with the emotions of the youngster that no one knows who is causing what — whether they or the youngster have initiated a particular action. Some mothers may feel that they are responsible whenever their youngsters throw a temper tantrum. Instead of saying "You're angry" or "You're misbehaving," the mother wonders what *she did* and immediately takes some apologetic stance to appease the child. This kind of confusion will not encourage differentiation of the child's sense of self. The growth-promoting parent must acknowledge the child's impact on the environment.

Children often tend to develop preferences for certain types of interests, or certain types of games or puzzles. These may include interactional games that are not completely to the liking of the parent. Nevertheless, the parent recognizes and respects individual differences in the youngster and goes along with him or her, at times, perhaps, insisting that the youngster play a game that the parent enjoys. Respect for the youngster's inclinations supports his or her emerging sense of uniqueness. In contrast, parents who overcontrol the youngster, or whose own conflicts undermine the autonomy and the individual uniqueness of the youngster, may disregard his personal inclinations.

Parents further need to respect the child's emerging capacities to delay gratification. At the same time as they provide a basic sense of security, they must also recognize that the child's newly emerging capacity for delay will not develop if his needs are immediately satisfied in concrete fashion. Particularly important in supporting representational modes is the need to strike a balance between the provision of support and limit-setting. The frustrated youngster's temper tantrums and other disorganized expressions of anger need to be accepted up to a point, so that these feelings and experiences can be elaborated on a representational level. Still, firm limit-setting (and, at times, suitable punishment) is also necessary if the youngster is to operate in a higher representational mode. The spoiled youngster who is given everything, and whose temper tantrums go unchallenged, may find little motivation for dealing with the world at higher levels of representation.

In contrast to the growth-promoting environment, the growth-inhibiting environment fails to support the development of representational capacities and/or fails to support representational capacities across the full range of age-appropriate experience in deep, stable, highly individualistic patterns.

At its most extreme, the maladaptive environment fails completely to engage the youngster representationally, either at the descriptive or the interactional level. There is no encouragement to use words to describe objects or people. The youngster's imitation of words, or attempts to use other symbols, are undermined by the caretaking environment. As the child begins to attach words to his toys or to kitchen utensils, the parents become preoccupied or withdrawn. Oblivious to their child's needs, the parents give them little or no feedback or support. Or, on the other hand, the parents may overcontrol the child, teaching or intruding excessively. They may insist that the child name everything in sight. In such instances, the bewildered toddler is likely to withdraw into a negativistic stance, refusing to use symbolic or representational modes even at the descriptive level.

More common are parents who do not encourage the representation of personal interactions. If they are willing to engage the youngster at all, it is around concrete modes such as holding or feeding. When the youngster says, "I want dinner now," rather than responding, "Not yet, you have to wait a little," the parent may ignore the youngster's verbal communication altogether, leaving the frustrated youngster to feel that he has no choice other than to resort to an earlier mode of behavior, crying or angry tantrums, much as he did when he was three or four months old and felt hungry. If the environment does respond to the child's symbolic communication of hunger, it may do so in an overly punitive, intrusive, and controlling way: "No, get out of here," accompanied by a spanking, so that the youngster finds representational modes of communicating highly unrewarding. In such instances, resorting once again to aggressive or earlier concrete modes of expression may seem to be the only way open to the toddler.

The growth-inhibiting environment may undermine emerging representational capacity in yet another way, by misreading or distorting the symbolic communication of the child. The child may come in smiling, saying the word "cookie" for his favorite food, and open his mouth in expectation as he or she points to the cookie jar in the symbolic mode. Instead of experiencing this as a way for her youngster to elaborate his or her wishes, mother experiences it as an assault on her freedom: "He knows I am reading my magazine. The little monster just wants to get my goat." Or the parent, uncomfortable with this kind of angry reaction, might simply respond with a non sequitur, "What a nice day it is outside," and a suggestion that the youngster look at the shining sun. Such lack of responsiveness, or distorted or unrelated responsiveness, may undermine the very foundation of the representational system. Jackson (1960), Lidz, Fleck, and Cornelison (1967), Lidz (1973), and Wynne, Matthysse, and Cromwell (1978) describe entire families whose members' failure to respond appropriately to each other lead to the faulty communication patterns that are hypothesized to be associated with such severe psychopathology as schizophrenia.

At a more specific level, we may see that the growth-inhibiting environment supports some areas of representational elaboration while undermining others. Parents with conflicts over aggression, for example, may be able to support the symbolic elaboration of dependency needs or pleasurable pursuits, whereas aggressive expressions may be met with misperceptions, withdrawal, or punishment.

The growth-inhibiting environment may fail to support the stability of representational capacities. Suppose that for some reason the youngster shows a regressive tendency to express his aggression in concrete fashion. If his parents cannot tolerate aggression, they may not structure their response so as to bring him back to the symbolic mode as quickly as possible. Instead, they may become aloof and withdrawn, seeing the youngster's aggression as a rejection of themselves. In other words, the growth-inhibiting environment supports the child's regressive behavior by matching it with regressive behavior of its own, rather than creating an opportunity for recovery. The youngster who, in the rapprochement phase of development, has just established some representational capacity may, after a brief separation from mother, cling or grab at her. Instead of cuddling the youngster to help restore his sense of security, the mother, frightened by the youngster's dependency needs, scolds the child loudly and orders him to act "grown-up." The youngster then responds with a temper tantrum. An opportunity to help the youngster see that it is possible to recover his higher level of representational functioning is missed.

The child's sense of individuality may be undermined by parents who find his expressions of uniqueness threatening to them. Instead of supporting the toddler's own style (e.g., the game he likes, the emotional expressions he prefers), family members in the maladaptive environment will find fault with each of these unique characteristics and insist that the youngster not play the game he has chosen but, instead, look at a book. If the youngster uses a certain gesture or facial expression to show his dislike for something, the parent will tell him it is inappropriate and insist that he smile instead. Perhaps even more overwhelming to the child is the parent who withdraws whenever the youngster's unique emotional style, personal interactive patterns, or preferences for special games or activities emerge. The youngster in such an environment may resort to chronic negativism as a means of maintaining a fragile yet stubbornly persistent sense of personal uniqueness; or, alternatively, he may become promiscuously imitative — acting one way one time and another way another time, chameleon-like, according to the needs of the environment.

The growth-inhibiting environment may give the youngster little substantive emotional feedback, and on the surface may seem to accept everything the youngster does. Yet at an emotional level it actually accepts nothing. This sort of attitude may leave the youngster confused as he tries without success to engage his parents emotionally. He may develop an "as if" style or give up altogether and become apathetic.

Another fundamental characteristic of the growth-inhibiting environment is its basic lack of respect for the person or the "self" of the toddler. There is, for example, little use of personal pronouns, few references to "you," what "you" want or what "you" feel, a premature sense of a collective family identity, or avoidance by the parents in expressing their personal wishes. In these cases one rarely sees a confrontation between parent and child in which the child says "I want this" and the parent says "I want that" and eventually some compromise is reached. Families that avoid the personal "you" or confuse the question of personal responsibility (or, indeed, avoid such questions entirely) may inhibit the child's sense of having an impact on the world.

Principles of Preventive Intervention and Treatment

A youngster may have negotiated the earlier stages of development — homeostasis, attachment, somatic-psychological differentiation, behavioral organization, initiative, and internalization — reasonably well, but, for a variety of reasons, may not be moving into the symbolic mode and/or elaborating symbolic capacities as a way of organizing experience. Perhaps his parents are still responding concretely, failing to encourage symbolic communication through language and play as a means of expressing more complex wishes, feelings, or interactions. They do not make available to the youngster those complex interpersonal interactions whereby concrete needs, to be held or fed, can be expressed and satisfied in symbolic form. (Of course, concrete modes continue to play an important role with respect to the child's age-appropriate regressions and continuing need for physical comfort.)

Where this is the case, the parents' inadequacies may be due to preoccupation with their own work, ignorance, conflicts around entering into the representational mode, or severe personality problems. Where the problem is a simple lack of know-how, didactic instruction (with follow-up support) may suffice. Modeling can be used as an important part of such teaching. But where parental conflicts are operative, the didactic approach must be combined with an approach that explores these conflicts and at the same time offers the parents the support they need to resolve their conflicts *in other ways* (other than at the expense of their growing toddler). With more severe parental pathology — major character problems and/or severe personality defects — it will be necessary to make use of a more complete psychotherapeutic approach, dealing with some of the causes of their difficulties while at the same time offering support and education. It is not always necessary for the parents to reach a total resolution of their difficulties before they can alter the environment to benefit the child. With a great deal of support and encouragement from a professional staff, willing parents often borrow the skills of the "other" to use with their children while they are engaged in resolving their own basic difficulties.

Another kind of challenge is presented where the child's failure to enter the representational mode and/or to elaborate this mode results from his failure to have acquired the capacities of earlier stages of development. The youngster who has not successfully negotiated the stage of behavioral organization, initiative, and internalization may bring with him fragmented rather than organized behavioral patterns and a tendency toward negativism rather than exploration. At the same time, however, this child is faced with a greater variety of more complex stimuli simply by virtue of his increased motor capacities and the increased discriminatory powers of his sensory equipment — that is to say, by virtue of the maturation of his central nervous system to an age-appropriate level for a 36-month-old child. Thus he is faced with the tasks of the phase of representational capacity when he has not yet acquired certain capacities of the previous developmental stage. In such cases, the basic principle of intervention is to assist the child in negotiating these earlier issues by means of the techniques outlined in Chapter 4 while at the same time encouraging the development of his newly emerging representational capacities. That is to say, behavioral organization can now be fostered in the representational mode as well as the more concrete modes.

Where residual difficulties remain from the stages of homeostasis, attachment, and somatic-psychological differentiation, the principle is the same: Assist the child in negotiating these earlier issues while at the same time encouraging the development of representational capacities. The youngster who has not developed the capacity for internal regulation and is either hyperexcitable or excessively irritable may require swaddling and a good deal of physical holding even at 20–24 months, and, at the same time, experiences that are consistent with his newly emerging representational capacities. An example of such an exercise might be work with a puzzle. Interest could be aroused by making the puzzle intriguing in color or design, and by combining

verbal encouragement with physical closeness. If the youngster begins to throw the pieces about, physical limitations,
including holding, may be appropriate.

The youngster who is only superficially and imperson-
ally involved with another person—shallow in his attachments—may require extra wooing. Many of the exercises
described in Chapter 2 for the stage of attachment can be
used at this higher level. But while the youngster may need
to be wooed partly through direct cuddling and pleasurable
physical activities, he can also be wooed through his now
more developed symbolic modes: through participation in
enjoyable, interactive games and/or play with dolls. Talking with such a youngster, showing one's interest in him,
helping him to interact with other people, but now at the
level of words and symbols, can help him overcome the earlier lack of attachment. Of course, the emotionally shallow
youngster may be taxing to his parents or to the staff of the
therapeutic infant center. Disinterested and aloof, he may
cause them to feel rejected. Therapeutic responses may then
be organized in equally impersonal modes, often involving
the inappropriate use of behavior modification programs.
Limit-setting and clear consequences are often essential but
must serve the more important goal of intimacy. The natural tendency to lose sight of this goal often requires a great
deal of intrapersonal vigilance on the part of the therapeutic
staff.

If a basic sense of causality has not been established in
the stage of somatic-psychological differentiation, the child
can be helped to understand his or her impact on the world
by the use of the representational mode. The youngster who
does not have a sense of causality, and who evidences disorganized, aggressive behavior or disorganized and promiscuous sexual behavior, may need to be shown that each of these
behaviors has its consequences. Very specific, direct patterns
of feedback at a more elementary level may need to be employed in both the symbolic and concrete behavioral modes.

It may also be necessary to set limits when the youngster becomes physically or verbally assaultive. But when this youngster reaches out for human contact and compassion, it is important to respond immediately, again through verbal and symbolic modes, as well as the concrete mode, to establish for this youngster the sense of consequences that may not have been established previously.

As a general rule, when youngsters at the stage of representational capacity have had difficulties in earlier stages of development, they will often show conflict at the symbolic level, as well as specific inadequacies. A 24-month-old child, whose earlier patterns of intimacy and attachment have not been established, may begin to play with one doll, establish a nurturing scene, pick up another, dropping the first abruptly. The scene may then deteriorate into a disorganized tossing around of pieces from the doll house. Intimacy, rejection, disorganization, and frenetic activity have all been pictured at a symbolic level. Not only is the child unable to integrate his play experiences because of a lack of a secure sense of intimacy, he is also showing us, at the representational level, the earlier experiential basis for not having established this sense of intimacy. Perhaps his intimate encounters with his parents may frequently have been abruptly interrupted, these interruptions then provoking his own disorganized protests and aggressive responses. The child may often show this same pattern in his relationships with other toddlers as well as with adults — intimacy followed by increasingly disorganized aggressive behavior (often precipitated by the adult caretaker's even temporary distraction). To some extent, these conflicts can be worked through in preventive therapeutic sessions, the staff working with the youngster to help him experience intimacy at the symbolic as well as the concrete level.

The staff may find that they will have to deal with some of the youngster's sequential expectations if he is to participate successfully in this new learning experience. The emerging capacity for language permits the youngster to rework some of his obvious concerns. For example, as one watches the child repeatedly play out the scene with the dolls, one can, if the youngster is sufficiently verbal, voice the sequence, and by simply putting it into words, give him a higher-order symbolic capacity to deal with what is happening. He can now "think" about it. One could then point out to the youngster how negative expectations can sometimes be self-fulfilling. Obviously, one cannot do this as one would with an adult, or even an older child. One can, however, manipulate the scenario with the dolls into different sequences to show the youngster the alternatives. Thus one can interrupt the developing sequence by changing the scene so that the baby doll pursues the adult doll, saying, "Come back, come back" and then show the adult doll returning and re-engaging the baby doll. At first the youngster will be confused because the plot has been changed. At the same time, however, he learns that there is another way to pursue what he wants. As he gets older and is able to use personal pronouns and express certain basic feelings such as "mad" or "happy" or "sad," one can attach these words to the scene being played out. In time, what the youngster may learn is that, in terms of real relationships, his former expectations need not be self-fulfilling. As he becomes cognitively and affectively more mature, he may even learn about his "feelings."

One may hear this youngster referring to the doll that represents himself as "icky," a sign that his frantic disorganization and uncontrollable aggression is already associated in his mind with a negative picture of himself. Through dramatic play, one can clarify for him that there is actually a connection between what may seem to him to be separate islands of experience, e.g., the disorganized aggression and the feeling of being "icky" or bad. Again, this may not be possible until the youngster is a little older, closer to age three.

It is not appropriate here to go further into the techniques of psychotherapeutic intervention with very young toddlers, since the magnitude of this subject requires separate treatment and will be the focus of a future work. We do want to point out that "psychotherapeutic" interventions — in the sense of work with conflicting tendencies and emerging properties of self and objects — can be done even before the representational stage (e.g., in the stage of behavioral organization, initiative, and internalization). We would like to suggest that a preventive intervention program for youngsters who have evidenced difficulty in earlier stages of development and are now evidencing further difficulties in establishing their representational capacities and/or elaborating them should include more than giving advice to parents. The program should endeavor to help parents alter the environment by means of a combination of didactic, supportive, and other therapeutic experiences. Staff should also consider working with the youngster directly or through the parents to help the child change his own maladaptive expectations and related experiences as they have become a part of his personality. It is important to be aware that by this age (24 months) aspects of experience are already internalized. Experiences from the very first day of life play their part in forming the personality of the toddler.

(As a brief side note it should also be emphasized that our direct work with toddlers and young children suggests that "deficiencies of experience" are almost always accompanied by conflict, even in a prerepresentational form. Both aspects of the toddler's experience must be considered.)

Youngsters with difficulties in this stage of development often exhibit the most extreme symptoms. They may be totally withdrawn and apathetic, looking and acting as if functionally retarded, or they may be overly aggressive, with chronic patterns of biting, kicking, or other highly disorganized behavior. These extreme situations require an appropriate structuring of the environment to deal with the kind of behavior manifested; e.g., sufficient support and wooing to bring out the withdrawn child; limit-setting as well as engagement for the overly aggressive youngster. The more specific patterns of care would be based, as described above, on what is diagnosed as the cause of the current difficulties and the possible unresolved issues of earlier stages of development.

Where the difficulties are more limited, another pattern of preventive intervention is required. There are youngsters, for example, who are developing and elaborating their symbolic and representational capacities, yet show marked constrictions along certain dimensions. They may lack a sense of exploration or curiosity, or be overly passive and compliant, or only aggressive and negativistic. Our task, then, is to see which issues are preventing elaboration in the constricted areas and to develop a program to help encourage and support symbolic elaboration in these areas. It may be found, for example, that the parents are uncomfortable with pleasure and dependency, and are strongly focused instead on success and assertion. At times these parents may simply need to be taught how to support development of representational capacity in these underused modes. At other times, however, parental conflicts will have to be dealt with directly before the parents can learn to support the child in these areas.

Many of these more subtle limitations in symbolic capacity and elaboration will go unnoticed. The youngster generally appears to be competent. Yet many "competent" youngsters do have limitations in the way they experience pleasure, dependency, and security. Because such youngsters may be bright and assertive and leaders among their peers even as toddlers, they are often praised by parents and teachers while their limitations go unrecognized. Often these limitations do not surface until adolescence or early adulthood when the challenges of life suddenly become more complicated. Only close scrutiny will disclose that whole realms of experience are not represented in their behaviors, their symbolic play, and their interactive communications. If the parental environment is not overly conflicted about these areas, preventive intervention can be relatively easy and extraordinarily effective. Similarly, lack of stability or personal uniqueness of representational capacity can be addressed therapeutically with relatively good results.

Clinical Illustrations

CASE 14

Mrs. N. was a rather assertive, warmly engaging mother with limited intellectual capacity, who tended to relate to her own emotional needs in a very concrete fashion. There were breaks in her capacity for organized thinking and reality testing. Although she tended to use denial and avoidance around emotional conflict, she was able to maintain a reasonable relationship with her husband, whose personality was organized along similar lines. When Jennifer was born, Mrs. N. was very excited and, in an obsessive way, wanted to make sure that Jennifer would have just the right food, just the right temperature in the house, just the right clothing, and so on. She seemed to be very concerned with providing appropriate physical care. An older daughter was having learning and behavioral problems in school and Mrs. N. felt that the way to guarantee a better adjustment for her new daughter was to make sure that she fed and clothed her properly.

Whenever she discussed her feelings, she would quickly bring the discussion around to such concrete needs as food and appropriate medication. In spite of these limitations, she was able to achieve a rich emotional involvement with her infant and to derive satisfaction from it. She responded quickly to Jennifer's fussiness or discomfort and, later, when her infant was able to crawl and push and throw things, she demonstrated some moderate overprotective tendencies. Otherwise, she did not interfere and was basically able to support differentiation and subsequent behavioral organization, initiative, and originality. While she did not often speak to her youngster, there was sufficient verbal interaction that language development proceeded reasonably well. By 20 months her little girl was able to string together a number of words and occasionally use a personal pronoun.

At this point we noted that little Jennifer was attempting to engage in symbolic play. She would bring dolls to her mother and attempt to develop some interaction between one doll and another, asking mother to hold one doll while she held the other. Or she would bring a toy telephone and say "hello" and "goodbye," wanting her mother to play a reciprocal role. We noted that, whenever Jennifer attempted to play these games with mother, Mrs. N. rather abruptly shifted gears and suggested that perhaps her daughter was "hungry or tired and needed to sleep." She tended to respond to her daughter's symbolic communications by bringing them down to a concrete level, at which she was obviously more comfortable. Her daughter, in reponse to this, became negative and aggressive, beginning to kick and bite and to give up her symbolic activity, using fewer words, playing with blocks more than dolls, and in general imitating the mother's use of the concrete mode.

At this point our therapeutic approach with Mrs. N. had two goals: To help her support the developing symbolic capacities of her very competent toddler, and to help her deal with whatever discomfort her daughter's evolving symbolic capacities were obviously causing her. Part of our approach was educative. This mother, who wanted to do well and who had been able to perform adequately up to this point, needed support, assurance, and some education with respect to the importance of language and other symbolic communications to her daughter's development.

At the same time, even talking about this in an abstract way clearly made mother anxious. She would frequently shift to another topic. When her avoidance of these more symbolic ways of engaging her daughter, and, for that matter, the therapist, were pointed out to her, mother began to express fears of "things getting out of control." She clearly felt that unless she maintained a concrete orientation she would lose control. With repeated exploration of this fear, mother was able to see that there was some anxiety on her part about engaging in these more complex symbolic activities. With this insight, mother became more responsive to our educative and supportive approaches. With the support of our staff, she was able to permit her daughter to take the lead in developing complicated games and to let herself enter into them. Over time she became somewhat more comfortable with her daughter's symbolic games and even experienced moments of satisfaction. There was still a good deal of nervousness and tension present, but no longer the avoidance and regression to the earlier more concrete mode of interacting. To date, the therapist is still exploring with mother exactly what it is that would "go out of control," and at the same time offering support, structure, and education as to how to relate to her daughter in a more complex, symbolic way.

Jennifer, too, is doing well with this approach. Symbolic development has resumed, and Jennifer is now an alert little girl, precociously verbal and imaginatively interactive for her age.

In this case mother, because of her own intellectual and cognitive orientation, and because of certain fears that are still not clear, was unable to support development in the area of symbolic elaboration. Structure and support from the therapist, and her own awareness of the problem, permitted her to engage her daughter, albeit "nervously." She no longer needed to use avoidance and regression to the more concrete modes that had begun to undermine her daughter's development.

It should also be mentioned that during the therapeutic work with mother, play sessions with Jennifer were also begun. An attempt was made to help her deal with her mother's nonsupport of her own symbolic capacities. It was interesting to observe that during this period of regression, when dolls were offered to Jennifer, she would play out certain themes. One that emerged repeatedly was that of one doll hitting another. Occasionally she would join in the fracas by throwing blocks at both dolls. We reasoned that her anger was in part related in a very general sense (we are not speaking here of specific dynamic issues) to the lack of maternal support for her emerging representational capacities. Based on our clinical experience, it appears that general frustration and anger will be manifested when a youngster is not being met at the developmental level at which he or she is capable of operating. Supporting this little girl while she played out her rage helped to limit her regression and allowed her to be more receptive to her mother's eventual support of her symbolic capacities. It is also possible that Jennifer was providing a picture of what it was that might "get out of control" during these symbolic interactions.

In this example we again see the importance of a clinical therapeutic approach in making parent and child more available to each other. This very specific therapeutic program would not have been possible without a center at which this dual approach could be carried out.

And again, just as we saw that the development of an attachment between therapist and caretaker will foster a growing capacity for attachment between caretaker and infant, and just as a therapeutically assisted capacity for self-observation on the part of the caretaker will encourage the development of her capacity for interacting in a more differentiated way with the infant, so too will the capacity for symbolic relatedness to the therapist parallel a developing capacity for symbolic relatedness to the youngster. When we encourage the verbalization of feelings and the elaboration of fantasy as a substitute for action, we often see growth in the parent's capacity to support symbolic activities in the youngster.

CASE 15

Direct therapeutic work with a toddler is illustrated by the case of Janet, a frail, wide-eyed, eager-looking 17-month-old girl who experienced a great deal of intermittent neglect from her borderline psychotic mother. Janet, whose weight gain and sensorimotor development had been severely compromised early in the first year and who had barely avoided being hospitalized for failure to thrive, was able, with special patterns of care (designed to facilitate somatic-psychological differentiation), to catch up cognitively. At 17 months, however, she was indiscriminate in her object relationships, flat in her affect, and conveyed a sense of affect hunger. She tended to victimize herself in relationships with other toddlers.

She was brought in daily to our Infant Center where part of her time was spent in a group with other children and staff in a consistent and secure environment (in contrast to the chaotic one at home) and part of her time (one hour) in a one-to-one therapeutic relationship with an assigned staff member. The goal of these individual sessions was to help Janet communicate her concerns so that her emotional development could progress.

The highlights of the process are instructive: First, simply the availability of an empathic adult behaving in a consistent way encouraged Janet to play, vocalize, and otherwise communicate, leading to a noticeable shift in Janet's overall emotional life. As she vacillated between states of passive withdrawal and chaotic play in which the baby doll was thrown around, torn up, etc., in her therapeutic sessisons, she slowly became less promiscuous in her relations to the staff. In fact, she became cautious and reserved.

With the growth of a special affective tie to her therapist (and to another key staff person), this quality of cautiousness with others increased. Simultaneously, she began using the baby doll to express both her needs and fears. Babies were pictured as helpless, crying, needing to be picked up, held, and fed. Yet there was a hidden lion who could "bite," wolves who could "hurt," and chaotic bedtime scenes with the doll being thrown around and torn apart. Janet became excessively vigilant in response to sounds in the room (the heat going on, for example), startling easily.

Shortly after this (Janet was now between 24 and 30 months), there was a thematic shift to what appeared to be an age-appropriate concern with the human body. Dolls were undressed. Curiosity about "peepees" was fervently expressed. Her special fears were also communicated, however, as people were "cut up." Themes of damage and injury were pervasive.

The therapist empathized with Janet's concerns, often putting into words what she communicated in play and encouraging elaboration of her symbolic play by offering herself in an intuitive manner to act out an implied role or to talk for one of the dolls or animals. A consistent affective tie within these sessions appeared to be very reassuring to Janet as she played out the various themes with which she was concerned.

During this time two important shifts occurred. Janet switched from using only the baby doll to express her concerns and began using the boy and girl dolls which clearly suggested children of Janet's age or older. At the same time, Janet was more relaxed with staff and other children. Her cautiousness lessened somewhat and a capacity for trust (e.g., she would ask for help) and at times even hints of empathy (if another child hurt himself, Janet would try to be comforting) emerged. At times she took the lead with other children in activities. Most important, Janet no longer evidenced affect-hungry, promiscuous, impersonal relationship patterns, and her pattern of setting herself up to be victimized was lessening. Interestingly, receptive and expressive language blossomed (even beyond age expectations) at this time.

As Janet approached age three, it was felt she would do

well in a regular day-care center, continuing her therapeutic sessions twice a week. As she anticipated the change and partial separation, themes of aggression and apprehension related to the unknown again emerged. Interestingly, the frightening "hidden" lion was now intermittently wrapped in a blanket and cuddled like a baby and then allowed to roar in anger and so forth, suggesting a greater sense of confidence in handling aggression. Subsequent sessions focused on controlling the "wolves and barking dogs."

Janet is doing quite well in her new setting. Her therapeutic sessions continue to be productive, now focusing on integrating her home life with the world she has come to know through her therapeutic program. She is now emotionally available to her mother whose own progress, while slower, has enabled her to at least support Janet's development. While her affective expression is still mildly subdued, she is in an overall sense a warm, engaging, competent, quite verbal three-year-old. She now has a remarkable ability to explore her concerns by means of language and the symbolic elaboration and differentiation of mental representations.

This case, of course, also illustrates how early deficits (caused by neglect with Janet) invariably lead to conflict (here, over aggression). Both the defect and the resulting conflict must be dealt with in a supportive, nurturing, consistent environment that permits skillful exploration of feelings and conflicts as part of a comprehensive approach to the child.

Representational Capacity: Phase II

Representational capacity: phase II is marked by the gradually increasing ability to learn by consequences again — that is, to differentiate means from ends — but now at a level of psychological representation. Parallel to what Mahler describes in terms of "on the way to object constancy," there is, both in the cognitive impersonal realm and in the emotion-laden interpersonal realm, a growing ability for reality testing. The youngster slowly ceases making the inanimate animate and begins to rely more on secondary-process thinking than on primary-process thinking as he heads from two toward and into four. This evolving capacity for accurate representation is made possible through learning by consequences at the representational level. Experience is not only represented internally, but is the vehicle for learning (e.g., trial and error). The greater capacity for memory and for discrimination is part of this process but will not be dealt with here.

This material originally appeared in slightly different form in the author's *Intelligence and Adaptation: An Integration of Psychoanalytic and Piagetian Developmental Psychology* © 1979, International Universities Press, New York, New York.

Not only can the youngster now organize experience, i.e., internal and external stimuli, in psychological representations, but he can, through his evolving capacity for means-ends differentiation, discriminate relatively better between those organizations that are predominantly determined by events based solely on his internal experiences and those based on his external experiences. In other words, the youngster has the ability at the psychological level, as he had before at the somatic level, to differentiate, in a relative sense, self from nonself. That this advance occurs together with the consolidation of object constancy is not surprising; the youngster's ability to hold representations of the object, even when separated from the object and in the face of up-surges from drive-affect organizations, indicates this greater capacity for differentiation of self from nonself.

With this new capacity, anger at the mothering figure for going away does not necessarily mean that she has disappeared permanently. The child feels some assurance that she will be back — even if the separation is *imagined* — because he has learned that his mother returns regardless of what he has been feeling toward her. Nevertheless, some youngsters retain strong fears, and that these fears influence the structure of secondary-process thinking is not surprising. Such fears are multiply determined, and some parents may reinforce their youngster's fantasy. The mother who withdraws every time her youngster is angry, for instance, may facilitate an organization that intrudes upon and influences secondary-process thinking. The youngster remains fearful that his anger or assertiveness will in fact result in the loss of the object. This situation may form the nucleus of a depressive organization later in life.

Let us consider only optimal development for the moment. With the differentiation of self from nonself, there is greater flexibility to tolerate and deal with a wide range of internal and external experience. Not only does the child have the capacity for psychological representation of these events or situations, but he can maintain these representations under the pressure of other internal and external events and can differentiate internally derived representations from externally derived ones. His capacity is therefore greater than earlier in life, since the child now assimilates, accommodates, and conserves a greater variety of stimuli, ranging over time and space, in relatively stable and permanent organizations.

We are not posing here a simple dichotomy between internally and externally derived representations. All representations of external reality are a product of human experience, or internal intelligence, and vice versa. But at this age there is a greater capacity than before for distinction between representations colored by primary-process thinking and the evolving capacity for secondary-process thinking. This new capacity is evidenced by the ability first to delineate the difference between self and nonself and then to organize means-ends relationships in terms of basic principles of causality.

6

Representational Differentiation and Consolidation (30–48 Months)

Following the capacity to organize internal mental representations, another differentiation occurs at the new level of mental representation or psychological life. Earlier we referred to somatic-psychological differentiation at the sensorimotor level. A similar differentiation in terms of means-ends relationships now occurs at the level of mental representation, as is evidenced by symbol formation and corresponding capacity for language development.

As noted above, between 18 and 30 months we see the ability for organizing representations. Initially these representations exist in the young child in the context of "magical thinking" or "primary-process thinking." While the child is capable of symbolically representing experience, he cannot yet connect these representations in logical fashion. Thus, while the toddler can *behave* in an organized, realistic way, what he or she says may seem disjointed or illogical. The illustration given earlier was of a child who confused time. Unable to represent remembered events in a logical time sequence, he talked about a birthday party with friends as though it had happened yesterday when in fact it had taken

159

place two weeks earlier. This same child also talked about a train ride that was to be taken later in the day as though it had already happened the day before. The two events—party and train ride—were thus connected in his mind in a way that defied our usual conception of time. Another example would be the youngster who develops a make-believe game with animals where the distinction between the real or make-believe is not wholly clear. Even though he says "This is pretend," he doesn't always act as though it were. Indeed, he may be frightened of a toy bear, having been afraid of the real one who growled at him in the zoo. This confusion of the inanimate and animate is typical of primary process thinking, in which symbols are not organized into *cohesive* structures of experience. Thus, a party for "me" is confused with a party for a friend, the animate world confused with the inanimate world, yesterday confused with today, and so on.

To use a metaphor, if we were to picture the mind as a balloon, it would be as though there were little balloons filled with experiences floating around within the larger one. Initially, these experiences would not be connected in a "logical" structure. As time went on, however, they might be connected from moment to moment according to temporal or spatial relationships or the wishes and urges of the youngster rather than according to adaptive or reality demands. Yet, paradoxically, this same youngster is often able to behave in a reasonable way, that is, follow instructions, respond to implicit wishes of his parents, and comprehend complex interpersonal situations. This sort of "behavioral" reality orientation, already demonstrated between 12 and 18 months when the youngster showed the capacity for organized and innovative behavioral patterns, has no parallel as yet at the level of mental representation.

Along these lines it is interesting to speculate for a moment about adults one observes in various states of disorganization. There are those adults who "talk crazy," yet behave adaptively, e.g., the psychotic individual who is able to take physical care of himself. He is careful in crossing the street, makes sure he eats well, bathes, dresses appropriately, etc. All the while that he complains of "crazy thoughts" or "intruding voices" he behaves in an organized way. In contrast, there are psychotic or sociopathic individuals who seem to be able to hold coherent discussions, but who behave in a very disorganized way. One might hypothesize that individuals who "think crazy" but behave in organized fashion have developed disorders during the phase of representational differentiation, whereas individuals who behave in a disorganized fashion may have disorders of the much earlier phase of development when behavioral capacities for differentiation are supposed to be established.

Let us return now to our metaphor of the smaller balloons within the large balloon. Over time, the islands of experience represented by the smaller balloons will begin to cluster together as the child begins to connect them appropriately. We notice that the child between 30 and 48 months begins to frame a number of sentences in order to present a cohesive idea. We notice a sense of cause and effect beginning to emerge in his thinking. The youngster is capable of realizing "I did this, therefore you got mad at me." He may then voice his concern or behave emotionally in a way consistent with this concern. The capacity to separate "I want" from what is, the animate from the inanimate, and, to some degree, the past from the present, becomes more evident, in part because of central nervous system maturation, in part because of supportive environmental interactions. Thus, internal representational experience becomes more organized, becomes *differentiated* along a number of dimensions. To use our metaphor once again, we can picture a lattice-like structure of balloons now interconnected according to certain organizational principles, some having to do with self and nonself, some with cause and effect, some with the animate and inanimate.

This is another way of saying that as the potential of the brain grows through the further myelinization of the central nervous system, experience is used to further differentiate reality along a number of dimensions. The most obvious, and the clearest to track, would be the differentiation of those experiences which pertain to the self from those which pertain to the nonself. The young child who has developed rich internal imagery at the animate, inanimate, and interactive levels during the phase of representational capacity and elaboration now begins to differentiate those experiences which pertain to the self — feelings, fantasies, thoughts, wishes — from those perceptions which pertain to others — mother's feelings and thoughts, the inanimate world, etc. Concomitant with this differentiation is a differentiation at a representational or psychological level of various feeling states and behavior. One example of the culmination of this process is the establishment of libidinal object constancy (Mahler, Pine, and Bergman, 1975). These differentiated organizations form the foundation for such basic ego functions as reality testing, regulation of impulses, and the organization and regulation of thought and affect. As time goes on, the sense of self reaches a stage of relative stability, where self/nonself differentiation is not undermined by brief separations or intense feeling states such as anger or jealousy.

We can understand how certain basic ego functions rest on the more fundamental capacity to differentiate self from nonself in terms of the child's capacity for means-ends differentiation, by which he differentiates the acting self from the consequences of those actions on the world. The capacity to regulate impulses, for example, is based in part on a sense of personal responsibility for one's impulsive actions, a sense of responsibility for what one does. If one relies heavily on projection, or engages in paranoid distortion, one may not feel responsible for one's impulses and thus not responsible for regulating them. As this "causal" self leads to greater differentiation of self from nonself experiences, we see greater stability of moods, another basic ego function.

The isolated islands of affect or emotion of the earlier representational stage (suggested by the youngster's shifting rapidly from one affect to another, from one island of experience to another island of experience) unite with one another into larger units to form a more stable emotional pattern, what we commonly call a mood.

Not only do these islands of affects come together to form moods, but islands of affects become united with islands of thought, ideas, or wishes and we see a greater integration of thought and affect, another basic ego function. During the earliest phase of representational capacity and elaboration it is not unusual to see a young child express an idea and follow it with a seemingly incompatible affect, giggling as something hurtful is happening to someone else. We do not think twice about such an event, since it is intuitively consistent with our image of early childish thinking. We may point out to the two-year-old that it is not nice to laugh when mother has hurt her hand or baby brother has fallen from the crib. From such interpersonal exchanges, the child slowly develops a concept of what emotions are appropriate in various circumstances. Based on these experiences, his perceptions and thoughts at the descriptive level (e.g., baby brother just banged his head) are eventually connected to certain affect organizations. This is not to say that the earlier more undifferentiated organizations cease to exist or that there are not different conflicts to be considered. Certainly the example of sibling rivalry suggests just such a conflict, but there is an important distinction between the person who is capable of integrated thought and affect expression — "Oh my, that's terrible" — accompanied by a look of fear or concern versus the person who says, "Oh my, that's terrible," and who cannot control an inappropriate giggle. In the latter case, the interconnections of the islands of affect and thought have not occurred.

With the organization of the self comes a certain sense of personal intentionality. As one experiences a sense of self, not only is there an accompanying responsibility for impulses, but there is also a sense of *self-intention*, implying a capacity for at least short-term future planning. From this evolves the experiential basis for the basic ego function of being able to focus and to concentrate, which we observe consolidating around three-and-a-half to five.

Many other basic ego functions — the "sense of reality," for example — are also based on the distinction between what is inside and outside. They have been described by a number of authors, including Bellak, Hurvich, and Gediman (1973), Greenspan and Cullander (1973), Greenspan, Hatleberg, and Cullander (1976), and we shall not go into them further except to point out that they are all more or less based on this fundamental differentiation of experiential organizations.

It is interesting to note that this phase of representational differentiation and consolidation corresponds to what has been described as the early phallic and beginning phallic-oedipal phases of development in the psychoanalytic theory of psychosexual development. It is generally accepted that the youngster during this time shows greater interest in his or her sexual body parts. Both boys and girls have a particular interest in being powerful. One has only to observe the drawings of towers, space ships, admired TV figures, etc., to see this special interest. It is possible to speculate that this phallic focus furthers and supports the overall development of representational differentiation and consolidation (Greenspan, 1980) as the youngster focuses clearly and in a highly differentiated way on a particular aspect of his or her body. It is also possible that the earlier phase of representational capacity and elaboration is associated with the anal phase of psychosexual development, when organizational units are not clearly differentiated from one another. During the anal phase, the interest of the youngster is focused on the retentive and eliminative modes related to the sphincter — holding in and giving out — which is consistent with a much more undifferentiated bodily focus. What at one moment is inside the body can at the next moment be outside the body. There is thus an interesting parallel between what is being postulated in our developmental structuralist approach and psychosexual as well as psychosocial theory (Erikson, 1959).

The Child's Capacities

The adaptive child at this stage of development is able to organize and differentiate imagery pertaining to the self and nonself, and shows a capacity to begin the manipulation of these now delineated organizations in terms of simple cause and effect determinations (cognitive insight). The adaptive youngster's now more differentiated experiential organizations are stable in the face of stress. In the global sense, the adaptive capacities of a toddler are evidenced in the growing capacity to differentiate what is real from what is not — to gradually develop a reality orientation. The foundation for this, as described earlier, is the child's growing capacity for means-ends differentiation, now at a representational level. The toddler's use of personal pronouns in his communications illustrates this emerging capacity. For example, the toddler who comes running to mother and says, "I broke the dish. Are you going to spank me?" can represent the expected consequences of his own activity and can differentiate his activity from the expected activity of his mother. His response is quite different from that of the earlier developmental phase in which, after breaking the dish, he slaps his own hand as though magically to excuse the act, or comes in giggling rather than feeling apprehensive about whether mother will punish him. The toddler may also be able to describe more accurately an interaction between himself and a friend. He can say to mother or father, "Johnny hit me. I have a boo-boo on my leg," and show his parents the injury to his leg caused by his friend. Again, one sees a capacity to describe a complex interaction with cause-and-effect components.

One also observes in the adaptive toddler the differentiation of animate and inanimate. The toddler on the way toward reality orientation may still be scared of the toy bear that looks like the real one he is frightened of but can say, "This is like the one in the zoo, but this one cannot hurt me." His differentiation of the inanimate bear from the animate suggests a recognition of the different consequences that can occur by being in the presence of each. The youngster who has not yet fully consolidated his reality orientation may still show some apprehension in relationship to the inanimate bear, and if sophisticated enough, may even be able to add, "But I'm still scared."

Even more impressive is the capacity for differentiating inner from outer, self from nonself, real from unreal, as it is conveyed in numerous ways at a nonverbal level. The toddler organizes his behavior, can carry out tasks, and can function in interpersonal relationships in ways that suggest an organized sense of self and nonself, and an understanding of cause and effect in relationships. In play, for example, the toddler might string together a number of themes in a cohesive way. The toddler who makes one doll feed another doll may then expand this theme and have the Mommy doll rock the baby doll to sleep after it has been fed, then actually put it to sleep, all the while describing these actions in words. The Mommy doll is then seated and a book placed in its hands as if it were a real parent. As we observe the stringing together at the representational level of a series of complex symbolic activities in a cohesive and organized way, we must be impressed with the growing organization of the youngster's representational world.

As the toddler learns to dress himself, come downstairs, sit down, and eat his breakfast, and then get his favorite games to take to pre-nursery school, we see an organized pattern of behavior coordinated by a sense of intentionality. This can be clearly distinguished from purely imitative, remembered activity by the fact that the youngster can integrate differences into this preparatory sequence. If, for example, there is to be a party at school that day and the youngster is bringing a gift, he will frequently remember and say before he leaves for school: "I need the present." Of course, at this stage there may still be a desire to have the present for himself so that one will see the youngster struggling with his wish to open it and then saying, "No, this is for Jane." The youngster is also able to follow implicit rules and regulations in the household. He does not have to be told repeatedly not to touch the ashtray, not to touch the plate, not to touch the candy in the living room. He can form a generalized construct that there are many things in the living room he must not touch.

To a parent who comes in preoccupied or upset and who ignores him by sitting and reading the newspaper, the youngster may say, "What's the matter?" If the parent responds, "I'm tired, I've had a rough day," the youngster might sit next to the parent, put his head on the parent's shoulder, and repeat, "Mommy tired, sleepy." Some youngsters may still insist that mother or father play a game with them. Others, if feeling fairly good that day, may be able, after a moment or two of sitting next to the parent, to go off and play the game alone, then return to the parent to say, "Still tired? Play with me now?" This capacity for complex interaction implies a recognition of the mood states, needs, and tensions of the other, the needs of the self, and a cognitive understanding of what is going on which permits the negotiation of complicated processes.

To most observers such processes seem to occur automatically at an intuitive level and are consistent with their expectations that the child will begin to move toward reality orientation. The complexities of the processes may go relatively unnoticed except when they are *not* occurring, when the youngster cannot recognize the needs of the other, cannot see them in relationship to the needs of the self, and cannot take appropriate steps to negotiate his perceptions.

All these processes continue until a point of stability is reached at which the youngster's capacity for reality orientation and complex integration of representational configurations can withstand illness, anger, upset, or brief separation from the parents. In the most adaptive young children we observe their moods gradually becoming more stable, their capacity to focus and concentrate increasing, and their future expectations as well as past experiences guiding them. We also see greater integration between what they say and what they feel (integration of thought and affect).

In more specific ways, we can look at the degree of the youngster's adaptive capacity for representational differentiation and consolidation. The most adaptive youngster can employ these new strategies across the full range of experience. Thus we see complex interactions with parents in which the sense of personal causality is appreciated in a pleasurable game or an affectionate interactive teasing. Or utilized in exploration or self-assertion, sorting out a new puzzle or game, being taken to a new surrounding, or trying to figure out what is going on with the people and things around. Even when the youngster is angry, he is able to say, "I am mad. You didn't give me my cake," or to get angry at the parent for forgetting to bring home the promised present. In the most adaptive circumstances a youngster may still cry, scream, or throw a temper tantrum, yet later will calm down. He can complain and express his anger in an organized fashion. The adaptive youngster can use these new capacities to explore and begin to understand his or her body and its functions. The interest in "the bottom," the "penis," in feces, erections, and "excited feelings" begins to become organized as aspects of the child's physical, sexual, and emotional self. If representational differentiation is occurring adaptively, the emerging understanding of these types of experiences helps the youngster organize his wishes, sensations, and curiosities without becoming overwhelmed by fears (which remain at manageable levels during normal development). As indicated earlier, there is a parallel course in psychosexual and structural development. Most likely both are interrelated, mutually reinforcing processes.

We can also look at the depth and stability of differentiated representations. There is an increasingly rich expression of feeling, wish, and thought in the various domains of dependency, pleasure, assertiveness, curiosity, protest, and anger. When the adaptive youngster is angry, he does not lose his capacity for representational differentiation, immediately projecting his own wishes onto his brother, mother, or father to say "You want to hurt me" or "I'm scared of you." The youngster maintains the ability to recognize the difference between his own angry feelings and those of others.

These adaptive capacities for differentiation also take on a more personal tone. Thus we see preferred games, preferred modes of expression for various emotions, and the like. The sense of personal uniqueness is enriched rather than compromised as this greater capacity for differentiation is employed.

Of course, the fact that differentiation is occurring does not mean that the youngster will still not regress, will still not engage in fantasy, magical thinking, or regressive temper tantrums. These modes of relating to the world will all be present in the adaptive youngster. But now the youngster can distinguish these modes from the reality-oriented mode. When he is angry, the child may not listen to the parent or permit the parent to speak to him. Once he is calmed down, however, rather than remaining in the regressive mode, rather than blaming everyone else for what went wrong, the child will be able to appreciate what he did that brought about the undesirable reaction from others. The youngster who is involved in a fantasy game, a tea party, at which he gets all the candy and cake he ever wanted, can, if he wishes, make a clear distinction between this and "really getting candy and cake." Frequently, after this elaborate game, the youngster may ask for the real candy or cake. If the parent teasingly says to the youngster, "But you just had your tea party," he can reply, "That was just play." Indeed, one frequently sees in the adaptive youngster such confidence and security in his reality orientation that he can use regressive modes, fantasy, and play for satisfaction, without getting so confused in relation to his reality orientation as to become alarmed. In contrast to the youngster whose capacity for differentiation is not fully consolidated, who may still be overwhelmed by his fantasies, the adaptive youngster can play out aggressive and frightening games — monsters eating little children, people shooting one another — and see it as make-believe, without becoming overly fearful or anxious.

We also see less polarization of emotional themes. A play activity will not be totally negative (shooting, biting) or totally positive (feeding, hugging). Rather, we are likely to see a wide variety of affects as a youngster in a single play session acts out with dolls a scene in which cops are in hot pursuit of the robbers. The scene then shifts as the policeman goes home and hugs his children and puts them to sleep. We see the full range of emotional polarities — aggression, love, tenderness, and dependency — expressed in one drama.

As the youngster moves closer to the final stages of representational differentiation and consolidation, we observe this integration not only in play, but also in the actual interactions of the youngster with others. Assertiveness, intimacy, and aggressiveness can all be part of a complicated personal interaction. A youngster can be angry and frustrated, then assertively insist on what he wants. He can then accept that he is not going to get what he wants and be available for a tender and intimate exchange with his parents. Usually the complexity of this configuration will go unnoticed; it will be considered normal for a healthy four-year-old. In a younger child, however, we would notice a less smooth transition from one theme and its affective expression to another.

The most severely maladaptive tendencies in toddlers at this stage of development are consistent with the patterns later exhibited by adults or older children with borderline psychotic personality organizations. While there may be some capacity for organized internal psychological life, there is little or no differentiation. Where differentiation exists, it is extremely vulnerable to stress. Under such stress, or where differentiation has not occurred at all, islands of organized representational activity exist in isolation from one another. The personality has no cohesion. In essence, primary process thinking predominates.

The most severely disordered youngster in this phase may have a capacity to describe in words what he sees and to engage in complex interactions, but does not develop cause-and-effect reasoning capabilities. He lacks the sense of "I did this to cause that" or "Because you did this, I did that," and so on. When strong feelings exist, he is confused about whom the feeling comes from. These tendencies often gain the attention of parents or pre-nursery-school teachers or play-group leaders. The youngster may, because of chronic, unmodulated projection of his own aggressive feelings, see the world as dangerous, and be chronically apprehensive and fearful; or may tend to withdraw for the same reason. The youngster may be impulsive and disrespectful of other children's property and even their bodies; his own needs are not differentiated from those of others, and this inability to differentiate his needs manifests itself in problems of impulse control. Strong affect states may so threaten his representational capacity as to lead to even more regressive forms of behavior, such as chronic, negativistic, aggressive, withdrawn, or totally disorganized behavioral patterns. Under the most severe circumstances, relationships may be totally relinquished as autistic patterns take over and relatedness to the inanimate world replaces relatedness to the animate world. Language is given up as an instrument of communication.

Just as when, in earlier stages of the development, a new capacity was not mastered, severe regression may occur. The child will experience difficulties with respect to *specific* tasks of development. That is to say, regression may occur to those *specific* areas in earlier development in which the child experienced difficulty. Again, central nervous system maturation increases the variety and complexity of stimuli that confront the child. Unless he is equipped with age-appropriate representational capacity, these stimuli may overwhelm him.

(This notion of regression deserves further comment. In psychoanalytic terms, regression is often thought of as a simple shifting back to the inclinations and interests of an earlier developmental phase. Indeed, when we think of regression in terms of libidinal development, in terms of drives and their associated wishes, this is often the case. The well-known example of the shift to an oral way of satisfying one's sexual yearning by smoking a cigarette is an often used example. We may think of regression in a different sense, however, when we talk about the structural capacity of the personality. That is, regression occurs not only to an earlier stage of development, but to deviations in the mode of functioning at that earlier stage. Thus, when we talk about a regression to pre-representational patterns, we usually do not see the regressed individual mimicking the *normal* infant or toddler. Rather, we see the behavior of a *disordered* infant, toddler, or child. This pattern is then mixed with various combinations of adult-level functioning to make the picture even more complex. In other words, no regression is ever total; no regression ever involves all aspects of structural functioning. It may occur with respect to the animate and not the inanimate world, or only with respect to certain sectors of the animate, around pleasure or dependency and not around assertion or aggression.)

At a less severe level, we may see basic differentiation occurring but with major distortion in the personality, i.e., an overall inflexibility of the personality to engage fully in life's major endeavors. It is as though the child relinquishes an important domain of human experience (e.g., intimacy, anger) in order to preserve whatever differentiation has occurred. This may lead to the severe personality disorders of very negativistic, withdrawn, schizoid, paranoid children or very depressed, apathetic children.

Characteristic of the youngster who is not moving toward representational differentiation and the establishment of basic ego functions is that the shift from fantasy to reality is not taking place. Under emotional stress he may experience severe distortions in reality-oriented thinking. Alternatively, there may be a chronic lack of organization and regulation of emotions and impulses and chronic patterns of disorganized aggressive or regressive behavior. Negativism increases as the personality becomes more inflexible; withdrawal from human relationships increases; the ability to care for bodily functions does not become established; the tendency to blame others becomes more intense; and the fears of loss of self, security, or love and the fears of bodily injury are so severe that progressive development is perceived as dangerous, such that intimacy, assertion, curiosity, and self-control are relinquished.

Even where differentiation occurs, there may still be compromises in its consolidation. Regression, states of anxiety and depression, and more moderate impairments in the flexibility of the personality occur under the stress of separation. Clinging patterns, moderate obsessive-compulsive patterns, hysterical patterns, patterns of impulsive behavior, or patterns of externalization often result. Rigidities in the personality or distortions of character serve to keep the growing child from experiencing certain thought and feeling states, such as anger or intimacy, which, for dynamic reasons, may threaten the stability of the personality organization.

Thus we may find that the capacity for representation and differentiation is present but not across the full range of human experience. We may see a youngster who can operate at a highly differentiated level, who understands cause-

and-effect relationships as evidenced in his play or interactions when dealing with themes of pleasure and dependency. He may show how some dolls satisfy their dependency needs through another doll by asking to be fed. He may be able to tell mother how nice he has been and thus earn his special dessert. At night, he will be able, perhaps, to behave pleasantly, so that father will play a game with him. His implicit understanding of cause-and-effect relationships is represented in language and in complex interactions and expectations, all of which confirm an existing representational configuration. The same youngster, however, when angered, or when stirred into aggressive interaction by father's provocation (e.g., father may tease him by flicking his buttocks with a towel), is unable to deal with these feelings. That is, he does not have differentiated capacities in this realm of experience. Instead of grabbing the towel and retaliating, or telling his father to stop because it hurts, this youngster becomes paralyzed with apprehension. His face becomes blank and he begins verbalizing nonsense syllables, speaking words with no relationship to each other. Mother comes rushing to the scene, offers the youngster some comfort, and slowly re-engages him. The blank look fades and one can see him beginning to organize his interactions and beginning to talk coherently again. We are not suggesting, of course, that father's provocation may not be traumatic. The child's behavior does, however, show the degree to which the youngster is unable to cope with aggressivity. For another youngster, just the opposite might be the case. The child would be capable of differentiated functioning around competitive and aggressive activities, but would either avoid intimacy or, when forced into intimate situations, become disorganized.

We also look for the circumstances under which the youngster relinquishes his uniqueness, his personal style in this more differentiated mode. Under stress of illness, separation, or strong affect, does the youngster who seems to have taken to a special game, or used to have a special facial expression, or to have a special way of showing his emotions, begin to mimic mechanically what he sees mother and father doing?

We may find youngsters with less maladaptive tendencies at this stage of development using either of two options. In one, we may see the regression described above, where basic ego functions are relinquished temporarily and states of stress are related to a vulnerable area of an earlier stage. Relinquishing his impulse control, for example, the youngster may begin to project his own feelings onto mother, so that he cannot distinguish who is going to hurt whom, and so on.

On the other hand, another choice is open to the youngster at this stage of consolidation of representational capacities. He may learn that it is safest to *avoid* those areas of experience in which he is vulnerable to regression. Thus, if assertion and aggression lead to dedifferentiation, or to an undermining of his sense of control and security, or to loss of reality orientation or impulse control, he may learn to avoid these areas. The youngster becomes passive, compliant, superficially affectionate, and avoids any experience that has to do with assertion and aggression. In addition, some projection may still occur, even with the avoidance, and the youngster may experience his own aggression in terms of frightening fantasies of being attacked, engulfed, or swallowed up. In such states of dedifferentiation the youngster who wants to leave and abandon the other may fear being abandoned himself. As the boundary of self and other becomes blurred, the associated frightening fears may emerge. Similarly, another youngster may avoid experiences of dependency and intimacy at a deep level because it is these experiential realms which are associated with his vulnerability to dedifferentiation. Where this occurs we often find characterological constrictions and/or inflexibility of personality. We might also find secondary symptomatic reactions. Persons who are incapable of asserting themselves for fear of dedifferentiation may be more prone to depression as they continually experience frustration in their efforts to achieve satisfaction. Others who experience sadness or depression as dangerous for them may limit themselves to patterns of impulsivity and pseudo-mastery. In essence, then, severe character limitations may form quite early in life as a way of protecting the integrity of fragile ego functions. It is as though the child says, "What I don't experience can't disrupt me and be dangerous."

Mild difficulties at this stage do not usually interfere with further development as it moves into the triangular, or phallic-oedipal, phase of development. Frequently, the final crystallization of these more moderate character distortions and symptoms reflects a condensation of these early experiences with the experiences in this next phase of development.

Environmental Characteristics

The growth-promoting environment at this stage of development is able to achieve four major goals. First, it is able to help the youngster move toward reality orientation, that is, toward a differentiation of inner and outer, self and nonself, and means and ends. Second, it is able to help the youngster deal with intense interpersonal experiences and affects and such events as separation in a way that does not compromise representational differentiation. Third, it provides those interpersonal experiences that help the youngster resolve the developmental tasks of the stage of representational differentiation. Fourth, it prepares the youngster to move on to higher levels of development at which a more differentiated psychic structure and new, expanded relationship patterns are possible.

Differentiation is enhanced by the environment's capacity to read and respond to the symbolic communications of the growing child at the cognitive and empathic levels, and in an appropriate temporal sequence. Responses of the environment to the youngster's symbolic communications must be selective and differentiated if they are to help the youngster differentiate his own internal world. For example, the youngster who assembles a puzzle because he wants to do it "better than Mommy" may be symbolically communicating his assertiveness and competitiveness. In trying to prove himself, he works tensely and somewhat successfully, finding the various parts of the puzzle and placing them correctly. Smiling gleefully, he says, "See, I can do it," and may even say, "You can't do it." At the cognitive level mother may appreciate this communication and respond by entering into the competitive play, saying, "Okay, now I'll try." Or may support the child: "Gee, that's terrific." Or may simply let the child's message register, giving him the satisfaction of her own careful observation and her sharing in his pleasure. Whichever her response, the mother has correctly interpreted the event at the cognitive level.

In contrast, some mothers or fathers may misperceive the meaning of the child's communication at this cognitive level. They may interpret his statement, "I can do it faster," or "You can't do it," as "My son is hyperactive, he tries to do things too fast. He doesn't concentrate well." Then, acting on this cognitive misperception, they might take the puzzle from him and say, "Watch me. Pay attention. Slow down." They might even smack his hands if he tries to hold onto the puzzle. Still other parents may misinterpret his communication in this way: "He is obviously asking for help from me." And even further, if preoccupied, the parent might not hear the communication at all and suggest to the child, "Let's play something else." In this case, the parent has completely failed to register the child's intense desire to show off his skills in putting the puzzle together. These examples of misreading cues at a cognitive level are related here to emphasize by contrast the growth-promoting environment's ability to read the child's communications correctly. As we have also shown, while the environment can choose to respond appropriately in any one of several ways, it must first be able to interpret the child's communications accurately.

Not only must the cues be read accurately at the cognitive level. There must also be an empathic understanding of the youngster's communication. For example, if the child's assertiveness and competitiveness are misread at the emotional level, the parent may preconsciously suppose that "he is trying to overwhelm me"; "he is too competitive"; "he is really not being competitive, but is just showing me how infantile he is"; "he is exaggerating his strength." If these are predominant emotional responses, they will color the affective interchange between mother and child. Thus, while mother may say, "Gee, that's terrific, Johnny," there may be a look of panic in her eyes reflecting her fear that her son is growing up too quickly. Or if she actively enters the fray and says, "Okay, let's see if Mommy can do it as fast as you can," she may get so involved with winning that her child's initiative and assertiveness will be buried under her own competitive strivings. In other words, for there to be a real understanding of the child's symbolic communication, it must be understood at both the cognitive and the empathic levels. Otherwise, these cognitive and emotional responses will not foster the child's own integration of cognitive and emotional representations.

It is through those interactions in which one's symbolic communications are read and responded to accurately that differentiation occurs. Just as earlier in development, when infant and parent's reciprocal responses fostered a sense of differentiation — that is, the infant learned that actions have consequences — so there develops here a differentiation at the representational level and the consolidation of these differentiated representational capacities as they are experienced operationally in interaction with the real world. Just as the solution to an arithmetic problem strengthens the concepts used to solve the problem, and just as answering questions about a book strengthens one's understanding of that book, similarly, receiving appropriate responses to one's symbolic communications strengthens those communications and increases their orientation to reality. In essence, the child's communications can be differentiated from their impact on the outside world. In this way, the self, which is the *means* by which appropriate responses are given, learns the kind of *ends* it can produce in the environment. In other words, means-ends differentiation begins to take place.

The growth-promoting environment responds appropriately in a temporal, flexible, and highly individualistic manner. Whether to simple communications such as "I want my milk" or to more complicated communications such as "Why did you talk that way to Daddy?" the environment responds flexibly, individualistically, and in a temporally appropriate manner. The environment will encourage the use of words or symbolic play or behavior and will try to orient the child's requests to reality. When the youngster says, "I want 23 presents by 12 o'clock tomorrow," and begins whining seriously, the growth-promoting environment might take his communication seriously and respond in kind, "No, you can't have 23 toys by 12 o'clock tomorrow," thereby helping the youngster to see that his demand is unrealistic and to see the connection between his unrealistic demand and the effect it produces on others. Or, if he then pulls out his toy pistol and says, "Or else," the parent might see that the youngster is teasing — he has a glint in his eye, he knows that he is being unrealistic — and might tease him in turn by playfully asking him to name all the 23 presents he wants. Or the parent might ask where he would put all those different presents. At this, the youngster might laugh gleefully, enjoying the fact that his mother has indulged his fantasy. In this case, too, the child receives appropriate, highly individualistic, flexible feedback from the environment. He begins to see a connection between what he thinks and expresses, and begins to be able to differentiate the one from the other. These examples of reading the child's communications as serious or teasing show how important it is that the parent be able, at an empathic level, to pick up the real intent of the youngster. The youngster who is jesting and yet responded to as serious, may come to feel that his fantasies are dangerous because they always make his parents angry. The youngster who is serious and yet whose parents always laugh at his demands, may come to feel either that his demands or wishes are not to be taken seriously and, therefore, that he should not take them seriously, or that they are too frightening to be taken seriously. The same message from different children may have different meanings; different messages may at times have the same meaning, depending on tone of voice, context, etc. To the degree that the parents are especially sensitive, selective, and differentiated in their responses, the youngster begins to differentiate the various nuances of his communications. Thus, the parent who can respond differently and appropriately to playful teasing, serious teasing, a careless request, a serious demand, mild competition, serious competition, mild curiosity, assertive curiosity, will encourage the differentiation and consolidation of these representational modes in the youngster. To the degree that parents can repond only in a non-differentiated way, and lack the ability to see the subtle differences in the youngster's verbal, emotional, or facial expressions, the youngster may not get the feedback he needs for differentiation and consolidation of subtle representational modes.

A special point should be made about appropriate temporal responses. In most instances, an empathic emotional response, whether it be a facial expression or a verbal communication, should be made within a reasonable time, so that the youngster can connect it with his or her own communication. This does not suggest that learning to delay is not important. Teaching a capacity for delay and tolerance of frustration is vitally important at this stage of development. Sometimes this capacity must be taught through verbal communication: "Tommy, you must wait." After repeating this several times, one may choose to ignore the subsequent constant requests for candy or to be played with. These issues, then, are best confronted directly, best explained to the child rather than ignored. The child must understand that tolerating delay is often necessary. In selected circumstances, of course, the strategy of ignoring the child may also be appropriate.

The growth-promoting environment responds to the child across various representational themes, from pleasure and dependency, to assertiveness and curiosity, to aggression and negativism, and the like. It responds to the child's interest in the animate and inanimate world, and encourages his complex interpersonal communications with a variety of individuals, parents and other significant adults, siblings and friends, etc. Thus, various developmentally appropriate themes are elaborated by the youngster in a variety of contexts, as the representational mode, through the child's continual experience of having an impact on the environment, undergoes its own pattern of differentiation.

The optimal environment not only reads and responds appropriately to the child's communications, but also tries to stay half a step ahead of the youngster, leading him or her to more differentiated capacities. The environment that does not distinguish between a teasing request and realistic request may eventually impede the youngster's ability to appreciate the difference between a wishful fantasy and a serious demand. In contrast, the optimal environment not only reads the child's intentions accurately, but tries to take them one level beyond (but only one level beyond) his present capacities. Thus, when the youngster says, "I want 23 toys by 12 tomorrow," the environment, in response, may decide not to assume that this is a serious demand, nor yet a completely teasing demand, but a demand whose serious or teasing quality the child himself is not entirely sure of. Thus, a middle course might be taken that would help the youngster understand a subtle behavioral distinction which he has not yet clearly demarcated for himself. Because he lacks this awareness as yet, and is therefore unable to signal clearly whether he is teasing or not, the adaptive environment might respond, "Is this a pretend wish or what you really want?" At first the child may be confused by this, but eventually he may be able to laugh and say, "Just pretend." Later on he may be able to say, "Just pretend, but I do want five presents on my birthday." The youngster thus shows that he appreciates the difference between a make-believe request and a real one by making it clear that he would like at least part of his fantasy to come true at an appropriate time — his birthday. Again, we see a highly differentiated capacity on the youngster's part.

Yet, the growth-promoting environment must also be able to engage the youngster in complete fantasy. When the child temporarily suspends his reality orientation and the dolls and animals become real and even frightening to him, the parent must be able to engage the youngster at this level. Thus, when the child asks the parent to be a wolf, and then asks the parent to save him from the wolf, the parent, moving back and forth in his roles (as protector and as wolf), is able to elaborate this bit of fantasy for the youngster. Or if the child wishes to play the wolf, the parent will run in fear, showing the youngster the other side of the drama. But when the youngster tires of this game and wants to look at one of his favorite books, the parent will be able to shift out of the fantasy mode and will engage the youngster at the more realistic level.

It must be emphasized that parents must be flexible in determining the circumstances under which indulging the child's fantasy will be appropriate. When the youngster takes the role of wolf and snaps at his younger sibling as if to hurt him, and comes a little too close for comfort, the parent must bring the youngster back to reality, ending the game and explaining that such "seemingly" playful behavior can hurt baby brother. The child thus learns to make a subtle distinction between acceptable and unacceptable forms of fantasy expression, between play with his parents and play with his vulnerable younger brother.

A belief exists among some parents that to set limits for the child in his play would interfere with his fantasy life. On the contrary, by making these distinctions clear, by setting and explaining limits, the environment actually provides a greater sense of security for the youngster and permits him to enjoy a richer, more varied, and deeper fantasy life. He acquires the ability to distinguish clearly those of his fantasies which may, in fact, hurt people, and those which are purely in the realm of fantasy. One three-year-old boy, for example, wanted to play a skipping game with his father while his younger sibling slept in the same room. The father agreed, provided that he would do it quietly. While each time he started quietly, he slowly began to thump his feet more and more loudly, particularly when he drew closer to his sleeping brother. At first the father responded, "Be quiet, or we can't play the game." And each time the older sibling agreed, only to thump louder once again as they got closer to the younger brother's crib. "We're just playing," he said, encouraging his father to continue. After this pattern had been repeated a few times, the parent, in frustration, said, "I don't think you care if you wake your brother; maybe you even want to." At this, the older sibling began to giggle and no longer insisted on playing the game. As this illustration highlights, a youngster's own clear intent will often be quite different from that of his parent. The parent's recognition of this intent and firmness in opposing it helps the youngster to understand not only that his behavior has consequences that he intends, but that his intentions can be recognized by the other and may, indeed, be in direct opposition to the intent of the other.

Of course, these kinds of interactions between parent and youngster go on automatically and on an intuitive level, without much thought being given to them. Just as the child has matured through the various stages of development, so too has the parent's capacity to respond flexibly and accurately to increasingly more complex communications. Still, the environment must occasionally examine its own behavior as to whether or not it is fostering the child's adaptation. Some environments may note that they respond differentially around pleasure and dependency, and not around aggression and negativism; or around curiosity and assertiveness, but not around pleasure, and so on. The parent may see that during a calm, pleasurable game with the child, he or she reads the child's cues quite accurately and responds contingently. The same parent may notice that when it comes to a rougher game, where the youngster is belligerent or demanding, he or she withdraws or retaliates by becoming nonverbal, aggressive, punitive, or scolding. This behavior obviously lacks the subtlety and contingency of the earlier response to the calm, pleasurable game. We are not suggesting that firm limits are not useful; they are. But they can be set in a context of contingent and differential responses to the child's symbolic behavior. Sometimes parental communications may also have to be reinforced with concrete physical limitations (such as holding).

Some parents have just the opposite problem. Around competition, assertion, and aggression, they are able to respond to the youngster differentially. When the youngster is teasingly provocative or seriously provocative, they know when it is appropriate simply to say "No." They are comfortable enough to then be able to reverse themselves somewhat and say, "Maybe this one time, but that's all." They are comfortable enough to then back up these limits with physical restraint, if necessary. Yet these same parents may become anxious and tense and withdraw when the youngster looks for physical intimacy, or touches on themes of dependency or closeness. Here, for example, they may misread the youngster's need for security as excessive dependency. When the little girl climbs up into Daddy's lap, he becomes uncomfortable because she has aroused his sexual feelings, and says to his wife so that his daughter can hear, "She is too dependent; she is going to be a baby all her life. Why don't you show her how to work a puzzle."

The growth-promoting environment helps the youngster stabilize his capacities for representational differentiation in the face of intense internal feelings or intense interpersonal experiences. Even when the child is under stress — frightening experiences of separation, for example — the environment helps the youngster maintain his capacity for representational differentiation and the representational capacity itself, in spite of the stressful experience.

This "coping" capacity is promoted in several ways by parents. One is to show the youngster that they are not afraid of engaging the youngster around intense affects. They do not withdraw, become fragmented or disorganized, or excessively aggressive, but tolerate and engage the youngster in intense interpersonal affects, setting firm limits when necessary. The child learns from the natural give-and-take of the interaction that his own anger does not frighten the world nor cause its disorganization. He learns as a consequence that such intense feelings are no more dangerous to himself than they are to others. Stability of representational differentiation in the face of these intense affects should then result. Similarly, when the youngster has strong feelings around sensual urges or dependency needs, no matter how intense, the adaptive environment will remain engaged around this issue, at times setting appropriate limits (e.g., the aggressively clinging or demanding youngster who clutches the mother's leg as she leaves the house will be redirected to an activity with the babysitter and told that mother will be back). The parents' firmness indicates to the youngster that they can tolerate this type of dependent yearning, the anger that accompanies it, and the demandingness. When the mother or father returns as promised, the youngster consolidates the capacity to tolerate this separation, no matter how

painful it may feel for the moment. Or perhaps the youngster who is overwhelmed by excitement as he wrestles with
his father, can find with the father's help that he can calm
down, redirect his activities, and structure them until he is
in peaceful harmony with himself. As the child begins to
lose control, the parent gradually takes the youngster in
hand, directing his attention to a quieter activity, perhaps
involving play with dolls or a puzzle. Here the father is
careful not to disengage prematurely from the activity because of his own problems with pleasurable interactions. He
continues to engage the child physically and departs from
the wrestling activity only when the child begins to lose control. He then shows that the child can regain self-control by
focusing on something less stimulating.

Most important of all, perhaps, the child must consolidate his capacity for representational differentiation in the
face of his own angry feelings. The projection of these feelings is often seen in the kinds of fears youngsters may experience between the years of two and four, ranging from early
fears of being attacked by monsters to the later fears of robbers stealing their most important possessions. These projections of their own angry feelings are often indications of
their own inability to deal fully with intense anger. A certain amount of projection is normal, of course, and to be expected in nightmares, night fears, and ordinary daydreams.
At times, however, when it becomes excessive, the youngster
may be too frightened to sleep, or if he does, may awaken
startled and frightened, and insist on coming into the parents' bedroom for security. While all types of fantasies may
express the child's fear of outside aggression — with competitive themes, lustful themes, or themes of outright aggression
— it is crucial that the youngster become secure in his capacity to deal with the inner wishes and affects that lay behind
his fantasies.

Almost all youngsters evidence such feelings in their behavior. Even those who have already inhibited direct ag-

gressive behavior and have become more passive will show passive-aggressive symbolic communication (e.g., by knocking things over, or spilling things, seemingly by accident). The growth-promoting environment actively confronts the child's intense anger and aggression. It uses these opportunities to set limits, and neither withdraws from nor overreacts to the youngster's provocations. Through the appropriate setting of limits, consistent with parental values and culture, the youngster begins to understand that he can set appropriate internal limits for himself, and begins to feel more secure about his capacity to handle his upsurges of intense feelings. Such upsurges do not then lead to a dedifferentiation of his representational capacity.

Of course, it is not always easy for the environment to engage the youngster across the various thematic modes, engage his fantasy life, and be the firm limit-setter all at the same time. Yet it is vital that parents show this flexibility if they are to help the child stabilize his capacity for differentiation. As the youngster gradually internalizes this flexibility himself, he can permit himself a depth and range of internal fantasy and feeling as he develops a stable, secure self-regulating structure of his own. He can then comfort himself when he feels overwhelmed and depressed, re-organize himself when he is disorganized, and limit himself when he is angrily aggressive. Indeed, the consolidation of the child's capacity for representational differentiation becomes the foundation for the basic ego functions of reality testing, impulse regulation, mood stabilization, self-esteem maintenance, and focused concentration.

While it is not absolutely necessary, the optimal environment tries to help the child move from dyadic to triadic relationships in this stage of development. During this early period of life, most youngsters are involved primarily in two-person relationships in which the other person is the fulfiller of needs, the setter of limits, or the partner in a variety of activities. The two-person system, for reasons we shall see, does not afford as much flexibility as the triangular system that later emerges.

During the dyadic stage, the individual is not yet able to use rivalry and intrigue as a mode of coping. In this earlier stage, the child may substitute one parent for another when frustrated or angry, chiefly as a means of getting his needs met. There is not the complex, triangular love affair that we see later on. Since it is primarily mother who satisfies dependency needs, it is not easy for the child to deal with intense feelings directed against her. To be too angry at mother may mean the loss of her support. Anger, therefore, becomes frightening and is associated with abandonment or withdrawal. Many mechanisms are used to handle such intense feeling states so that they will not be so dangerous. Often (and this is consistent with the youngster's not yet being fully capable of differential representations) it is easy to project such anger, so that it is not the child who is angry at mother but the mother who is angry at the child. These types of projections are seen in all kinds of fearful fantasies. Often the anger that they think mother feels at them is displaced onto "the monster." These mechanisms of projection, incorporation, and displacement are consistent with primary process thinking, and consistent with the early phases of representational capacity in which there is little or no differentiation of self from nonself or means from ends. They are also consistent with only partial states of differentiation. In these instances, the youngster achieves differentiation in certain realms of experience, but, under pressure of strong affects or wishes, has islands of undifferentiated activity on which these projections, incorporations, and displacements run rampant.

In order to foster the youngster's shift to the three-person system, it is necessary that a significant other be available, so that the intensity of wish and affect is not directed toward one person only. When there is a second significant other available, the youngster can then be angry at mother and fantasize mother being angry in turn, but still feel that he or she is relatively secure because father is available. As the youngster moves from two to four, the relationship to the significant "second other," usually the father, may become more intense. Mothers will often comment that their children (especially their daughters, but also their sons) become more involved with fathers as they get older. Many fathers who have not been "involved" find that the child begins to seek them out more actively at this stage of development.

It is not by chance that the youngster seeks out the significant "second other." The optimal environment makes such a figure available. When the father has been involved in a nurturing role from the very beginning, it may make this seeking out even easier for the youngster. The father may notice, for example, that the youngster now uses him in a new way — not just as a simple substitute, but in a more complex pattern: "You are on my side while I am angry at mother." This beginning capacity to use the significant other as an ally permits the youngster to develop an internal sense of security while he deals with his intense affects. It is especially important at this stage of development where such affects exist in relatively undifferentiated form so that the child is often not certain as to exactly *who* is being aggressive. Having an ally permits the youngster to feel that it is not so dangerous to have intense feelings toward a person. Even if the fantasy is so intense that the child imagines that his feelings could overwhelm and destroy him or lead to a separation or severe retaliation, he is able to hold onto the thought that there is still another person available to him: His world won't be totally destroyed. This permits the youngster to tolerate more intense affect states without resorting to distorting mechanisms. Indeed, the child's tentative experimentation without the use of these primitive undifferentiated mechanisms helps him to give them up. He learns that his realistic affects are much less dangerous than they would have seemed were the ally not available. We are not suggesting that children in families without fathers do not develop appropriately; it may, however, be more difficult for them. Of course, many children of single-parent families do have significant available others — a grandparent, a boyfriend of the mother, another relative, or an older sibling. Where present, however, the warm, supportive, and engaging father is the most appropriate ally for the child. (Naturally, in families in which the mother works and father performs the primary nurturing role, mother will become the significant "second other.")

Having an ally present also helps the youngster separate from his dyadic partner. Up to now, the youngster has been dependent primarily on one parental figure. If he is to become more interested in peers, school activities, and expanded relationship patterns, he must pull away from this earlier primary relationship which held so much inherent satisfaction for him and, at the same time, so much frustration and rage. The ally helps him pull away, helps him move out of dependency to a more individuated state. At the same time, of course, the ally should not overplay his role so as to create in the child even more frightening fears that the primary caregiver in his life will be destroyed.

Finally, the ally's presence sets the stage for the more complicated, triangular relationship patterns of the phallic-oedipal stage of development. As has been discussed elsewhere (Greenspan, 1979), the youngster at this stage acquires the capacity for derivative representational systems. That is, the youngster will develop new representations which, while tied to the original representations, can alter the nature of wishes and feelings. This occurs in the context of three-person relationship patterns in which two very different and separate significant others can be played off in various configurations. Thus the number of possible combinations are far more varied than they were earlier. This complexity in relationship patterns, with all the intrigues, rivalries, and hidden agendas it makes possible prepares the youngster for group activities and for the expanded relationship patterns that will be part of school life and later development. Along these lines, it is interesting to note that when two-, three-, or four-year-olds play with one or another friend, they can often do quite well, developing elaborate dramas and themes. Place these same children in a larger group, however (e.g., at a birthday party), and they will often play by themselves, or in diffuse, less differentiated group activities. It is rare, in a large group, to see children develop a complex drama which involves three or four children unless the teacher structures it for them. It is as though youngsters in the larger group are slightly overwhelmed and function in a slightly more regressed mode. While this has implications for how we set up our pre-nursery and day-care environments, it is pointed out here to illustrate the lack of triangular capacity in the stage of representational differentiation and the way in which the availability of the ally helps the youngster reach the point at which this triangular capacity becomes possible.

The growth-inhibiting environment at the stage of representational differentiation and consolidation will misread or respond non-contingently or unrealistically to the emerging symbolic communications of the youngster, thereby undermining reality orientation. It may be overly permissive or punitive. As the child shows increasing tendencies toward differentiation, the growth-inhibiting environment may regress and respond to the child in concrete, non-symbolic modes only, even if it has previously engaged the child in the symbolic mode. Denying the child a response in the symbolic mode generally occurs in particular realms (around pleasure, for example). The growth-inhibiting environment denies or is fearful of the changing phase-appropriate needs, communications, and related developmental patterns of the growing child.

The most fundamental flaw in the growth-inhibiting environment is a basic deficit in reading the youngster's symbolic communications at a cognitive and empathic level. Thus the mother who projects her own inner experience onto her youngster and misreads his signals is likely to respond inappropriately in a way that undermines reality orientation or capacity for differentiation. When the youngster expresses a complex symbolic communication and is responded to inappropriately or not at all, means/ends differentiation along realistic grounds does not occur (or it may occur along distorted lines of development). For example, the child playing with dolls shows how the mommy doll hugs and kisses the baby doll. The child then says to her own mother, "Mommy, I love you," and reaches out to be picked up. Moving from symbolic play to direct verbal communication with mother, the child expresses her expectation that her need for affection will be satisfied. The growth-inhibiting mother then sees this as an attack on her autonomy and thinks that her child is trying to control and engulf her. In a conversation with one such mother, she elaborated the fantasy that her child wanted to sit on her lap so that she could bite her or put something in her mouth to poison her. This paranoid distortion led this particular mother to slap her child and order her to return to playing with her dolls. In a similar case of paranoid distortion, another mother simply stared glassy-eyed at her daughter. She felt paralyzed, not knowing what to do, aware at one level of the child's expectation for closeness, and petrified at another level by her fearful projections. These are examples of the most severe types of distortion. The youngster, as a result, does not experience the appropriate consequences of his or her symbolic communication: Means are not associated with appropriate ends.

Another severe deficit in the growth-inhibiting environment is its tendency to incorporate the child's communications as if they were its own. The youngster who has hurt himself may come to mother to report his hurt and show his injury. When the emotionally needy child shows his mother the sore, cuddles up, and puts his head on mother's shoulder, saying, "Mommy make better," an inappropriate reading of this signal might lead mother to feel injured herself. Instead of responding with a comforting remark, "My little boy is hurt, let me kiss it and make it feel better," or, "Come and let Mommy hug you," or just simply an understanding look and a hug, she may begin to cry and pull away and show the child an earlier injury of her own. The youngster, confused and horrified, runs away in a panic. A more subtle version of this occurs when the youngster looks at mother in a way that indicates some internal discomfort and a wish for comforting. Instead of responding appropriately, mother suddenly begins to offer her own complaint of various bodily aches and pains and tells the young child that what she really needs is a nap. In each of these instances, the mother has left the youngster confused about the impact on the other of his own sense of distress, and wondering whether the distress is really his own. The differentiation of self from nonself remains blurred. The means — the child's symbolic communication — are not associated with the appropriate ends — a sense of having an impact on the environment.

At times, entire families may function in this way. The members of what have been referred to as schizophrenogenic families may take turns misreading communications or may unconsciously conspire to misread them. In the example given above, as one member of the family, the little girl, begins to express a need for comfort and nurturance because she has hurt her leg, the mother and older sibling get involved in a heated discussion about whose headache is worse, ignoring the little girl's needs. Is it any wonder that the girl is confused as to who is in pain? Is it she, her sibling, or her mother?

This kind of distortion can also occur at a much more subtle level. An angry child who begins to signal his anger with facial gestures and the like may, in some families, immediately cause other members of the family to behave in an overtly angry and aggressive way. This incorporation of

feelings leads to clear dedifferentiation of existing bounda-
ries between self and nonself, inner and outer, and means
and ends.

The use of "projective identification," whereby an attribute of the parents is projected onto the child and the
child is then responded to as though he embodies this attribute, has been widely discussed in the literature (e.g., Shapiro and Zinner, 1975; Greenspan and Mannino, 1974). A
youngster who is basically gentle and sweet and comfortable in his dependency may be perceived by parents as a
competitive, aggressive "little tiger." In all kinds of subtle
symbolic intercommunications the parents assign these "tigerish" attitudes to him and reward him accordingly. The
youngster, who is not really inclined to be this way at all,
may nevertheless soon take on these tigerish attitudes, which
may actually be part of some other family member's personality. There may be an unspoken collusion among an entire
family to attribute these attitudes to the newest member of
the family. If such use of projective identification predominates, there may be a distortion of the self/object boundary
and basic interferences with means/ends differentiation.
Where the pattern is not so strong, there may be some vacil-
lation in the youngster's self-image, consistent with character pathology rather more than with a basic deficit in differentiating capacity.

Individual members or the whole family can undermine representational differentiation in yet another way:
not so much by specific distortions as by a general disorganization in the capacity to receive and respond to the youngster's communications. Whenever the child develops an organized play theme around, let us say, two dolls feeding
each other, or two cars racing each other, or a wolf attacking the baby doll, mother, father, or older sibling will go off
in a totally irrelevant direction. There is no specific distortion per se; whoever may be the interpersonal partner in the
game simply goes off on a tangent, talking about whatever is

on his mind in a somewhat disorganized manner. Mother may begin talking about having dinner together with a friend, and how her little girl would like to meet this friend. Even when the child begins to look perplexed, mother still rambles on about this meeting and then from one subject to another, totally confusing the youngster. The child perceives the environment as having the type of thinking that the youngster had experienced only a few months before in her own development, those isolated islands of internal representations bridged only by illogical connections. If the environment remains disorganized and fails to respond appropriately to the child's affective behaviors or speech, the youngster who would ordinarily become more integrated (by learning to see relationships between one subject and another) begins to picture his world in terms of these disorganized themes. Some youngsters then take on the same rambling, disorganized quality in their own behavior. Other children may withdraw into relationships solely with the inanimate world. Still other youngsters may be fortunate enough to find other adults from whom they can get realistic feedback for their communications.

The youngster's capacity for differentiation is further undermined by the overly intrusive or overly withdrawn environment. The youngster's symbolic game in which, say, a wolf chases a little girl is interrupted by mother's demand that she play a tea-party game, perhaps because mother is anxious about the implied aggression in the child's original play theme. If this switching of themes is repeated too frequently, the youngster may hold back from further development of the symbolic mode or may begin responding aggressively and impulsively in pre-symbolic modes. Parental withdrawal will have a similar effect.

Some growth-inhibiting parents may not undermine differentiation in general, but only in particular ranges of experience. The environment may be incapable of offering differentiating experiences around pleasure or dependency, or assertiveness and curiosity, or aggression and negativism. Examples of these special problem areas were given when we talked about the growth-promoting environment. In essence, it is because the environment feels uncomfortable around these modes that it cannot promote their differentiation. Even when it does permit their use, it discourages anything more than their shallow expression. Similarly, there are some parents who become anxious around fantasy modes and cannot foster the elaboration of such modes.

The stability of the child's capacity for representational differentiation may be undermined in families who cannot structure a situation when the youngster becomes disorganized, offer warm support when the youngster is feeling overwhelmed, or set firm limits when the child is angrily aggressive. The environment is afraid to face up to its responsibilities. The father who is so angry that he fears his own aggressiveness will avoid angry confrontations with his young son. The mother who is so guilty about working that she cannot empathize with her child when he feels apprehensive about separation may insist instead that the child grow up and fend for himself. Or she may overindulge the child and be unable to set limits, as if to make up for having been away all day. In such cases, the child never learns that he can recover from disorganization in the face of stress and retain his capacity for differentiation. Conversely, when the youngster goes out of control, running, jumping, and yelling frantically, the frightened parent may go so far as to take a strap to him, which only increases his frenzied state. Another parent might turn up the music to drown out the child's noise, leaving the youngster to become even more disorganized. In cases like these, where the youngster is left with the feeling that the environment is unable to help him structure his behavior from without, there is no model to imitate, no source of strength through which he learns to internalize a sense of structure. Contrast this with the optimal parent who can use whatever means is necessary to help quiet the child and redirect his attention.

The growth-inhibiting environment also fails to respond to the developing uniqueness of the child. The environment does not support the youngster's growth in preferred modes of behavior — assertion, for example — by engaging the child when he is curious. Rather, it immediately intervenes and forces the child to be more creative and sensitive instead. If the child shows an interest in music or other artistic expression, the parent wonders aloud if the youngster is showing effeminate qualities and tries to shift his activity to more aggressive games. The optimal environment, in contrast, not only tolerates these individual differences, but helps foster their further differentiation by encouraging the youngster in his or her preferred modes, while at the same time helping the youngster to build flexibility into his personality structure when he seems to become locked into one or another mode.

The growth-inhibiting environment will not support the child's movement from dyadic to triadic relationship patterns. The primary nurturing figure might have a vested interest in maintaining dependency and may be conflicted, as a result, about letting the child go. The youngster whose parents have not set appropriate limits for him may, because of a basic confusion as to what is acceptable and what is unacceptable behavior, feel very worried about hurting the significant other in his life, and may therefore find it hard to separate. Separation is viewed as an act of aggression against the loved one rather than as a mutually satisfying and beneficial growth experience for both. In general, where movement beyond the dyadic relationship is undermined, maturation to more differentiated ways of dealing with the world will not occur.

As we have seen, the presence of a significant "second other" — an ally — not only helps the child separate from the primary nurturing figure, but also helps him express his aggressive feelings toward that figure without the use of primary process mechanisms. Where an ally is not available, we almost invariably find difficulty in negotiating this stage of development. At times, the youngster may seem to leap out of the "symbiotic waters," but at the expense of a later capacity for intimate loving and empathic sharing. At the other extreme, the youngster may remain totally undifferentiated along certain dimensions of personality. The isolated dyadic unit is fortunately a rarity. In most cases a significant "second other" is available.

But even where a father is present in the home, he may not adequately perform the ally function. He may be so withdrawn and emotionally unavailable as to be experienced as nonexistent. He may be so involved in competitive and aggressive battles with his wife that the role of ally too closely approximates his angry feelings toward his wife, causing him to shy away. Or he may so embrace the alliance that the child is frightened that the primary caregiver will be utterly destroyed.

Principles of Preventive Intervention and Treatment

Generally, intervention approaches at this stage of development focus on helping the severely growth-inhibiting environment correct gross distortions in its perception of the child's communications so as to enhance its capacity to offer reality-oriented feedback. The mother who projects her own feelings onto her child, or who incorporates the child's feelings as her own, must be offered appropriately structured support and, if necessary, medication to permit her to read and respond to her growing child in a more adaptive manner. Similar recommendations would hold for other family members who constitute the immediate environment of the youngster. If the primary caretaker evidences borderline personality characteristics which interfere with his or her capacity for communication, obviously a supportive psychotherapy or even an intensive dynamic program in psychotherapy will not alter this pattern overnight. Often, many years of treatment are necessary and, even then, results may be only modest. But by offering a supportive approach and by helping the parents achieve a reality orientation of their own (that is, by providing an opportunity for the parents to engage in close relationships in which their signals are correctly understood), the therapist can help them operate at the more developmentally advanced end of their personality structures. Most adults who employ the projective and incorporative modes to distort their perceptions of others will shift back and forth from these to more realistic modes depending on the degree of their anxiety or depression, or other disruptive affects. Thus therapeutic approaches must initially be supportive, concerned with concrete issues (resolving a housing crisis; offering an ongoing consistent human relationship; offering empathic understanding of underlying concerns), while at the same time pointing out and supporting solutions to the problems they confront with the child.

The therapeutic approach should focus on those particular signals of the child that the parent may be distorting. Some of the child's signals may be more threatening to the parent than others. Some parents may become disorganized around intimacy and dependency, others around themes of aggression, still others around themes of separation. And since not only single individuals within a family, but the whole family as a unit may be involved in a distorted pattern of communication, family therapy approaches can be directed toward examining threatening developmental themes. Some families whose styles of communicating are based on themes of merger and dependence will have difficulty with the young child at this particular age as he heads toward a more independent, reality-oriented way of operating. Other families will have trouble in making themselves available to the youngster shifting between dependency and independence.

Where the environment does not grossly distort, misread, or misrespond to the communications of the growing child, where, in other words, it is generally quite able to support reality orientation, it may still evidence conflicts and anxiety around specific developmentally appropriate representational communications of the child. Thus, the parent who is conflicted about a youngster's curiosity and assertiveness tends to be more supportive when the child is in the passive and dependent modes. Or perhaps the environment cannot shift back and forth smoothly and comfortably between the youngster's dependency needs and his need for independence and assertiveness. As the anxiety level rises, one or more inappropriate responses may occur. For instance, the environment may disengage itself temporarily, become overly controlling, overstimulate the child sexually, or cause the child to be caught up in family differences and conflicts. In each of these well-known examples, the individuals in the family as a whole respond to the youngster's cues more or less appropriately, and more or less in a temporally appropriate contingent manner, so that the youngster does get feedback for his symbolic communications. But he does not get the same rich, engaging feedback in some thematic areas as he does in others. Thus certain sectors of his personality fail to develop as fully as others. Conflict and anxiety dominate these sectors and characterological constrictions may result.

Such situations can be dealt with in a number of ways. At one level, the family may not be able to engage the youngster because of misguided notions about how to rear children, or lack of information about what is an appropriate interest for a child (for example, that it is normal for a youngster to be interested in his or her sexual body parts between the ages of three and five; that it is normal for a youngster to vacillate between independence and mastery and dependency and need). Supportive and educational approaches which explain to parents these age-expectable developmental behaviors can be very helpful.

Along these same lines, educational approaches that focus on the individual differences of the child may also be helpful. Just as infants have proclivities toward passivity or excessive irritability, so too do some youngsters at this stage of development evidence a greater capacity for differentiated communication in some realms more than in others. If the parents are flexible, they can be taught to engage the youngster in highly differentiated representational communication that encourages a more flexible behavioral repertoire in the child. In order to do this, parents and other family members must take stock of their child. In what areas has the child already developed his capacities for an appropriate differentiated representational system? Which areas are now in the process of developing? Where is the youngster not developing? They can then begin to encourage more depth and flexibility in the areas that are not developing properly.

Similarly, where the youngster is failing to consolidate his representational capacities and shows tendencies toward anxiety and depression, or a lack of stable ego functions, the parents can foster stability by effective limit-setting for the youngster's provocative and disruptive anger, warm support when he feels overwhelmed, and structure when he feels disorganized. Examples were given in the section on the environment. Here, too, otherwise competent parents can be helped by simple educational approaches.

It often happens, however, that parents will be unresponsive to such approaches because of their own earlier experiences and resulting limitations in the flexibility of their personality structures. A parent who has never developed a differentiated representational capacity around intimacy and dependency may have a hard time relating to his child's expressions in this mode. The parent who has never developed an appropriate reality orientation toward assertion or aggression may find it difficult to help the youngster negotiate the appropriate balance between fantasy and reality or to understand cause and effect in these realms.

Where the parents' difficulties are related to their own inner conflicts or limitations, a combination of educational and therapeutic intervention measures may often be necessary. In some instances, supportive measures alone may suffice. In these cases, the parents' conflicts can simply be pointed out to them without deeper, more intensive work. The parents may, with the ongoing support of a therapist, learn how to engage the child in areas where they themselves had never been engaged. But where the parents' conflicts are more severe, a more intensive intervention approach may be necessary which helps them resolve their own conflicts and connect those conflicts to their limitations with their children. As we have suggested, there may be a special motivation in such instances for the parents to refrain from involving their children in their conflicted patterns.

One can also work directly with the child. Children having difficulty in developing a reality orientation and/or consolidating representational differentiation may also have had difficulties in earlier developmental phases. As we discussed in the last chapter, a youngster's history of developmental difficulties will now be represented intrapsychically. His fears and concerns about assertion and aggression, for example, will now be internalized so that he cannot fully engage in these areas. Since youngsters at this age are still quite free in their use of play or other unstructured communications, interaction with a skilled worker can be quite helpful. Hour-long sessions several times a week in which the youngster's communications are paid attention to and he is encouraged to put his concerns into words or other symbolic modes can aid the child to rework some of these concerns. The skilled worker can foster the child's expression of previously avoided thematic areas.

One tends to shy away from the thought of doing therapy with youngsters between the ages of two and four-and-a-half. Yet, within this time frame, the personality structure has not yet consolidated to such a degree that these children are fixed in their behavioral patterns. Most of these young-sters are still open to trying new experiences. With a skilled worker, they will engage in the formerly feared or disorgan-izing realms of experiences through symbolic play and other forms of communication. By elaborating on the child's anxi-eties, conflicts, and fears, and offering him or her the kind of feedback which might not ordinarily be forthcoming from the environment, or which the child might ordinarily ingen-iously sabotage, the skillful worker can facilitate the child's development and help him make it easier for his parents to be helpful to him.

A youngster, for example, who is anxious about intima-cy may, when developing a play theme in which these feel-ings start to emerge, become disruptive and disorganized, throwing toys and dolls around. Perhaps this occurs imme-diately after the child pretends that one doll is feeding an-other doll. When the youngster becomes similarly aggressive and disorganized at home, the parents punish him. They may feel they are responding (somewhat naturally) to the youngster's provocation and are setting appropriate limits. The skilled worker, however, realizes that the youngster is being provocatively aggressive as a way of avoiding further involvement with the themes of feeding, nurturance, and intimacy in general. The worker assumes that the child is anxious and conflicted about this experiential domain. An activity may then be structured so that the youngster will not be able to indulge in his aggressive disorganization. The worker brings him back to the original feeding scene, but now points out that one of the dolls is scared. The doll being fed has "become scared of something," the worker may say, and wonders aloud what could have scared that little doll. The youngster may then be able to fantasize (using play) the frightening imagery that will reveal the reason for his disruptive behaviors around scenes of feeding and intimacy. By creating repeated opportunities for the child to replay those issues which tend to disorganize and disrupt him, he will be able to gain better coping capacities in these experiential areas. Eventually, perhaps not with words but through play acting alone, an explanation for his fears around feeding and intimacy may become apparent. As the worker continues to interact with the child around these themes and offers him more intensive feedback, including differentiating responses, than he had received earlier in his development (when these conflicts may have first arisen), the child gains some understanding of his conflicts and, finally, a new way of experiencing feeding and intimacy. It is the worker's own consistency and tolerance for certain affects and themes that, in time, helps the child rework these dramas and achieve a level of development more appropriate to his age.

Examples similar to the above could be cited for youngsters with difficulties in other experiential realms in which differentiated capacities are not developing. The important point is that at this age, and often in a relatively brief period with a skilled worker, a youngster's coping capacities can be improved. In an interaction with his mother he will no longer be driven to jump off her lap precipitately and begin throwing his toys around. He may not only tolerate sitting on her lap but enjoy it. His parents, if they are basically comfortable with this kind of intimacy, may comment that "He is now fun to be with," or "He is so much more loving and responsive than he ever was before."

A clinical observation of some importance has been made that by the time youngsters are capable of symbolic elaboration they are already in part the "directors" of their own behaviors. Sometimes, if they can modify their inclinations, life may be made much easier for their parents. One often assumes that the parents are at fault, that it is their rigidities that cause the problems. Yet some parents who are flexible enough to respond adequately to an engaging youngster will be overwhelmed and disorganized by a youngster who is not able to engage them effectively. This is similar to the observations we have made with respect to infants, some of whom are so engaging that even a depressed mother can become interested in them, while others are so withdrawn that they may further depress the dejected mother.

The diagnostician must try to assess in whom the greater flexibility lies. Ironic as this may seem, in many families the greater adaptive flexibility may lie in the child. Helping the child to be a more effective communicator may then secondarily lead the parents into more adaptive interaction patterns.

Clinical Illustrations

CASE 16

Cindy, just under three, was a bright, energetic little girl who was waking up with panic-provoking nightmares. She insisted on being comforted by her mother, often for hours before she would return to sleep. As the nightmares grew in intensity, mother was required to be with her for increasing lengths of time until finally mother and father sought consultation. Her history revealed that Cindy had been quite slow in developing sensory, motor, and cognitive capacities but had seemed to accelerate between 18 and 24 months. Cognitively, she was well ahead of the 3-year-old range, and during the day, at least, was able to deal appropriately with a variety of routine activities.

We learned that when Cindy was about 22 months old, mother, who had been working part-time, rather precipitously decided to return to full-time work. Father was coming home progressively later, at eight or nine o'clock in the evening, leaving this little girl in the care of a baby-sitter (whom she knew quite well). The night terrors had begun shortly after the mother's resumption of full-time work. Mother felt that she had given up her career long enough and now needed to jump back into it before it was too late. Mother was a highly competent, assertive, matter-of-fact woman who seemed unable to relax and uncomfortable about showing the more dependent, passive, intimate aspects of her personality. Father was similar. A very obsessive man, and very invested in his daughter's cognitive development, he angrily demanded of the evaluator that we find out what was wrong.

Observing mother and daughter in a play session together showed mother interacting at a descriptive representational level, helping her daughter name objects. But when her daughter tried to interact symbolically around an emotional theme, mother usually returned to the descriptive symbolic level. This avoidance of emotional interaction was not absolute. That is, mother was able to engage her daughter to some extent in certain symbolic themes but not in others. When they were playing with dolls, for example, and Cindy wanted mother to hold one doll while a second doll fed it, and a third doll nurtured yet a fourth, mother was able to cooperate. But when Cindy tried to play out an aggressive scene, and pretended that an animal was going after mother's nose, mother abruptly grabbed the animal and started attacking her daughter. This seemed fairly characteristic of their relationship. While mother was reluctant to engage in differentiated symbolic activity in a general sense, she was particularly anxious with regard to aggressive themes. Whenever the theme turned to aggression, mother would take charge immediately and put her daughter down. She would then return to a descriptive level. Cindy was tense throughout the play session with mother and showed little range of affect.

It seemed, therefore, that this little girl's symbolic elaboration and differentiation were being somewhat supported in certain areas of emotional experience, but being compromised rather dramatically in others.

Her history revealed further that there were almost no power struggles, stubbornness, or negativism on her part during the day. Nor was there much opportunity for this little girl to engage her parents along the more assertive domain as long as they were out of the house. Thus, the power struggles seemed to occur at night when she would waken frightened and demand that mother stay with her. Mother, not knowing what else to do, yielded to her daughter's demands.

It was explained to the parents that perhaps they should give their daughter an opportunity for a fuller range of experiences during the day. Mother's sudden decision to return to work was explored. It seemed that, in addition to her desire to resume her career, mother wanted to avoid the very kinds of entanglements that her daughter was now capable of creating. She unconsciously wanted to see Cindy as "slow," whereas, in fact, Cindy was an assertive, cognitively competent little girl who could indeed challenge her equally assertive mother. Interestingly, father would only engage his daughter on the level of her "intelligence," constantly trying to compensate for her "slow start." In response to supportive advice, mother was willing to reduce her working hours again and engage her daughter during the day by exposing herself fully to her daughter's potentially rich emotional life. Mother seemed capable of working through her own anxieties about her daughter's assertiveness, and Cindy began to transfer some of the power struggles to the daytime hours. The night terrors slowly diminished and were finally given up entirely. In addition, Cindy began evidencing a broader range of affective and thematic communication patterns.

This case illustrates what may occur when a youngster's symbolic capacities are engaged in one area, and not another. This little girl's assertiveness and aggressiveness, it may be hypothesized, was so frightening to mother that it led to premature separation.

When we look at Cindy's symptoms, we can see that they were adaptive to the extent that they allowed her to engage her mother in the only time she was available to her. While this was hardly an optimally adaptive situation, it did provide her with the opportunity to express her assertive and aggressive inclinations. Once further opportunities were made available during the day, she was flexible enough to deal with her full potential for emotional and behavioral experience in the symbolic mode.

In this case supportive counseling for mother and father seemed to be sufficient. In other such instances, where the difficulties are less reactive in nature (mother's abrupt return to work), or where there is a general failure to engage the child because of parental personality limitations, or where overall early development has not been so favorable, a broader program incorporating a number of elements described earlier may be necessary. In one case, for example, a little boy was having occasional nightmares at age two-and-a-half and became fearful of going outside because of "the monsters" he was seeing at night. His fears could be related to certain family dynamics. His early development had not been as favorable as Cindy's. He had been excessively labile as an infant, was severely punished for his impulses as a toddler and perceived as a "little monster" by his parents who related to him, off and on, in an impersonal manner. A combined program of working with the parents and the youngster was begun. During these regular sessions, the little boy could play out his fear of monsters and his concerns with separation and with impersonal responses with a skilled therapist. He soon returned to a more appropriate developmental pattern.

CASE 17

Barbara was a physically and cognitively very competent little girl whose overall social and emotional development (as best as could be understood from her history) seemed appropriate up to age two. At that time she had begun to become, not unexpectedly, more negativistic and demanding. Her history revealed that her emotional expression had then become flat and constricted. She did not show the variation or responsiveness that she had shown earlier. For example, she tended to look bland even when given a special candy treat or a new game, a pattern her parents ignored. By the time Barbara reached two-and-a-half, she had begun to develop obsessive rituals. She insisted that mother wash her hands several times before she would eat. When mother taught her about brushing her teeth, she insisted that her teeth be brushed over and over again before she would go to sleep. She was successfully toilet trained and insisted that she be wiped by her mother repeatedly. She became more stubborn and her negativism intensified. In addition, she began to get up early in the morning and would sit downstairs by herself.

At age three, when she was in a pre-nursery school class, Barbara came to the teacher's attention when she began to steal things from the other children. She took their new crayons, toys, and occasionally shoes and coats. Alarmed, the parents sought consultation. Her teachers went on to confirm what the parents had sensed but not fully acknowledged, that Barbara was very constricted and flat in her emotionality, and demonstrated patterns of ritualistic behavior.

In clinical assessment, it was also noticed that Barbara tended to talk in a rambling, somewhat free-associative style. These were islands of disconnected verbal activity. When she came into the session, she grabbed a doll and began pulling an arm off, and then switched to talking about wanting candy, and switched again to drawing lines with a crayon, showing the therapist an approximate circle. While this is not entirely unusual for age three, there was more randomness than one ordinarily expects at this age. Indeed, Barbara was more like a precocious two-and-a-half-year-old in her verbal ability and in her ability to organize these verbal segments into a cohesive pattern. Themes that continually emerged had to do with hunger, aggression, and danger. While her affect was noticeably flat, there was a hungry quality about her. Near the end of her session she wanted to take some toys home with her.

In the meeting with her parents it was found that father was a passive man who had tried to make himself available to Barbara, but had felt confused by her behavior and had decided that it was best to leave her care to her mother. Mother was an extraordinarily controlling, obsessive woman who felt that she had to win Barbara over in a series of routine power struggles. In reaction to Barbara's early morning rising, for example, mother would tell Barbara that she would spank her if she got up before her parents did. Nevertheless, Barbara would get up and go downstairs. Mother would then scold her and often spank her. Mother felt she was being manipulated by her daughter. As mother described it, "In every little activity during the day she challenges me and tries to make me back down." In short, there seemed to be almost no islands of pleasure, spontaneity, or warmth in any of her interactions with Barbara. Instead, there were desperate battles.

While mother seemed to be a competent, assertive woman, it was noticed that when she talked about Barbara she became anxious so that her own associations became mildly tangential. When she spoke of her concern about Barbara's stealing, she would, after a few sentences, with no apparent causal linkage, change the subject to her younger son (not without dynamic implications). Mother seemed to be quite ambivalent toward him, admiring his masculinity on the one hand and yet indicating a great deal of fear of his breaking things now that he was walking.

Our initial impression was that mother and Barbara had both begun having difficulties during the phase of representational elaboration and differentiation. Barbara had reached a level where she could use representational capacities and show a range of balanced affects and appropriate social capacities. Mother, while having her own internalized difficulties, nevertheless appeared able to support development to that point. Then, for reasons that were not apparent in the initial diagnostic sessions (though they were related in part to the pressures of the younger sibling's activity and competence — a pressure which exerted its impact both on mother and Barbara), the relationship between mother and Barbara had become organized solely around power struggles.

It was then that mother and daughter both began to demonstrate difficulty in organizing their representations into differentiated, cohesive, purposeful communications. The entire pleasurable component of representational elaboration and differentiation was missing. It was not surprising, therefore, that Barbara was frightened by her own ideas. She had little capacity to distinguish reality from fantasy. Yet cognitively she was a bright little child and was proceeding appropriately in differentially representing the non-emotional world. Because of her cognitive capacities, of course, she was also able to generate more and more complex and potentially frightening fantasies.

A program of exploratory treatment was begun with both Barbara and her mother. With mother the treatment focused on what made her anxious, how this anxiety led her to become disorganized in her thinking, and what went on in particular between Barbara and herself that made her anxious. Barbara's treatment focused on trying to understand what conflicts were inhibiting her orientation toward pleasurable experiences and her ability to use her cognitive capacities in her emotional life.

Over time, as Barbara was permitted to play out some of her concerns, themes of closeness emerged, with mothers feeding babies, followed usually by bodies falling apart and body parts being pulled from one another. A notion that intimacy resulted in bodily damage was verbalized. Barbara soon become able to engage in more pleasurable modes and her communications took on a more differentiated quality.

Exploratory treatment with mother resulted in a warm, trusting, supportive relationship between the therapist and herself. Mother had had a younger sibling who had been killed in an automobile accident at two years of age, when mother was three-and-a-half. She had avoided revealing this during the initial diagnostic evaluation, and when now it finally emerged spontaneously, she was asked how it was that even when there was a specific discussion of her own upbringing and family life, she had neglected to reveal this event. She said, "It was like she never existed. I don't remember her very well, and I never really considered her a part of the family."

The mother gradually arrived at the possibility that somehow her sister's death at age two had interfered with her capacity to continue supporting Barbara's development at this same age and that perhaps some of her unresolved feelings toward her sister did not permit her to engage Barbara fully. Perhaps mother's tendency to disorganize in her thinking, particularly in talking about her daughter, was also related to the as yet unresolved conflicts related to the death of her sibling.

At this point, of course, the full implications of mother's childhood experience were still largely unknown. We did know, however, that Barbara's age at the time that difficulties arose was the same age as mother's sibling had been when she died. With this information, and the therapeutic relationship that had developed, mother was able to take some distance from her angry power struggles with Barbara and to try to engage her in other types of interactions. She also demonstrated a greater capacity to maintain her thinking in an organized form. Meanwhile, even without a deeper understanding of her problems and even without appropriate working through, Barbara's symptomatic behavior began to disappear. She stopped stealing at school, was more cooperative with other children, was more relaxed with pleasurable pursuits, and was able to achieve a more appropriate reality orientation.

The fact that we were able to help Barbara and her

mother without the need for a full understanding and resolution of each of their conflicts illustrates the usefulness of a preventive intervention approach at the first sign of difficulties. It also highlights the importance of understanding the structural levels of personality organization. As the youngster becomes capable of representational differentiation, the environment must be able to support the full elaboration of this capacity. Conflicts which narrow the range of parental affect are of a different order than conflicts which result in an inability for differentiated communication. The former may lead to restrictions in the young child while the latter may interrupt a major line of development.

There is often a reluctance to engage youngsters of two-and-a-half to three in therapeutic play or other interactive activities. This reluctance is probably due to a lack of specific training in this area of clinical experience. Clinicians who are experienced with this age group report their marvelously adaptive communication skills — their use of a mixture of words, symbolic play, and gestures to convey their ideas. Children of this age are open to seeing alternative ways to resolve conflicts before they are fully internalized. While the youngsters are being encouraged to play out their difficulties, the clinician can help the parents to work at engaging the youngster in a developmentally more appropriate way.

Earlier we discussed our observations on the parallelism of changing relationships: how regularity in the caretaker-therapist relationship may predict to some degree good homeostatic development; how a rich attachment with the therapist correlates with an attachment with the youngster; how the capacity for an "observing ego" seems to facilitate the parent's ability to read the signals of the youngster in the stage of somatic-psychological differentiation. We can also see that as the youngster becomes more organized and challenging in his emotional and behavioral communications, the ability of the parent to maintain the self-observing function during this stage of wider affective experience is necessary if development is to proceed properly.

With the growth of the youngster's capacity for symbolic elaboration, differentiation, and consolidation, we need to look for symbolic capacities in the parents and for those conflicts that interfere with such symbolic elaboration. That is, if the parents are to facilitate symbolic elaboration and differentiation in their youngsters, they should do more than simply observe their own feelings. They should be able to develop fantasies around specific affectively charged issues in a range of intra- and interpersonal areas, including dependency, love, pleasure, assertion, aggression, and competition. If parents can develop their own fantasy life in these areas and at the same time maintain a reality orientation, they can then support the same capacities for symbolic elaboration and differentiation in their youngster. Where the parents are anxious about a particular thematic area such as assertiveness, they are likely either to avoid this area entirely, retreat to concrete, non-symbolic modes, or resort to other devices that will undermine their ability to engage their youngster in these experiences.

7

Discussion of Clinical Applications

We can now conceptualize a system for therapeutic intervention at both the service-system and clinical levels based on the stage-specific structural capacities we have outlined. In general, intervention approaches operate at two levels. At the first level, we seek to establish a safe, protective, regular, and consistent environment in which the child can develop. Thus, we attempt to help parents with respect to certain basic concrete needs — housing, nutrition, medical care, and so on. We also seek to minimize the regressive functioning that often results when parents are confronted with crises around these issues. The coordinated efforts of the various social services (including the educational system, the health and mental health systems, legal services, and protective services) are often necessary at each stage of development to insure that the environment is able to function in a safe, protective, and consistent way.

At the same time, however, we have also found that with more disordered environments such approaches at the service-system level are not enough. We thus seek to establish a regular and consistent relationship between the primary caretaker and the therapist. Our initial goal here is a modest one: to create a therapeutic relationship in which the therapist's availability to the caretaker serves as a model for the caretaker's availability to the child. We often find that the parent's difficulty in providing such a relationship for the child is symptomatic of a larger inability to form such relationships generally. We then further seek to create a therapeutic relationship in which the clinician's empathic understanding of the patient's feelings of negativism, ambivalence, or avoidance makes an affective bond possible and sets an example for the patient's relationship with the child. Again, we should emphasize the importance of coordinating clinical efforts with efforts at the service-system level.

The personal relationship that results from the regular empathic availability of the therapist to the primary caretaker then becomes the basis for our subsequent clinical approach. Here we attempt to help the caretaker understand the underlying psychological issues that may be associated with the less than optimal development of the child, either generally or with respect to certain areas of experience (though, of course, we have already seen how failure to develop in one area can lead to overall failure of development). Essentially, our subsequent approach focuses on understanding. But it is important to emphasize that because of the special incentive parents have with respect to their children, it is often not necessary for underlying psychological issues to be fully elaborated or indeed worked through before the parents can interact in more optimal fashion with their children. Indeed, we have often found that the provision of support, education, and a regular relationship is sufficient to foster the necessary improvement in the caretakers. Even when these do not prove sufficient, however, the identification of certain *specific* patterns of engaging the therapist may help the caretaker understand how similar patterns of engaging the *child* may be interfering with his development. With practice, parents can learn to distinguish these patterns and substitute more adaptive ones. Thus, while these parents may still have a tendency to regress in their relationships with their spouses, by projecting their own needs and so forth, they are able to control this tendency with respect to the child. Of course, whenever possible, we attempt to foster a full working through of the identified emotional problems.

Working through involves a number of principles which should be highlighted in our discussion of the therapeutic program. It must first be recognized that forming a therapeutic relationship may itself take months or even years. Gradually, a satisfying sense of mutual involvement (attachment) progresses until it can sustain itself in the face of anger, separations, etc. Thus, forming an intimate attachment may tax the skills and empathic capacities of a clinical team; outreach efforts, especially, may be rejected or only occasionally responded to. A second principle is that—in the context of this attachment—the exploration of emotional issues occurs at a number of levels. Initially, the therapist is seen as a helping person with whom the caretaker can talk about his or her life. At the next level, the individual observes that he or she has become involved in causal sequences or patterns (e.g., his withdrawal leads to another person becoming angry). Such pattern recognition may at first be concrete or action-oriented and may only slowly accommodate complex sequences dealing with feelings (e.g., "When I feel needy and dependent, I become scared and precipitate a crisis."). Simultaneously, the individual begins to observe that certain emotional patterns and feelings occur not only in relationship to his or her family, or to other individuals, but to the therapeutic person or team as well. A pattern that has existed in the past, and exists in outside relationships, also comes to be manifested in the therapeutic relationship proper. This identification of patterns and the continuing exploration of their existence in relationship to the infant and in the relationship to the therapeutic situation and other interpersonal relationships is especially useful.

218 STANLEY I. GREENSPAN

At subsequent levels in the therapeutic work with parents and families, the goal is for these and other relevant patterns to be further elaborated in greater emotional depth and richness (e.g., more examples, memories, and a greater range of affect). The continuing re-examination of these patterns in relationship to the growing child, other relationships, historical relationships, and the therapeutic relationship facilitates working through and overall emotional growth. New patterns reflecting more advanced levels of social and emotional development emerge and are experimented with for the first time.

Of course, the infant's and toddler's developmental momentum presents new challenges for the parents which may then trigger unresolved issues in their own development. The infant's development thus provides a useful context in which to highlight maladaptive patterns. For example, the infant's insistence on physical intimacy at four to eight months or autonomy at 12 to 16 months will challenge the ability of parents with difficulties in supporting these capacities. An opportunity as well as an incentive for new learning is thereby created. The active encouragement of the staff and the learning achieved through modeling approaches further support the caretaker's capacity to engage in new realms of experience essential to fostering the child's development. Our approach to therapy with the caretaker is thus consistent with our theory of development. Psychological growth, in our view, depends on the accomplishment of certain phase-specific developmental tasks, conceptualized in terms of the acquisition of certain characteristic experiences. Where severe conflicts, fears, and chronic maladaptive patterns inhibit the active exploration of these potentially facilitating experiences, these conflicts, fears, and patterns must be understood and worked through in a psychotherapeutic context so that *new* experience can become the basis for new learning. Where a simple lack of education has prevented access to certain experiences, educational approaches alone may suffice. But usually a combination of approaches, addressing both the issues of intrinsic limitations tied to conflicts and fears as well as lack of education, is required.

In considering these levels of intervention, we have obviously focused on work with the environment. But, of course, the child can also be worked with directly. As we have seen, it often happens that by strengthening the child's capacities, he can then help his parents help him. The youngster who is a weak sender at eight months, or whose parent does not adequately read his signals, can learn through work with an infant specialist how to strengthen his signals. As he then relates more readily to his depressed caretaker, the caretaker will be drawn out of his or her depression and relate to the infant in more adaptive ways. Similarly, the youngster who at 22 months already has a history of prior developmental difficulties and who shows a tendency for negativistic avoidance and fragmented aggressive behavior can, by means of his available symbolic modes, explore through play and other symbolic communication the repetitive maladaptive patterns he may have learned as a way of dealing with his situation. Even at a nonverbal level, these patterns can be played out symbolically and alternatives to them can be presented. In our case history of the youngster who caused the doll to run away all the time, we saw that the worker took the doll and showed it moving more assertively toward its parent doll — reaching out to the family rather than avoiding it. Naturally, it is always preferable to have the parents in the therapeutic program as well, actively supporting the child's development.

With these general considerations as a context, we can now briefly outline the intervention approaches specific to each developmental stage. The *basal* approaches, common to each stage, though relatively more important at earlier levels of development, involve service-system assistance with respect to concrete needs. Thus, at the stage of homeostasis, it is critical that the infant receive adequate nutritional, medical, and overall physical care because it is precisely his body that is the source of his knowledge of the world, and it is precisely his body that he must regulate in order to achieve this knowledge of the world. But as development progresses, first through the stages of somatic intelligence and then through the stages of representational intelligence — as the child's behavior, in other words, becomes more and more "psychological" — the importance of service-system approaches must be viewed in balance with approaches that address the child's more complexly organized capacities. That is to say, while assistance with respect to concrete needs continues to play an important role in producing a consistent environment for the child, the very fact of the child's growing capacities for "psychological" behavior makes other, more specialized approaches necessary. Now the child's capacities challenge even further the capacities of his parents. Obviously, when the parent's tendency for projection is the source of the child's difficulties in differentiating his representational world, this tendency can only be addressed in the context of additional, specialized therapeutic approaches.

Thus, the service-system must assist the family in providing adequate pediatric care, appropriate housing, nutrition, and, when necessary, legal protection for the infant in the stage of homeostasis; in fact, all the services that enhance human development. Service-system planning at this level of development needs to be based not on the easiest, but the most difficult case, that is, the multi-problem, hard-to-reach family. Indeed, it often happens that an infant comes to our attention only after a second agency — protective services, for example — has been asked to assist in the case of another member of the family. Coordination between the various relevant agencies is, again, essential.

In addition to the service-system approach, we have found that in an Infant Center to which the most vulnerable multi-problem families — often with severe psychopathology in the caretaker — can come on a daily basis is most useful not only in the homeostatic phase but in all other developmental phases as well. Here the very disordered caretaker can be provided with structure, and offered support for the infant. The infant can himself be worked with in the context of an active and expert environment. Other adults are available to meet his needs for physical care and protection and, just as important, to encourage his capacity for engagement and regulation. An outreach program in which home visits can be made, on a daily basis if necessary, is a useful substitute or supplement for Infant Center care where families, for whatever reason, cannot leave the home. An integrated pattern of service-system and Infant Center approaches provides the necessary alternative to the often inadequate foster-care system of the present day.

It should be emphasized that the service-system and clinical approaches outlined here must be able to succeed at a minimum in creating a degree of interest in the caretaker to use the program to help sustain a protective and consistent environment. The availability of the therapy team to the caretaker is essential to the creation of this interest, so that the clinician should be encouraged even if he is only occasionally let into the participant's home and even if he is only called on in times of crisis.

The same service-system approaches are necessary at the stage of attachment, supplemented again by skilled psychotherapeutic support for the parents and complementary care for the infant. A regular and consistent therapeutic relationship with the parent will provide him or her with an experience of intimacy and a model for affective interaction with the infant. The earlier interest in the therapeutic program can now develop into an affective interest in a primary clinician. And again, skilled infant-care workers can help the child become more interested in the animate world.

At the stage of somatic-psychological differentiation, caretakers must be helped to read the signals of their infant and respond emotionally and empathically in a reciprocal manner. Relatively sophisticated clinical approaches are necessary for the most impaired caretakers if they are to learn to respond adequately to both the cognitive and emotional communications of their infant. In order for them to be able to observe their own growth-inhibiting patterns of engaging their infants, it is often necessary that they first observe the similar patterns with which they interact with the therapist. Thus, the development of a capacity for self-observation is the goal of therapy with parents at this stage. Success in this goal is predicated on the establishment of a warm, trusting, and regular relationship between caretaker and therapist. The therapeutic relationship must be able to accommodate negative feelings without fear of interrupting the regular course of the relationship. The service system must be able to provide the kind of sophisticated therapeutic approach that will enable the parents to work toward this self-observing function. Sometimes simple support, combined with educational approaches, will help the parent learn to read the signals of the infant at the cognitive level. Our goal, however, remains to foster contingent interaction at the emotional level as well.

During the stage of behavioral organization, initiative, and internalization, the family is called upon not only to read the child's simple emotional and cognitive signals, but to interact in a more organized and complex reciprocal manner. They must now not only support the toddler's new behavioral organization and emerging ability for greater autonomy, but also his continuing dependency needs. Here the capacity for reading more complex emotional signals is of prime importance. The parent must be able to walk the fine line between encouraging the child's growing assertiveness and independence and the continuing need to be available to him. Parents must now be able to maintain the self-observing function over a wide range of affective experience and complicated behavioral patterns. As we described in one of our cases, a woman with an underlying thought disorder was capable of maintaining a self-observing function and reality orientation with respect to simple communications. But once the emotions within these communications became more complicated (e.g., a mixture of love and aggression), her self-observing function and ability to read signals deteriorated. In such a case the individual requires an even more sophisticated therapeutic approach than we have seen before. Not only must there be a regular therapeutic relationship in which negative feelings are tolerated and a capacity for self-observation encouraged, but this capacity itself must be strengthened enough so that the patient can observe his or her own emotional signals in greater complexity. Only then will the caretaker be able to tolerate the highly complex and ambivalent emotions of the child. Again, educative as well as dynamic approaches will help the parent learn to observe and understand his own feelings and communications as well as the child's.

As we have emphasized from the beginning, it is often not necessary for parents fully to resolve all their own difficulties (including conflicts, characterological limitations, tendencies toward fragmentation, etc.) in order for them to observe those aspects of their own emotional lives that impinge on their infants' or toddlers' emotional lives. If they can understand those areas of feelings that relate specifically to their relationships with their infants and toddlers, and the parallel aspects of their relationship to the therapist, other non-related areas can be dealt with later.

At the next level of development, our approaches seek to foster the child's growing capacity for symbolic elaboration. We often note that if we can help *parents* represent their own experiences in words, fantasies, and rich mental imagery, they can then engage their growing child in this representational mode. Where this is not possible, parents often maintain a concrete way of relating which undermines the natural development of the symbolic capacities in their toddlers and young children. Here the clinical approach seeks to establish a therapeutic relationship of sufficiently long duration to help parents use the representational mode without becoming disorganized. Or where the parent's capacity for mental imagery is restricted due to characterological limitations or conflict, therapy attempts to "liberate" it, at least in regard to the relationship with the toddler. This requires complex therapeutic work in which the parent's own fantasies are permitted to emerge. The parent is then encouraged to observe his or her own way of handling fantasy and mental imagery in the relationship with the therapist and, thereby, in the relationship with the child.

The capacity for reality orientation and differentiation of representational capacities takes us to the sixth stage of the child's development. Here the task is not simply to help parents develop and elaborate mental imagery, but also to be able to differentiate fantasy from reality. With this differentiation they can begin to understand how to facilitate a similar reality orientation in their youngsters. It permits them to make pivotal judgments as to when limit-setting is important, when it is important to point out the reality of a situation, and when it is important to encourage the make-believe play of the toddler or child. These judgments are not easy to make, yet healthy, competent parents make them intuitively.

When parents have characterological constrictions, severe conflicts, or tendencies toward fragmentation, intensive therapeutic work may be required. The establishment or strengthening of these capacities in the caretakers may then serve as a foundation for the establishment in the child of such basic ego functions as reality testing, impulse regulation, mood stabilization, and capacity for focused concentration and attention.

The Special Role of the Infant's Own Development on Parental and Family Functioning

It is impressive to note the degree to which an infant's

developmental accomplishments and developmental needs may lead to disequilibrium in the parents and/or family. (Of course, in healthy families, these same accomplishments and needs often lead to further growth.) Some mothers, for example, may be quite comfortable in the early months when the infant's capacities and requirements involve his being held, cuddled, fed, protected, calmed, and sensitively engaged with the world. The infant's fundamental dependency is satisfying to the mother. When the same infant, often due to extraordinarily competent early rearing, becomes an active, explorative "crawler" at eight months, begins to toddle by 11 or 12 months, and begins to use the mother as a secure base from which to curiously explore his environment, this same mother may become quite anxious, possibly threatened. At this point a number of symptoms may begin to appear, including mild depression and withdrawal from her very competent toddler. These symptoms can be due to a variety of factors. The mother may find it hard to deal with the more complicated demands her toddler is now placing on her. She must now balance his need for nurturing with his need to become independent. Or it may be hard for the mother to deal with the youngster's increased motor or verbal capacities, now as they are enlisted for assertive behavior. The youngster can insist on what he wants. He can take mother by the hand, point, and "demand" an object. If that is not enough, he can scream in order to make his wants known. This is quite a contrast to the three-month-old infant who can also cry in protest, but without the quality of assertiveness, of directness present in the healthy 15-month-old.

Caretakers who have difficulty with such assertiveness become aggressively controlling and punitive, or passively apathetic, withdrawn, and depressed. More subtle symptoms, including psychosomatic problems and difficulties in other areas of the parents' lives, may be the first sign that they are experiencing problems in relation to their young-

ster's developmental progress. In some cases we have noticed that as a youngster moves into the stage of behavioral
organization, initiative, and internalization, and evidences
the increased assertiveness, originality, and curiosity that is
expectable at this stage, a mother who has, until now, been
quite competent, begins to have social difficulties. For example, one mother began to have arguments with her boyfriend over her independence. It was as though she were
identifying with her youngster. Suddenly she "wasn't going
to take it anymore." In this case, the mother's sudden shift
from a compliant attitude to one of "I'll show him" would
not have been surprising if it did not so directly parallel her
youngster's own movement toward independence. It was also striking that this new behavior on the mother's part also
began to cause problems for her at work. As her relationships and activities outside the home thus began to change,
mother became so caught up with them that she ceased being available to her young son. What merely appeared to be
an increase in mother's own assertiveness, then, emerged as
an interference in her relationships with her son, her boyfriend, and her fellow workers. Only a close examination revealed that what had set all this in motion was her difficulty
in dealing with the new development in her son. Our first
impression was simply that she had become more assertive.
No longer so passive and compliant, her own growth appeared to be causing some strain. But the identification of
the defensive aspects of this "pseudo" growth suggested otherwise.

It is essential, then, when one sees a change in a pattern
of parental behavior, no matter how substantive or superficial, no matter how apparently growth-promoting or growth-
inhibiting, that this change be viewed in terms of whether it
has actually been precipitated by an inability to deal with
the youngster's new developmental accomplishments and
requirements.

Another example of this dynamic involved a mother,

referred to earlier, with an underlying thought disorder. When her daughter, with the support of our program, began to exhibit a capacity for more organized behavior and a capacity to verbalize her needs, wants, and assertive demands, mother precipitously separated from her by sending her to live with a relative for two months. This led to a severe regression. This bright, curious, assertive youngster became withdrawn, apathetic, disinterested in people, and even gave up her capacity to use words, all because of this abrupt separation. A casual appraisal would have made it appear as if mother were overwhelmed by problems with friends, family, and work and that, because she was overwhelmed, she had had to send her daughter away. Closer scrutiny, however, revealed that the mother's primary anxiety was related to her daughter's development, to a point where mother found her relationship to her daughter disorganizing. When her daughter would communicate complicated emotions and behave in an organized and complex manner, it was difficult for mother, with the underlying thought disorder, to process the child's messages. When, for example, the daughter shifted rapidly from loving to assertive responses, the mother would become mildly loose in her own associations. Mother later described this in these terms: "I would have the feeling that I would bleed and my body would fall apart." Step by step, mother's acute anxiety over becoming disorganized led her into difficulties in other areas of her life, and finally to decide to send her daughter away.

We have been impressed with similar occurrences even in the first few months of life. A mother abruptly returns to work when her baby is five months old, even though she had planned to stay at home until the baby was 12 months old or more. This abrupt switch in plans is often related to the beginning capacities for differentiation that the baby is evidencing. At other times, even in the first month or two, we may see difficulties in caretakers, related to the total dependency and nurturing needs of their child.

The point we are making here is that, no matter how strongly it may appear that work, family relationships, or other factors are causing the disequilibrium in the caretaker, the clinician should first rule out the possibility that it may actually be caused by a reaction to the youngster's development. We are not suggesting that this will always be the case. But a thorough check creates the opportunity for working on a primary difficulty rather than overlooking it.

This approach makes special sense, indeed, when we realize that the affective bonds between caretakers and their children are likely to be extraordinarily powerful. Even with seemingly indifferent caretakers, there is often a strong affective bond. The bond may be so strong, even overwhelming for some, that it leads to denial and avoidance and the observed aloofness. Having children is such a biologically unique experience and the relationship between the infant and his caretakers is so profound that it would be hard to conceive that strong affective bonds do not exist. That these bonds exist in a variety of forms, and may be masked at times or even denied, is not surprising, given the flexible defensive and coping strategies of adults. In any case, it makes sense to look at this bond in assessing parental disequilibrium, whatever the appearance to the contrary. Indeed, it is usually the most important, most affectively laden relationships that give rise to these states of disequilibrium in the first place.

This model of looking first at the relationship between the infant's developmental stage and parental functioning can be carried over to older children as well. Changes in family functioning when the youngster is between four and six, seven and ten, or in the teenage years, are often related to the youngster's development. That is to say, the youngster's rapid development during these years brings new issues to family functioning. Each step toward adulthood brings further changes in family interrelationships, from early dependency, to beginning tendencies toward independence and mastery, to later interests in sexual issues, to a shift outside the family circle toward peer relationships, to the changes of early adolescence, to rebellion during the second individuation of middle or late adolescence, etc. Each change not only shifts the family equilibrium, but also represents an opportunity for the parents to reactivate aspects of their own early growth and development. While at times this can lead to exceptionally constructive adaptive reactions in parent and/or family, at other times it can lead to maladaptive, disorganized patterns. A well-known example is that of the four- to six-year-old child who begins to show an interest in the parent of the opposite sex, along with an increased sexual curiosity in general. This leads, in turn, to family disequilibrium as rivalries and alliances are altered. Other developmental issues may similarly lead to disequilibrium involving more than one person, including siblings and, at times, even grandparents or other extended family members.

In this context it is important to emphasize that while difficulties between mother and father may frequently be related to the development of their child, parental conflicts will at times be displaced onto the child (e.g., the frustrated mother uses her child as a substitute for her spouse). Such patterns are usually the work of both parents, with the parents and children engaged in varying degrees of covert and overt collusion. Thus, couples therapy and family therapy may at times play a significant role in the overall treatment plan. Helping a couple deal more directly with each other rather than displacing their conflict onto their child cannot help but facilitate more appropriate development.

Finally, it is important to point out that each family member will himself be confronted with the developmental tasks of his own stage of life. The tasks of middle age or of mourning for the death of a loved one are typical examples. Thus, the rapidly changing developmental accomplishments and demands of the infant or toddler have their effects in what is itself a dynamic developmental context.

Additional Implications of a Developmental
Structuralist Approach

A framework has been presented for understanding human development during the early years of life. The developmental stages that we have delineated are compatible with what has been learned about physical, cognitive, and affective development in infants and young children in clinical observations, hypotheses derived from reconstructive work with adults, and empirical research based on observations of infants and young children in experimental as well as in naturalistic settings.

This framework allows us to suggest clinical landmarks for early development that can be used as the basis for therapeutic planning and for evaluating therapeutic progress. Such a framework is obviously open to constant revision and, as with any framework that attempts to order complex events, based on conceptualizations that are approximations, approximations in the service of systematization. We have tried to strike a balance between attention to the complexity of development and the need for such systematization.

We have found this framework to be useful in translating complex clinical phenomena into quantitative measures for research purposes. Based on the developmental landmarks and the clinical features that illustrate each stage in development from homeostasis through symbolic elaboration and differentiation, we have been able to develop clearly defined behavioral indicators representing the increasing complexity of child and caretaker interaction patterns. (See Appendix 1.) These patterns can be scored with a high degree of reliability (Greenspan and Lieberman, 1981). We have also found that they closely parallel a consensus among clinicians regarding the youngster's developmental status.

Particularly striking about the research use of this framework is that the indicator behaviors are scored from only ten minutes of free play between the child and his caretakers and without any knowledge of earlier history, overall clinical course, or data from other observational settings. The indicator behaviors were selected based on a combination of our theoretical perspectives and clinical reasoning (i.e., what do we use to make our clinical judgments).

This research approach is also useful in judging the subject's interactions and behaviors as a whole. In addition to scoring short intervals, an overall clinical rating may be given to what has been observed in different segments of free play. This, too, can be done reliably, with results consistent with clinical judgments based on access to greater amounts of data.

A framework which allows for clinical complexity and which is based on the youngster's structural capacity offers greater promise, it seems to us, than reductionistic approaches based only on molecular behavioral assessments. It is important to recognize that by focusing on the structural capacity of the youngster we are focusing on the youngster's unique way of organizing and differentiating experience rather than on a single cross-sectional experience. Because this structural capacity is based on the youngster's history, our current observations incorporate aspects of his constitutional make-up and his experiential history.

There may be special value in such an approach for longitudinal studies and for assessing outcome. We are more likely, for example, to observe the continuity of development with our approach than we would with an approach that focuses on specific referent behaviors. While a youngster who shows highly flexible adaptive structures early in life may continue to show highly adaptive structures and while a youngster who shows basically maladaptive structures may remain at these less adaptive levels, *specific* patterns of behavior may shift dramatically. The passive youngster may become aggressive; the aggressive youngster passive. The passive youngster who can integrate emotional polarities may remain relatively adaptive. The assertive youngster who cannot integrate polarities, who can deal only with the aggressive spectrum of behavior, may remain relatively maladaptive.

Similarly, in assessing outcome, the developmental structuralist approach affords a model for the "baseline" functioning of the personality — the context in which we can look for more specific symptomatic behavioral changes. In general medicine, if we look at a new medication designed to cure an infection, we use baseline measures of overall physical functioning (e.g., liver, blood, respiratory functioning, etc.) to make sure we do not cure the infection at the expense of other important bodily functions. In our approach to intervention for infants, children, and adults, however, we have not yet reached the point where we have an adequate series of baseline measures to assess overall functioning. We therefore tend to ignore the behavioral and emotional side effects and often look only for physical side effects. When we offer a behavioral or pharmacological approach to a youngster, we ought to know what this will do to his overall level of adaptation. Some approaches may cure the symptom but restrict the youngster's capacity for experiencing certain feelings, e.g., narrow the range of compassionate feelings he is capable of experiencing in interpersonal relationships. Some mechanical or charismatic therapies, for example, which may cure symptoms and lead to a feeling of well-being, may increase certain narcissistic limitations. The developmental structuralist approach affords a way of looking at the basic context (the stage, so to speak) of the child's specific developmental drama.

An important caveat should be mentioned here before we conclude this section. The developmental structuralist approach should not be seen as suggesting that predictions from earlier to later behavior can be made. For some aspects of development, an absence rather than the presence of a linear course has been documented (Kagan, 1978). Nor should the reader mistakenly assume that there is one optimal environmental response or infant pattern for each developmental phase. Rather, the developmental structuralist approach, in outlining the characteristics of the various levels of integration, provides a new way of looking at the relative adaptiveness of psychological structures and the many factors —

environmental, constitutional, developmental, etc. — which influence them at each level of development. As such, it provides a model for understanding those aspects of development which may be relatively more continuous and those which may be relatively less continuous. Similarly, it outlines a broad range of experiences that are postulated to lead to relatively more or relatively less optimal personality organizations at each stage of development, in the context, of course, of individually different constitutional, maturational, and experiential patterns. Thus, the construct postulated in this work, while strongly emphasizing the importance of early experience and early patterns of structural integration, nevertheless suggests that new experiences and, consequently, new levels of integration are possible at any age. If anything, by focusing on levels of integration, the approach leads away from efforts to find one-to-one relationships between specific early events or specific constitutional factors and later events. Rather, it creates a conceptual basis for understanding the far more complex relationships between levels of development.

Summary

We have presented a developmental structuralist approach for understanding adaptive and pathological personality patterns in infants and young children. We have considered the effect of the environment on the child's development and suggested certain principles of preventive intervention. In addition to providing a diagnostic and therapeutic scheme, the developmental structuralist approach proposes a high-order construct based on the level of integration of a variety of behaviors, rather than a construct based on isolated, less stable behaviors that may be more sensitive to minor environmental changes. Levels and patterns of integration, as indicated above, incorporate the history and meaning that the organism has given to events as well as the way in which it has organized these meanings into stable coherent patterns. Tables 1 and 2 summarize the developmental structuralist approach in schematic form.

TABLE 1

Stages of Development	Illustrative Adaptive Capacities	Illustrative Maladaptive (Pathologic) Capacities	Growth-Promoting Environment	Growth-Inhibiting Environment
Homeostasis (0–3 months)	Internal regulation (harmony) and balanced interest in the world.	Unregulated (e.g., hyperexcitable), withdrawn (apathetic).	Invested, dedicated, protective, comforting, predictable, engaging, and interesting.	Unavailable, chaotic, dangerous, abusive, hypo- or hyperstimulating.
Attachment (2–7 months)	Rich, deep, multisensory emotional investment in animate world (especially with primary caregivers).	Total lack of, or non-affective, shallow, impersonal involvement (e.g., autistic patterns) in animate world.	In love, and woos infant to "fall in love"; multimodality, pleasurable affective involvement.	Emotionally distant, aloof, and/or impersonal (highly ambivalent).
Somatic-Psychological Differentiation (3–10 months)	Flexible, wide-ranging, multisystem, contingent (reciprocal) affective interactions (especially with primary caregivers).	Behavior and affects random and/or chaotic, or narrow, rigid, and stereotyped.	Reads and responds contingently to infant's communications across multiple sensory and affective systems.	Ignores or misreads (e.g., projection) infant's communications (overly intrusive, preoccupied, or depressed caretaker).

Behavioral Organization, Initiative, and Internalization (9–24 months)	Complex, organized, assertive, innovative, integrated behavioral and emotional patterns.	Fragmented, stereotyped, and polarized behavior and emotions (e.g., withdrawn, compliant, hyperaggressive, or disorganized toddler).	Admiring of toddler's initiative and autonomy, yet available and firm; follows toddler's lead and helps him organize diverse behavioral and affective systems.	Overly intrusive, controlling; fragmented, fearful (especially of toddler's autonomy); abruptly and prematurely separates.
Representational Capacity, Differentiation, and Consolidation (18–48 months)	Formation and elaboration of internal representations (imagery) Organization and differentiation of imagery pertaining to self and nonself; emergence of cognitive insight Stabilization of mood and gradual emergence of basic personality functions.	No representational (symbolic) elaboration; behavior and affect concrete, shallow, and polarized; sense of self and "other" fragmented, undifferentiated, or narrow and rigid; reality testing, impulse regulation, mood stabilization compromised or vulnerable (e.g., borderline psychotic and severe character problems).	Emotionally available to phase-appropriate regressions and dependency needs; reads, responds to, and encourages symbolic elaboration across emotional and behavioral domains (e.g., love, pleasure, assertion) while fostering gradual reality orientation and internalization of limits.	Fearful of or denies phase-appropriate needs; engages child only in concrete (non-symbolic) modes generally or in certain realms (e.g., around pleasure), and/or misreads or responds non-contingently or non-realistically to emerging communications (i.e. undermines reality orientation); overly permissive or punitive.

TABLE 2

LEVELS OF DEVELOPMENT, CORRESPONDING SERVICE-SYSTEM REQUIREMENTS, AND THERAPEUTIC RELATIONSHIPS WITH ENVIRONMENT AND CHILD

Stages of Development	Service-System Approaches	Basic Goals	Therapeutic Relationship with Parents or Family	Direct Work with Infant where Clinically Necessary
Homeostasis (0–3 Months)	Basal capacities: health, mental health, social service, educational, legal systems working in an integrated fashion.	Regulation and engagement in world.	Develop a pattern of therapeutic availability that is predictable and regular.	Adjust range and intensity of environmental stimuli to encourage alertness and interest, and/or diminish disorganization (in context of regulating experiences tailored to individual constitutional differences).
Attachment (2–7 Months)	Add: special services (e.g., therapist for mother, homemaker, or temporary surrogate care) to support consistent caretaker-infant relationship.	Rich investment in human world.	Develop a therapeutic attachment that has pleasurable components and survives negative feelings.	Through interesting pleasurable and regulating sensorimotor and affective experiences, facilitate capacity for intimacy with human world and remove or alter factors associated with apprehension.
Somatic-Psychological Differentiation (3–10 Months)	Add: special educative and psychotherapeutic services (e.g., modeling, exploration) to facilitate reading of infant's communications.	Contingent responses to range of affective and behavioral cues.	Includes work on capacity for self-observation to facilitate reading of the "other," at least at a concrete, descriptive level.	Through practice with pleasurable feedback, increase range, organization, and intensity of infant's communication signals across multiple sensorimotor and affective themes. Facilitate discriminative capacity.

	Add:		
Behavioral Organization, Initiative, and Internalization (9–24 Months)	Add: skilled therapists for direct exploratory work with the toddler, and staff for remedial educational approaches, especially in perceptual-motor area.	Behavioral initiative and originality.	Further work on self-observing capacity to permit integration of affective polarities around dependency/aggression and passivity/assertiveness.	Encourage greater behavioral organization and initiative (e.g., practice complex games). Resolve inhibiting prerepresentational conflicts (e.g., toddler who is fearful of separation or aggression) using, as necessary, therapeutic relationship (e.g., play therapy). Selectively teach and support the uses of distal communication channels.
Capacity for Organizing Internal Representations (18–30 Months)	Add: special therapeutic, educational, and vocational programs for parents (e.g., GED) to provide new skills and capacity for encouraging emerging representational capacities of toddler.	Elaboration of evolving representational (symbolic) capacities across a wide thematic and affective range.	Work on capacity to use and elaborate fantasy in the service of self-understanding.	Use symbolic play and language to facilitate representational mode across themes and affective polarities; use therapeutic relationship to resolve conflicts that keep child tied to concrete modes.
Representational Differentiation and Consolidation (30–48 Months)	Add: services to permit, as appropriate, more independent functioning and new relationships (e.g., nursery schools).	Facilitation of representational capacity and reality orientation.	Work on capacity to shift between fantasy and reality and integrate wide range of affective and thematic issues.	Create opportunities both in therapeutic relationship and other settings (home, day care, nursery school) for balance between encouragement of fantasy and reality orientation.

Appendix

The following is an outline of clinical landmarks for adaptive and disordered infant and early childhood functioning, based on a developmental structuralist approach. It is intended for screening purposes only and not to replace in-depth evaluation. Each category of functioning is measured on a nine-point scale, with scores of one and nine representing, respectively, passivity and activity in the maladaptive function. A score of five represents optimal development. Ideally, this screening approach would be based on two sources of information — direct observation and history-taking. Ten minutes of observation of parent and infant will lead to an impression of the presence or absence of these landmarks. Subsequent questioning of mother or father regarding these landmarks will produce the necessary historical information (e.g., "Does your child like to look at people, or does he prefer looking at objects? Does he look away sometimes?" And so on.).

In order to properly use these clinical guidelines for screening purposes, the following should be observed: For each stage of development, all the prior categories of functioning should be re-evaluated. In other words, in assessing attachment, homeostasis should also be assessed. A youngster who during the stage of behavioral organization and initiative becomes impulsive and negativistic may be having recent difficulties at this developmental stage only. On the other hand, if compromises in his capacity for self-regulation or attachment are found, it may be hypothesized that his difficulties began much earlier and are now presenting an obstacle to continued development.

I. Homeostasis

1 Spends most of the day sleeping. Shows no interest in anything or anyone; does not respond to stimuli.

3 Apathetic. Responds a little to touch or movement, but not very interested in seeing or hearing.

5 Relaxed, and sleeps at regular times; cries only occasionally. Is very alert; looks at one when talked to; brightens up when rocked, touched, or otherwise stimulated.

7 Often upset and crying. Excitable. Gets somewhat distracted by things he can see, hear, or feel.

9 Always upset or crying; rigid. Becomes completely distracted by any sights, noises, touch, movement; gets too excited and cries.

II. Attachment

1 Uninterested in mother, father, and/or other primary caretakers (e.g., always looks away rather than at people); withdrawn; human approaches (i.e., holding) lead to rigidity and turning away or further withdrawal.

3 Occasionally looks at people or responds to their voices with show of interest, either a smile or putting hand out or kicking, etc.

5 Very interested in people, especially mother or father or other key caregivers; looks, smiles, responds to their voices, their touch with signs of pleasure and interest — smiling or vocalizations indicating pleasure.

Seems to respond with deep feeling and with multiple sensory modalities.

7 Clings to mother, father, or other primary caretaker; cries easily if not held; goes to strangers and holds on as if they were parents. Not very interested in playing alone.

9 Insists on being held all the time; will not sleep without being held.

III. Somatic-Psychological Differentiation

1 Seems oblivious to caregivers; does not respond to their smiles, voices, reaching out.

3 Responds occasionally to caregiver signal, such as smile or sounds, but hard to predict when; random rather than purposeful social responses, or limited only to one mode.

5 Able to interact in a purposeful (cause-and-effect) manner; smiles in response to a smile; alerting, smiling, or looking in response to a voice; able to initiate signals and respond to signals using multiple sensory modalities and the motor system across range of emotions; able to get involved with toys and other inanimate objects and have pleasure when interacting with a person.

7 Able to interact, but seems overly sensitive to any emotional communication of caretaker; looks sad and forlorn at slightest sign that caretaker is preoccupied; gets very easily frustrated if signal is not responded to.

9 Demands constant interaction, cannot tolerate being alone; has temper tantrums or withdraws if caretaker does not respond to his signals or initiate signals.

IV. Behavioral Organization, Initiative, and Internalization

1 Rarely initiates behaviors; mostly passive and withdrawn or excessively negativistic. Passive; compliant.

3 Can manifest a few socially meaningful behaviors in

narrow range (e.g., can only protest); involved only with interaction around inanimate world; no capacity for integrating pleasure, warmth, assertiveness, and anger in social context. Occasionally takes initiative, but usually only responds to other's initiative and may also be negativistic; little or no originality.

5 Manifests a wide range of socially meaningful behaviors and feelings including warmth, pleasure, assertion, exploration, protest, anger, etc., in an organized manner. Can play or interact with parents, stringing together a number of reciprocal interactions into a complex social interchange. Able to go from interacting to separation and reunion with organized affects including pleasure, apprehension, and protest. Initiates complex, organized, emotionally and socially relevant interactions, yet also accepts limits. Can explore new objects and new people, especially when parents are available.

7 Many behaviors and feelings manifested but in poorly organized, unmodulated manner; shifts behaviors and moods rapidly, only occasionally involved in organized, socially meaningful interactions. Takes initiative but is demanding and stubborn; tends to repeat rather than develop new behaviors or interactions.

9 Behavior and affect completely random and chaotic. Toddler almost always appears "out of control" with aggressive affects predominating.

V. Capacity for Organizing Internal Representations

1 No symbolic behavior or complex actions implying planning and anticipation, etc. Behavior fragmented or stereotyped.

3 Some symbolic behavior, limited to descriptive use of symbolic mode with little or no capacity for interactive use of thoughts.

5 Symbolic elaboration in descriptive and interactive

contexts. Uses words or wordlike sounds to indicate wishes and intentions; can use dolls or other objects to play out a drama. Symbolic elaboration appears to cover a range of emotions including love, dependency, assertion, curiosity, anger, and protest.

7 Symbols used, but often in chaotic, disorganized fashion; dramas have only fragments of discernible meaning.

9 Symbolic activity but totally disorganized and fragmented and used exclusively in the service of discharge-type hyperactivity; words or play activities *never* develop into an organized theme.

VI. Representational Differentiation and Consolidation

1 Withdrawn; unrelated to people; uses words or symbolic play only with things. If words or symbolic play with people are used, distinction of real from unreal is unclear. No sense of purpose or intention in social use of symbolic mode.

3 Relates slightly to people with words or other symbols, but in narrow range of emotions. Some purposefulness and reality orientation is present but vulnerable to the slightest stress.

5 Relates in balanced manner to people and things across a range of emotions (e.g., warmth, assertiveness). Is able to be purposeful, distinguishes what is real from unreal; accepts limits; can be self-limiting and feel good about self; switches from fantasy to reality with little difficulty.

7 Relates to people and things using words or play across a range of emotions and themes but in a chaotic manner, unrelated to reality; reality orientation only with structure.

9 Relates to people and things symbolically in totally chaotic, unrealistic manner; no reality testing or impulse control. Self-esteem and mood are labile.

The following is an outline of caretaker functioning

that can be used in conjunction with the assessment strategy discussed earlier. Once again, the scores of one and nine represent passivity and activity, respectively.

I. Homeostasis

1 Completely unavailable to comfort infant (e.g., aloof, self-absorbed, very depressed, etc.). Presents no interesting stimuli, animate or inanimate.

3 Intermittently available (e.g., can comfort for brief periods or when infant is not too upset); other times is withdrawn, aloof, or otherwise unavailable. Intermittently interesting to infant; gains his attention on occasion.

5 Excellent at helping infant become fully regulated and comforted; can use multiple sensory and motor modes — voice, vision, movement (rocking) — as well as a variety of affect states in ways that acknowledge the individual differences of the infant. Interests infant in a variety of animate and inanimate stimuli. Gains infant's attention in a relaxed, focused manner and helps infant use multiple sensory and motor modalities such as vision, sound, touch, movement to explore the human and inanimate world. Caretaker stress generally does not interfere, except temporarily, with this capacity.

7 Tries to comfort, but out of sync with infant; overly intrusive, occasionally hyperstimulating. Gains infant's interest, but intermittently chaotic and distracting (e.g., too many stimuli or too intense).

9 Grossly hyperstimulating and chaotic; undermines infant's own regulatory capacity.

II. Attachment

1 Totally unavailable; lacks emotional warmth (e.g., mechanical or disinterested; does not look at, smile at, talk to, or touch infant).

3 Intermittent emotional interest as reflected in some looking, cuddling, talking to, and/or stroking; may

be limited to one modality (e.g., looking only, or talking only). Whatever emotional contact does exist is very vulnerable to caretaker stress.

5 Optimal attachment with deep emotional investment expressed through smiles, looks, touch, talk, etc. Loving interest can accommodate occasional anger and disappointment, and survive caretaker stress (e.g., illness, tiredness, etc.).

7 Appears very interested in infant, but seems overly anxious and overprotective (e.g., always smiling, stroking, and worried that infant be "happy").

9 Slightly chaotic emotional investment; overwhelming, intrusive, hypomanic quality; seems impervious to infant's moods or states.

III. Somatic-Psychological Differentiation

1 Impervious to infant's communications. Fails totally to recognize or respond purposefully to infant's signals in any modality (e.g., no responsive smile; no responsive looks; no responsive vocalization; no appropriate reaching out in response to infant's inviting gesture).

3 Responds purposefully only intermittently or in one modality (e.g., only sometimes responds to smile or may totally misread entire areas of affect, such as assertiveness or tenderness, etc.).

5 Reads and responds causally and with empathy to entire range of infant's communications across all sensorimotor modalities and affect states. For example, reads and responds reciprocally to smiles, vocalizations, glances, facial expressions, motoric behaviors in context of pleasurable dependency, as well as to protest and assertiveness. This capacity is resilient to stress.

7 Overresponds and/or misreads some signals. When anxious, tends to confuse own feelings with infant's feelings. This is either limited to certain affects or

sensorimotor modalities or states of stress. For example, responds contingently to smiles but overresponds
to infant's protests by overfeeding child (i.e., sees
protest as hunger).

9 Misreads and overresponds to all signals. There is a
chaotic, intrusive quality.

IV. Behavioral Organization, Initiative, and Internalization

1 Unavailable to child as child is organizing complex
behavior (e.g., withdraws, feels "the child doesn't
need me anymore"). Unaccepting of any initiative by
child, however appropriate.

3 Can interact in organized manner around a few limited themes or when not under stress. For example,
will play organized, interactive games around love,
but withdraws as soon as aggression or assertion
comes to the fore. Intermittently unavailable to child's
initiative, depending on thematic area (e.g., will encourage initiative around play with puzzles but pulls
away from child's initiative around pleasure, including interest in the human body, etc.). Easily disorganized by stress.

5 Can interact in complex, organized manner and help
child organize one step further. Able to do this across
a wide range of themes (e.g., love, dependency, separation, anger, etc.). Can incorporate many themes
into one interaction sequence, including polarities of
love/hate and passivity/activity. Recovers well from
stress, tolerates frustration and child's negativism,
and is able to pursue and be available without being
overly controlling. Admires child's initiative, can follow child's lead, and at the same time set limits effectively to help child take initiative in self-control. Permits separation; remains available and knows when
to pursue child lovingly.

7 Tends to become confused and mildly disorganized

when child's behavior becomes complex. For example, cannot switch with child from one game to another or tends to switch and introduce new ideas too
quickly, confusing and disorganizing the child. Tends
to overcontrol and undermine initiative. Anxious and
intrusive.

9 Totally chaotic and easily disorganized by child; or
disorganizing to the child. Provides no opportunity
for child's initiative. Becomes physical in tendency to
overcontrol. Tends to do the initiating in all areas.

V. Capacity for Organizing Internal Representations

1 Lacks all capacity to engage child symbolically; engages child in concrete fashion only (e.g., can deal
with feeding and cleanliness, but cannot interact imaginatively [i.e., with words to describe feelings, or
through play with dolls to represent people, etc.]).

3 Some symbolic interactive capacity, but limited to
narrow thematic areas (e.g., only around dependency but not assertiveness, etc.) and to one or two sensorimotor modalities (e.g., can play symbolically,
whereas language use is concrete only).

5 Interacts in symbolic mode across a variety of age-appropriate themes using multiple sensorimotor capacities (e.g., can interact using language and/or symbolic play in all thematic areas such as love, pleasure,
dependency, aggression, competition, envy, hate,
curiosity, etc.). Can supportively pursue thematic
areas which may be mildly frightening to a child.
Can gradually develop richer and deeper symbolic
communications (e.g., caretaker can further child's
play sequence without assuming the initiative). Caretaker can maintain symbolic mode in face of stress.

7 Interacts symbolically but only along own agenda,
thereby undermining the child's capacities for elaboration; may do this in only some thematic areas.

9 Symbolic capacity supported in chaotic, fleeting, hy-

pomanic manner (e.g., mother keeps switching top-
ics, etc.). Often totally misreads child's communication.

VI. Representational Differentiation and Consolidation

1 Unable to use symbolic mode in logical or causal
manner. Depressed mother only interacts occasionally or, when child shows doll being "naughty," mother cannot finish sequence (even with child's encouragement) to show how child is either punished or
learns a lesson, etc. Mother cannot use language to
set limits and thereby help child see consequences of
actions; similarly, unable to convey through language a sense of pleasure or pride in child's accomplishments. In general, child initiates symbolic act
and mother is too preoccupied or depressed to respond, or does not understand the child's communication.

3 Intermittent compromises in purposeful symbolic
communications due either to stress, inability to deal
with certain thematic areas, or for other reasons
(e.g., no limit-setting in response to anger or explo-
siveness, yet occasionally able to interact meaning-
fully with child's symbolic expressions of dependency).

5 Able to interact symbolically in a purposeful (causal
and reciprocal) manner to a wide range of themes,
including love, dependency, pleasure, assertion, aggression, impulsivity, curiosity, etc. Can respond in
flexible manner, including support, encouragement,
empathy, and firm limit-setting. Stress does not interfere with functioning.

7 Interacts symbolically, but frequently not purposefully or causally. Tends to be disorganized in communication patterns.

9 Totally disorganized symbolic interactions (e.g.,
mother with severe thought disorder).

References

Ainsworth, M. (1973), The development of infant-mother attachment.
In: *Review of Child Developmental Research*, Vol. 3, ed. B. Caldwell & R. Ricciuti. Chicago: University of Chicago Press, pp. 1–94.
_____ Bell, S., & Stayton, D. (1974), Infant-mother attachment and social development: Socialization as a product of reciprocal responsiveness to signals. In: *The Integration of the Child into the Social World*, ed. M. Richards. Cambridge, England: Cambridge University Press, pp. 99–135.
Bellak, L., Hurvich, M., & Gediman, H. (1973), *Ego Functions in Schizophrenics, Neurotics, and Normals*. New York: John Wiley & Sons.
Bowlby, J. (1969), *Attachment and Loss*, Vol. 1. New York: Basic Books.
Brackbill, Y. (1958), Extinction of the smiling response in infants as a function of reinforcement schedule. *Child Devel.*, 29:115–124.
Brazelton, T. (1973), *Neonatal Behavioral Assessment Scale*. Philadelphia: Lippincott.
_____ Koslowski, B., & Main, M. (1974), The origins of reciprocity: The early mother-infant interaction. In: *The Effect of the Infant on its Caregiver*, ed. M. Lewis & L. Rosenblum. New York: Wiley, pp. 49–76.
Brody, S., & Axelrad, S. (1966), Anxiety, socialization, and ego formation in infancy. *Internat. J. Psycho-Anal.*, 47:218–229.
_____ _____ (1970), *Anxiety and Ego Formation in Infancy*. New York: International Universities Press.
Charlesworth, W. (1969), The role of surprise in cognitive development. In: *Studies in Cognitive Development: Essays in Honor of Jean Piaget*, ed. D. Elkind & J. Flavell. London: Oxford University Press, pp. 257–314.
Décarie, T. Gouin (1962), *Intelligence and Affectivity in Early Child-*

hood. New York: International Universities Press, 1965.

Emde, R. (1979), New research. Presentation at the training institute on "Clinical Approaches to Infants and Their Families" sponsored by The National Center for Clinical Infant Programs, Washington, D.C., December 5–7.

_____ Gaensbauer, T., & Harmon, R. (1976), *Emotional Expression in Infancy: A Biobehavioral Study*. [*Psychological Issues*, Monogr. 37.] New York: International Universities Press.

Erikson, E. (1959), *Identity and the Life Cycle*. [*Psychological Issues*, Monogr. 1.] New York: International Universities Press.

Escalona, S. (1968), *The Roots of Individuality*. Chicago: Aldine.

Fraiberg, S. (1977), *Insights from the Blind: Comparative Studies of Blind and Sighted Infants*. New York: Basic Books.

_____ (1979), Treatment modalities in an infant mental health program. Presentation at the training institute on "Clinical Approaches to Infants and Their Families" sponsored by The National Center for Clinical Infant Programs, Washington, D.C., December 5–7.

Freud, A. (1965), *Normality and Pathology in Childhood*. *The Writings of Anna Freud*, 6. New York: International Universities Press.

Freud, S. (1900), *The Interpretation of Dreams*. *Standard Edition*, 4 & 5. London: Hogarth Press, 1953.

_____ (1905), Three essays on the theory of sexuality. *Standard Edition*, 7:135–242. London: Hogarth Press, 1953.

_____ (1911), Formulations on the two principles of mental functioning. *Standard Edition*, 12:218–226. London: Hogarth Press, 1958.

Gewirtz, J. (1965), The course of infant smiling in four child-rearing environments in Israel. In: *Determinants of Infant Behavior*, Vol. 3, ed. B. Foss. London: Methuen, pp. 205–260.

_____ (1969), Levels of conceptual analysis in environment-infant interaction research. *Merrill-Palmer Quarterly*, 15:9–47.

Greenacre, P. (1969), The fetish and the transitional object. In: *Emotional Growth*, Vol. 1. New York: International Universities Press, 1971, pp. 315–334.

Greenspan, S. (1979), *Intelligence and Adaptation: An Integration of Psychoanalytic and Piagetian Developmental Psychology*. [*Psychological Issues*, Monogr. 47/48.] New York: International Universities Press.

_____ (1980), Analysis of a five-and-a-half-year-old girl: Indications for a dyadic-phallic phase of development. *J. Amer. Psychoanal. Assn.*, 28:575–603.

_____ & Cullander, C. (1973), A systematic metapsychological assessment of the personality — its application to the problem of analyzability. *J. Amer. Psychoanal. Assn.*, 21:303–327.

_____ Hatleberg, J., & Cullander, C. (1976), A systematic metapsychological assessment of the personality in childhood. *J. Amer. Psychoanal. Assn.*, 24:875–903.

_____ & Lieberman, A. (1981), Infants, mothers, and their interaction: A quantitative clinical approach to developmental assessment. In: *The Course of Life: Psychoanalytic Contributions Toward Understanding Personality Development. Vol. 1: Infancy and Early Childhood*, ed. S. Greenspan & G. Pollock. Washington, D.C.: Government Printing Office. DHHS Pub. No. (ADM) 79-786.

_____ Lourie, R., & Nover, R. (1979), A developmental approach to the classification of psychopathology in infancy and early childhood. In: *The Basic Handbook of Child Psychiatry*, Vol. 2, ed. J. Noshpitz. New York: Basic Books, pp. 157-164.

_____ & Mannino, F. (1974), A model for brief intervention with couples based on projective identification. *Amer. J. Psychiat.*, 131:1103-1106.

Hartmann, H. (1939), *Ego Psychology and the Problem of Adaptation*. New York: International Universities Press.

Jackson, D. (1960), *The Etiology of Schizophrenia*. New York: Basic Books.

Kagan, J. (1978), *Infancy: Its Place in Human Development*. Cambridge, Mass.: Harvard University Press.

Kernberg, O. (1975), *Borderline Conditions and Pathological Narcissism*. New York: Jason Aronson.

Klaus, M., & Kennell, J. (1976), *Maternal-Infant Bonding: The Impact of Early Separation or Loss on Family Development*. St. Louis: Mosby.

Kohut, H. (1971), *The Analysis of the Self: A Systematic Approach to the Psychoanalytic Treatment of Narcissistic Personality Disorders*. New York: International Universities Press.

Lewis, M., & Rosenblum, L., Eds. (1974), *The Effect of the Infant on Its Caregiver*. New York: Wiley.

Lidz, T. (1973), *Origins and Treatment of Schizophrenic Disorders*. New York: Basic Books.

_____ Fleck, S., & Cornelison, A. (1967), *Schizophrenia and the Family*. New York: International Universities Press.

Lipsitt, L. (1966), Learning processes of newborns. *Merrill-Palmer Quarterly*, 12:45-71.

Lourie, R. (1980), The National Center: Primary prevention in the earliest years. *Zero to Three*, 1:1.

Mahler, M., Pine, F., & Bergman, A. (1975), *The Psychological Birth of the Human Infant*. New York: Basic Books.

Meltzoff, A., & Moore, K. (1977), Imitation of facial and manual gestures by human neonates. *Science*, 19:75-78.

Murphy, L., & Moriarty, A. (1976), *Vulnerability, Coping, and Growth*. New Haven: Yale University Press.

Parmelee, A., Jr. (1972), Development of states in infants. In: *Sleep and the Maturing Nervous System*, ed. C. Clemente, D. Purpura, & F. Mayer. New York: Academic Press, pp. 199-228.

Piaget, J. (1936), *The Origins of Intelligence in Children*. New York: International Universities Press, 1952.

—— (1937), *The Construction of Reality in the Child*. New York: Basic Books, 1954.

—— (1962), The stages of the intellectual development of the child. In: *Childhood Psychopathology*, ed. S. Harrison & J. McDermott. New York: International Universities Press, 1972, pp. 157–166.

—— (1968), *Structuralism*. New York: Basic Books, 1970.

Provence, S. (1979), A service-centered study: Methods of intervention and outcome. Address delivered at the training institute on "Clinical Approaches to Infants and Their Families" sponsored by The National Center for Clinical Infant Programs, Washington, D.C., December 5–7.

—— (in press), *Early Intervention and Outcome in a Service Centered Study*. New York: Basic Books.

Sander, L. (1962), Issues in early mother-child interaction. *J. Amer. Acad. Child Psychiat.*, 1:141–166.

Shapiro, R., & Zinner, J. (1975), Family organization and adolescent development. In: *Task and Organization*, ed. E. Miller. New York: Wiley.

Spitz, R. (1965), *The First Year of Life*. New York: International Universities Press.

—— Emde, R., & Metcalf, D. (1970), Further prototypes of ego formation. *The Psychoanalytic Study of the Child*, 25:417–444. New York: International Universities Press.

Sroufe, L., & Waters, E. (1976), The ontogenesis of smiling and laughter: A perspective on the organization of development in infancy. *Psychol. Rev.*, 83:173–189.

—— —— (1977), Attachment as an organizational construct. *Child Devel.*, 48:1184–1199.

—— —— & Matas, L. (1974), Contextual determinants of infant affective response. In: *The Origins of Fear*, ed. M. Lewis & L. Rosenblum. New York: Wiley, pp. 49–72.

Stern, D. (1974a), Mother and infant at play: The dyadic interaction involving facial, vocal and gaze behaviors. In: *The Effect of the Infant on Its Caregiver*, ed. M. Lewis & L. Rosenblum. New York: Wiley, pp. 187–213.

—— (1974b), The goal and structure of mother-infant play. *J. Amer. Acad. Child Psychiat.*, 13:402–421.

Tennes, K., Emde, R., Kisley, A., & Metcalf, D. (1972), The stimulus barrier in early infancy: An exploration of some formulations of John Benjamin. In: *Psychoanalysis and Contemporary Science*, 1:206–234. New York: Macmillan.

Thomas, A., Chess, S., & Birch, H. (1968), *Temperament and Behavior Disorders in Children*. New York: New York University Press.

Waters, E., Matas, L., & Sroufe, L. (1975), Infant's reactions to an approaching stranger: Description, validation and functional significance of wariness. *Child Devel.*, 46:348–356.

Werner, H., & Kaplan, B. (1963), *Symbol Formation*. New York: Wiley.

Winnicott, D. (1953), Transitional objects and transitional phenomena: A study of the first not-me possession. In: *Collected Papers*. New York: Basic Books, 1958, pp. 278–294.

———— (1962), *The Maturational Processes and the Facilitating Environment*. New York: International Universities Press, 1965.

Wolff, P. (1966), *The Causes, Controls, and Organization of Behavior in the Neonate*. [*Psychological Issues*, Monogr. 17.] New York: International Universities Press.

Wynne, L., Matthysse, S., & Cromwell, R. (1978), *The Nature of Schizophrenia: New Approaches to Research and Treatment*. New York: John Wiley & Sons.

Yarrow, L., & Goodwin, M. (1965), Some conceptual issues in the study of mother-infant interaction. *Amer. J. Orthopsychiat.*, 35:473–481.

———— Rubinstein, J., Pederson, F., & Jankowski, T. (1972), Dimensions of early stimulation and their differential effects on infant development. *Merrill-Palmer Quart.*, 18:205–218.

Name Index

255

Subject Index